METAPHOR AND ART

METAPHOR AND ART

Interactionism and Reference
in the Verbal and Nonverbal Arts

CARL R. HAUSMAN

Pennsylvania State University

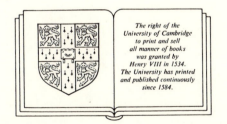

The right of the
University of Cambridge
to print and sell
all manner of books
was granted by
Henry VIII in 1534.
The University has printed
and published continuously
since 1584.

CAMBRIDGE UNIVERSITY PRESS
Cambridge
New York   New Rochelle   Melbourne   Sydney

PN
228
M4
H283
1989

Published by the Press Syndicate of the University of Cambridge
The Pitt Building, Trumpington Street, Cambridge CB2 1RP
32 East 57th Street, New York, NY 10022, USA
10 Stamford Road, Oakleigh, Melbourne 3166, Australia

© Cambridge University Press 1989

First published in 1989

Printed in the United States of America

Library of Congress Cataloging-in-Publication Data
Hausman, Carl R.
Metaphor and art : interactionism and reference in the verbal and
nonverbal arts / Carl R. Hausman.
p.   cm.
ISBN 0-521-36385-3
1. Metaphor.   2. Creative ability.   3. Arts – Themes, motives.
4. Symbolism in art.   I. Title
PN228.M4H28   1988
808'.001–dc19   88–16151
CIP

British Library Cataloguing in Publication Data
Hausman, Carl R.
Metaphor and art : interactionism and
reference in the verbal and nonverbal arts.
1. Metaphor. Semantic aspects
I. Title
415

ISBN 0 521 36385 3

Contents

Preface

The origin of this book lies in a suggestion I once made concerning the problems of explaining creativity.[1] I argued for accepting a strong sense of innovation, according to which creative acts and their outcomes are irreducible – both unpredictable in principle and not deducible within a system. Consequently, we should not expect complete explanations that conform to the empiricist and rationalist conceptions that have been dominant in our heritage. It was suggested that an alternative way of understanding creativity might be found in the use and study of metaphor. A relatively briefly stated proposal sketched the way in which the components of verbal metaphors could be subjected to analysis in terms of the ways they relate to one another so that new meanings enter language. I suggested also that the relations among the components of verbal metaphors were operative in the arts in general, verbal and nonverbal. It seems to me that the ways that words and larger linguistic verbal units function within metaphors and, in turn, within the contexts of metaphors, are comparable to the functions of the components of works of the visual arts and music. An exploration of the last suggestion is one of the chief concerns of this book.

The other main concern is with the sense in which creative metaphors are responsible for creating the referents of meanings as well as the meanings themselves. Thus, not only are new perspectives – new ideas, values, and ways of organizing experience – created, but also the new perspectives may be insightful and thus appropriate to the world. My interest in pursuing this controversial proposal was provoked in part by Max Black's equally controversial proposal – at least as he initially formulated it – that metaphors may sometimes be said to create rather than to discover similarities.[2] As in the case of my concern about how the components of metaphors function in contexts, this claim about reference is explored in regard to both verbal and nonverbal arts.

[1] *A Discourse on Novelty and Creation* (Albany: State University of New York Press, 1984, originally published, The Hague: M. Nijhoff, 1975), Chap. 3.
[2] Black's initial formulation of this point appears in "Metaphor," *Proceedings of the Aristotelian Society*, N.S. 55 (1954–5): 273–94. His qualifications will be discussed in the first chapter of this book.

This book devotes nearly equal attention to the development of each of these two main concerns. Concentration on the structures or relationships among components consists of an extension of what has been called "the interaction theory of metaphor." Discussion in the first chapter begins, then, with the seminal ideas of I. A. Richards and Max Black, who originated the interaction view as it is generally considered in current literature.[3] The development of interactionism emphasizes the place of tension, or difference, that integrates while differentiating, sometimes polarizing, the meanings that function in or in relation to metaphorically interpreted expressions. As I indicated, the extension I propose is not limited to verbal expressions but is concerned with nonverbal expression as well, and this cannot be pursued properly without engaging in a discussion of a theory of art that focuses on aesthetic meaning. The meaning at issue here is understood as the outcome of metaphorical interaction said to take place among the components of nonverbal and verbal expressions.

In anticipation of the other main concern about reference, let me say that the problems raised by this concern are philosophical in that they presuppose an ontology or metaphysics. Underlying the suggestions I shall make is the view that the world, language, and thought evolve. This evolutionary realism stems from my interpretation of Charles S. Peirce's philosophy, and the proposal concerning how creative metaphors can generate new referents and meanings relies heavily on a part of Peirce's philosophy in which he discusses the basic constraining conditions of semiotic processes.

It seems to me that my proposal regarding how metaphors may be creative raises a fundamental philosophical issue that is alive today. On the one hand, a view that affirms creativity in the strong sense requires us to interpret the mind, or human intelligence (where intelligence may be inclusive of more than intellectual activity), as active in the constituting of its objects. This view may take some form of idealism (objective or subjective) or, if pushed to one extreme, it may be construed as deconstructionism or a radical relativism. On the other hand, the view that affirms creativity in the strong sense may refuse to abandon the need for a condition that is somehow independent of mind-constituting activity and the objects it constitutes. This alternative may be thought of as a commitment to some form of Kantianism. For such a view, there is an independent condition, but it is unknowable in itself. My proposed evolutionary realism offers a way to mediate the two alternatives that seem to me to be at the root of current controversies over relativism and realism, or over objectivity as op-

---

[3] Richards's statement of the interaction view was set forth in *Philosophy of Rhetoric* (Oxford, England: Oxford University Press, 1936). Black's development of the view was originally formulated in "Metaphor."

posed to subjectivity with respect to interpretation. With the help of some of Peirce's statements about realism and about the way in which semiotic processes are not arbitrary, I wish to formulate an account that not only does justice to the fairly widely accepted conviction that there is an interpretive dimension constituting all thought but that also points to a basis for affirming the vital role of mind-independent objectivity in some if not all interpretation. It seems to me that this aim can be approached, or reached, through an extension of the interaction view of metaphor that I propose in this book.

University Park, Pennsylvania   Carl R. Hausman

Acknowledgments

All the individuals to whom I should like to express my appreciation for the stimulation and insights that aided my thinking about metaphor are too numerous to be mentioned by name. I shall limit myself to mentioning a few who belong to different groups that have been helpful in different ways. First are those with whom I have had particularly fruitful discussions about metaphor and figurative language in general over the past twenty or so years and those with whom I have had briefer but directly significant interchanges within the past two or three years. The first group includes Albert Rothenberg and Carl Vaught; the second group, Mary Hesse and Mark Johnson. Indirectly helpful have been my recent interchanges with Salim Kemal and Paul Weiss. I should not neglect to mention the excitement and stimulus provided by two graduate seminars that I held in 1982 and 1986. Many of the students in these seminars helped me see points at which I needed to bring my ideas into better focus. Needless to say, I alone am responsible for whatever problematic points the reader may find in my discussion.

I should like to acknowledge the generous support I have received from The Pennsylvania State University in the form of a sabbatical leave, and especially the support that has come from the College of the Liberal Arts and Department of Philosophy research funds, some of which made possible the helpful research assistance provided by Janis Guerney and Michael Olscheske.

Finally, I wish to express my appreciation for the opportunity of having earlier versions of chapters of this book appear in journal articles. Specifically, Chapters 3 and 5 are expanded versions of "Metaphors, Referents, and Individuality" and "Insight in the Arts," which appeared in the *Journal of Aesthetics and Art Criticism*, volumes 41 (1983) and 45 (1986), respectively. The Appendix is a slightly modified version of "Metaphorical Reference and Peirce's Dynamical Object," which first appeared in *The Transactions of the Charles S. Peirce Society*, vol. 23.

Introduction

Interest in metaphor has never been more extensive than during the last decade or so. This recent fascination with the topic probably stems from contemporary theoretical concerns about language, coupled with the long recognized problematic character of metaphor as a form of linguistic expression. That metaphors are problematic was seen clearly by Aristotle, who established the first theoretical framework for contemporary interpretations of metaphor.[1] Aristotle's view that metaphorical expressions depart from ordinary linguistic usage suggests that there is something paradoxical in them. This should not be surprising, for even some of the most "tough-minded" contemporary philosophers have regarded metaphorical expressions as paradoxical, emphasizing this fact in their own paradoxical and metaphorical descriptions. Nelson Goodman says that metaphors reassign labels in "an affair between a predicate with a past and an object that yields while protesting."[2] Max Black expresses the paradox when he says that "*taken as literal*, a metaphorical statement appears to be perversely asserting something to be what it is plainly known not to be." He also affirms the paradox in proposing that metaphors create the similarities that connect two disparate, literally interpreted concepts, although a created similarity seems prima facie self-inconsistent.[3] Finally, Monroe Beardsley points out that the problems in understanding metaphor arise because what may be construed as a nonsensical expression seems to make sense, and I. A. Richards points to the paradoxical dimension of metaphor in his seminal description of the "interactions" among the key terms of metaphors.[4]

The idea of paradox depends on the characterization of metaphors as at once nonsensical – or at least as apparently incongruous in some

[1] The most frequently cited discussion of metaphor in Aristotle's work can be found in *Poetics*, 1457b ff.
[2] Nelson Goodman, *Languages of Art: An Approach to a Theory of Symbols* (Indianapolis: Bobbs-Merrill, 1968), p. 69.
[3] In Max Black, "More about Metaphor," *Dialectica*, vol. 31, fosc. 3–4 (1977): 431–57. Reprinted in a slightly modified version in Andrew Ortony, ed., *Metaphor and Thought* (Cambridge, England: Cambridge University Press, 1979), pp. 19–43. All quotations are taken from the latter.
[4] Monroe Beardsley, "Metaphorical Senses," *Nous* 12 (1978): 3–16. I. A. Richards, *The Philosophy of Rhetoric* (London: Oxford University Press, 1936), chaps. 5 and 6.

way and in need of construal – and intelligible, having cognitive significance. It should be obvious, then, that my own and these authors' approaches reject the interpretation of metaphors as nothing but nonsense and consequently as nothing but a kind of ornamentation on language or as only interesting didactic prompters. As will be clear in what follows, this kind of intelligibility need not be identical with truth or falsity in some literal sense. The sense and extent to which the intelligibility of at least some metaphors is related to truth that relates expressions to the world will be a key issue later. At this point, what is important is that metaphors seem to be both intelligible and unintelligible, and this appears paradoxical and puzzling.

A quick glance at some examples may help illustrate the reason for this puzzlement. For the sake of emphasis and brevity, most of the examples are offered out of context and necessarily appear in a rather bare format.[5]

1. Man is the dream of a shadow.
2. The world is an unweeded garden.
3. The road is a rocket in sunlight.
4. The world is a machine.
5. The mind is a computer.
6. That is not my cup of tea.
7. He is in a sour mood.
8. Bolts pray from torn paper.
9. Noun furried is plus brown.

Each utterance, at least before we reflect on it, violates our expectations of language if it is regarded literally or if we expect it to conform to conventional usage and standards of factual truth. It should be noted that the sixth example is not, as a sentence, immediately a violation of literal interpretation, for it is a negation and is, in fact, literally true when it functions figuratively, for example, if I were to

---

[5] The first example is a variation on a standard translation of a metaphor in Pindar, *Pythian* 8, trans. Richard Lattimore. The variation on this translation was suggested by Erich Segal in a review of *The Oresteia of Aeschylus* by Robert Lowell, *The New Republic*, June 30, 1979. Segal thinks the varied translation yields a more powerful metaphor, and I think he is correct about this, regardless of the adequacy of the translation. I am indebted to James Daley for calling this to my attention. The second example comes from Shakespeare, *Hamlet*, act 1, sc. 2, lines 134–5. The third is from Albert Rothenberg's *The Emerging Goddess: The Creative Process in Art, Science, and Other Fields* (Chicago: University of Chicago Press, 1979) and was formulated by a poet he was interviewing for the research project on which his book is based. The fourth is a formulation of what S. Pepper calls a "root metaphor" in *World Hypotheses* (Berkeley and Los Angeles: University of California Press, 1948). The sixth is from Richard Boyd, "Metaphor and Theory Change: What is a 'Metaphor' For?" in Ortony, ed., *Metaphor and Thought*, pp. 356–408. The remaining examples are my own, all but the last two being drawn from my recollections of everyday speech.

say that rock and roll is not my cup of tea. The conflict with literal expectations in this case is the result of an incongruity or irrelevance of application of the sentence taken literally, that is, as denying the ownership of a cup of tea.

It is more important at the moment, however, to observe that we should be cautious about using the term *literal*. Not only is it difficult in many instances to determine what is and what is not literal, but there also are theorists who deny the distinction between literal and metaphorical language. At this stage of the study, I shall simply assume a commonsense recognition that there are times when we speak literally and at other times figuratively and that many of us recognize a figurative expression. I shall return to this issue later.

The point here is simply that all but possibly the last two of the preceding examples are somehow meaningful. The first seven do "say" something. Speakers of metaphors such as these presumably mean what they say in just that way of saying it. Not only are the expressions meaningful, but some of them are also profoundly significant. The first two examples suggest fundamental insights into the world and humanity, insights that are seen when we are compelled to surpass their so-called literal interpretations. The third example expresses a perceptual insight. The fourth and fifth say something that may contribute – indeed, have contributed – to philosophical and scientific ways of understanding the world and mental processes. These first five examples seem clearly to be creative metaphors. If they violate literal expectations, they do so creatively. The sixth and seventh examples, however, are not obviously creative. It is not even clear that they are metaphors, particularly if we think that an expression is not metaphorical unless it is creative. In any case, they have been so well established in our speech habits that they no longer seem striking. They may be readily paraphrased by obviously literal statements. If they are metaphors, they are "frozen" or "dormant." The eighth and ninth expressions also may not seem metaphorical, not because they do not violate our literal expectations of how language ought to be used, but because it is not clear that they say anything at all, or at least in the case of the eighth example, that it says anything significant. These examples, then, share with the others a nonliteral incongruous character, but they do not clearly share in being metaphors, dormant, frozen, or "alive."

One reason that the way language functions metaphorically is so puzzling is that we usually cannot depend on our interpretations of expressions, such as the preceding, apart from their contexts. Even the expression "That is not my cup of tea" might be literally interpreted in a context in which I am trying to find my own misplaced cup of tea. The eighth and perhaps even the ninth example might be

construed as meaningful in a specific context, for instance, if they are
formulations that follow a code.[6] And it is conceivable that they might
have been intended by someone as metaphors. To be sure, some
expressions are relatively context free. "Man is the dream of a shadow"
is significant when abstracted from its original setting. And it can be
understood in a variety of settings in which it retains a central affirmation about the universal condition of being human. But context
does not make a difference to many expressions if we want to know
why they are understood figuratively.

The relevance of context is not defined exclusively by the intention
of a writer or speaker. A metaphor, or what looks like one, may be
unintended or may occur inadvertently. We may find an expression
metaphorical when the speaker or writer is believed to have intended
it to be understood literally, as in the case in which the utterer is in
error, for example, if a child were to say that "the moon is a bright
disk," or in the case in which someone is groping for a way to describe
something, for example, if a child were to say, when its nose tickles,
"My nose is laughing." And someone might intend to formulate a
metaphor and succeed in constructing one that is so poor that we
would hesitate to call it metaphorical; for example, "My head is a bal-
loon this morning." For a context to be relevant, we must include
more than the speaker's intentions. It should be noted, too, that some
expressions that normally could be interpreted literally may be conjoined so that the result is a metaphor; for example, "The girl opened
the gate" and "Her tears could not be quenched."

This is not the place to examine these expressions further or to
explore the ways in which the terms of expressions function together
so that they seem both to be and to resist being meaningful. This
latter task will be undertaken later. The point of citing examples is to
indicate what provokes puzzlement about metaphorical expressions.
They illustrate Beardsley's remark that problems arise because, although metaphors may be taken initially as nonsensical, they also and
initially seem to make sense. The examples also illustrate that the paradox at the heart of metaphorical discourse is not equally intense in
all examples. At one end of the scale, literal incongruity or literal
meaninglessness is obvious, but the suggestion of insight is also clearest. At the other end, meaninglessness, if not falsity, is also obvious,
but the suggestion of meaningfulness, much less insight, at least at
first blush, is absent. Deviation from a literal use of language, or from
conventional or standard expectations of what counts as a significant
utterance, is not enough to guarantee that the expression is a meta-

[6] In connection with the problem of literal as related to figurative speech, see Owen
Barfield, "The Meaning of the Word 'Literal'," in L. C. Knight and Basil Cottle, eds.,
Metaphor and Symbol (London: Butterworths Scientific Publications, 1960), pp. 48–63.

phor, creative or uncreative. I shall later develop the point that something more is needed: first, an inner opposition between the complexes of meanings associated with the subject and what is attributed to it and, second, insight. A consideration of the conditions for these features of metaphors will be one of the main tasks of the first two chapters of this book.

Seeing the difficulties of understanding how metaphors function has led to some of the most extreme acknowledgments of the problematic character of metaphor: those that associate metaphorical expressions with mystery. For example, Robert Boyle says, "Among the mysteries of human speech, metaphor has remained one of the most baffling."[7] And in the words of the literary critic Murray Krieger, "The most exciting discussions of metaphor by recent critics . . . have invariably ended by invoking the miraculous."[8] Furthermore, the fascination with metaphor that has been provoked by its puzzling character has led to attempts to understand it that often are either too expansive or too constricted. Just as there has been a tendency to resort to proclaiming mystery, there also has been a tendency to insist on the pervasiveness of metaphorical language, even in what is ordinarily taken as literal speech. I. A. Richards's early study illustrates this in insisting on the omnipresence of metaphor.[9] On the other hand, discussions of metaphor in some philosophical circles, especially those that lean toward interpreting issues in terms of ideal languages, too frequently overconceptualize the topic; that is, theorists constrict the discussion by imposing the tightest possible rational framework on metaphor. This is most evident in those views that treat metaphors as having substitutable literal statements, which is to deny the possibility that metaphors offer irreducible cognitive content. This approach and its opposite will be considered in the first chapter.[10] For the purposes of these introductory remarks, it is sufficient to observe that neither of these extreme views seems convincing, at least without rather drastic qualifications. The discussion to follow will be directed toward a view that does not simply surrender to affirming the mysteries of metaphor or to treating metaphors as disguised literal statements.

[7] Robert R. Boyle, S. J., "The Nature of Metaphor," *The Modern Schoolman* 31 (1954): 257.

[8] Murray Krieger, *A Window to Criticism; Shakespeare's Sonnets and Modern Poetics* (Princeton, N.J.: Princeton University Press, 1964), p. 4.

[9] I. A. Richards, *The Philosophy of Rhetoric* (Oxford, England: Oxford University Press, 1936).

[10] I shall argue later that even Black's recent extension of his own view is couched in a conceptual frame that belies his own insights into the peculiar cognitive thrust of the phenomenon he studies. Indeed, in the final analysis, he too falls back on an interpretation of metaphor that is suspiciously close to the views he opposes. Thus his interaction view loses some of its force in advocating the possibility that metaphors are creative. See Black, "More about Metaphor."

What is the point of trying to understand a phenomenon that has long been so elusive? Why should writers devote so much effort to the topic? The answer may seem obvious to those who already have been drawn into a study of it. And the need to raise the question may seem pointless to those who have simply appreciated the power of metaphor or who have only wanted to create and use metaphors for poetic or other purposes. But to all who reflect on what fascinates them, the question is important to consider because even if in its general outlines the answer is obvious, what may not be so obvious is the extent to which both the question and its answers differ depending on the professional perspective. Even within philosophy and aesthetics the puzzle of metaphor raises different issues according to one's philosophical perspective. In any case, considerations of this question will help explain the direction of my study.

In his monograph-length work on metaphor, Douglas Berggren formulates, from the standpoint of metaphysics, perhaps the most fundamental answers to this question:[11]

Metaphor has always been one of the central problems of philosophy. Nor is this simply because metaphors are in fact used and abused in every area of human discourse. Even more important is the fact that metaphor constitutes the indispensable principle for integrating diverse phenomena and perspectives without sacrificing their diversity.

For Berggren, metaphor is of interest to philosophers because it has to do with a principle of integrating experience. To understand how language can be used metaphorically should help us see how we can understand the whole of things. Even a less ambitious philosophical aim would share in the hope of seeing how what is ordered and seemingly immediately understandable can be reconciled with what breaks out of this order. We want to establish coherence where there is diversity. This basic aim underlies the reason that a theory of metaphor has far-reaching ramifications for other fields.

Directly connected with one of the main concerns of my study is the importance of metaphor to poets, literary critics, and, as I shall argue later, art critics. In mentioning poets, I do not mean only lyric poets, or those who write verse; I mean anyone who writes with literary–aesthetic ends in view.[12] In fact, it may be said that every poetic artic-

---

[11] "The Use and Abuse of Metaphor," *Review of Metaphysics* 16 (1962): 237–58, and (March 1963): 450–72. The quotation is from p. 237.

[12] Just what literary–aesthetic ends are must be discussed later. For the moment, I appeal to our intuitive ability to know that a piece of writing, or an instance of the spoken word, is an aesthetic presentation – a work of art – rather than a treatise or a piece of propaganda or a sermon, each of which may have aesthetic quality but which does not permit this quality to play a self-sufficient role. But the point here is

ulation in language is, as a whole, a kind of metaphor. Certainly, metaphors are integral to literary, aesthetic expression. Gifted poets do create with and through metaphors, and if we are interested in poetry and how it works, we must be interested in metaphor.

If metaphors are vital to poetry, they are also necessarily important to literary criticism. Not only are metaphors in poems basic components to be interpreted, but also critics use metaphors to formulate their interpretations. Indeed, metaphorical speech in art criticism is, I think, the most appropriate way to interpret works that are thought to be creations, that is, to be the outcomes of creativity.[13]

The importance of metaphor extends beyond literary criticism to the understanding and interpretation of nonverbal arts as well. The point of this claim can be seen in a brief sketch of one of the main theses of the following chapters. The thesis is that verbal metaphors have a structure that is shared with nonverbal expressions. I shall try to show how the structure of metaphorical expressions can be characterized in terms of both the divergence and the convergence of meanings.

Divergence and convergence can be regarded as an internal order in which there is an interaction between or among components in the metaphorical expression. This can be seen most clearly in verbal examples. In "The world is an unweeded garden," the divergent concepts, world and garden, are brought together in an expression that takes the form of an identity statement. Insofar as the expression asserts an identity, the divergent concepts are made to converge, and the meanings relate to one another bidirectionally. The term *converge* is used to indicate that the divergent meanings are not merely put together in a nonsensical expression. Instead, the terms cooperate and direct divergent meanings toward a new significance.

The bidirectional action of metaphors can also be seen externally, as an interaction of the metaphor as a whole with its context. Shakespeare's unweeded garden that is a world is intelligible only in a particular context. In the context of drama, it is clearly not a mistake in the use of words (as it might be uttered by a creature from another planet learning the meaning of the word *world*). Nor should it be regarded as a mistake even when it is extracted from the drama by us, for it appears to require construal so that it can be understood as figuratively appropriate to the word in some context. Yet outside the drama, it asserts itself as a metaphor against a literal background. It is an intrusion, although when it appears in its original poetic context,

that metaphors are important to poets – metaphors are the heart of poetry; they constitute it.

[13] Hausman, *A Discourse on Novelty and Creation.*

it is a welcome one. Paul Ricoeur uses the word *impertinence* to suggest the way that a metaphor intrudes on expected norms of usage.[14] The divergence of meanings in metaphors and their characteristic way of intruding presents the interpreter with a special kind of tension, whose consideration will have a prominent place in what follows.

√ The convergence and divergence and consequent tension in question are also present in some nonverbal expressions. More generally, the structure of verbal metaphors is a fundamental feature of certain phenomena wherever meanings are exhibited or wherever there is intelligibility. Thus, my proposal is that metaphor is integral to the visual arts, music, and, finally, all art forms. It is also integral to philosophical discourse and scientific theorizing.

The metaphorical structure of nonverbal arts is most easily illustrated in paintings that show us obvious distortions of conventional perspectives on things. For example, in Picasso's *Woman Before a Mirror,* natural shapes are flattened and changed to help construct the composition that governs the painting as a whole. Or in a Cézanne still life, the stability of the shape of a vase is dislodged, and the vase's shape is transformed into another visual image — into a mountain or rocklike stability as it interacts within the tensions among the broken outlines, the tilting of the vase, the vibrant colors, and the unstable background. In music, metaphorical structure is exhibited, for example, in the transformations of main themes in the middle, or development, sections of movements in sonata allegro form. And it is illustrated in the way that patterns of sound in which components interrelate through dissonance and harmony, through tension and resolution, succeed in presenting themselves as more than sheer abstract sound. A passage in a Bach chorale may exhibit grandeur and hope and a soaring, religious outpouring far beyond the significance found in abstract sound and beyond the import sometimes found in verbal — including poetic — expressions that are intended as descriptions of the power of music. The common ground between music, or the nonverbal arts in general, and verbal metaphor, of course, will need to be seen against the background of an account of what an art object is. If my claim about the pervasiveness of metaphorical structure is correct, then the consideration of metaphor will be important to anyone who tries to interpret creative achievements in the visual arts and music as well as in poetry.

Yet the very peculiarity of metaphor, wherever it occurs, also attracts the attention of others who are not practicing artists or critics. It has been hinted already that the paradox of metaphor should pro-

[14] Paul Ricoeur, *The Rule of Metaphor: Multi-Disciplinary Studies of the Creation of Meaning in Language,* trans. Robert Czerny with Kathleen McLaughlin and John Costello, S. J. (Toronto: University of Toronto Press, 1975).

voke the interest of linguists. Closely related to this interest is the concern of philosophical aesthetics. And the characterization of the structure of metaphor as something that transcends diverse contexts of meaning, verbal and nonverbal, is a task that transcends the special disciplines or approaches appropriate to linguistics and art criticism. And the attempts to understand this structure, its conditions, its source, and, as Berggren saw, its significance for human existence are appropriate to philosophy.

This broader and more fundamental interest in metaphor is also appropriate to epistemology and ontology or metaphysics. If we were to understand how a phenomenon can exhibit intelligible meaning within articulations that depart from accepted standards of intelligibility, then we would understand a problem in epistemology. A theory of knowledge, after all, should be relevant to the apprehension of intelligibility wherever it occurs, especially when it originates in situations that include something that violates our expectations of intelligibility.

To attempt to understand the structure of metaphor is to attempt to understand the structure of something that contributes to the intelligibility of the world. I. A. Richards had a glimpse of this when he spoke of the "deeper problem" with which his theory of rhetoric deals: "What is the connection between the mind and the world by which events in the mind mean other events in the world?"[15] Such questions of epistemology and metaphysics clearly extend the topic of metaphor beyond the domain of aesthetics. Nevertheless, my immediate context is aesthetics, and the following account is intended to be adequate primarily to the aesthetic role of metaphor. Consequently, the ontological implications that must be considered will be viewed primarily in terms of their significance for art.

There is a specific issue that joins my general ontological considerations to aesthetics. This issue arises in the way that metaphorical expressions are paradoxical. The point that metaphors are puzzling because they are at once nonsensical and meaningful suggests a more fundamental consideration, the paradox of creativity. This point should be obvious if it is granted that at least some metaphors are creative because they articulate new insights. Thus, what is puzzling about such metaphors is that they are significant even though what is significant about them is unfamiliar and not readily traceable (if traceable at all) to what was familiar. If metaphors are creative, then they must display at least some of the distinguishing features of achievements that are new and valuable and that contribute to their traditions. As new, they contrast with results that are based solely on antecedent rules

[15] Ibid., p. 28.

and conditions. Presumably this is one reason that Max Black stated that a metaphor may be cognitively significant and may "create the similarity" rather than refer to "some similarity antecedently existing."

The paradox of creativity is not one that is amenable to ready resolution. Nevertheless, many interpreters of creativity share with many interpreters of metaphor the assumption that they deal with a set of problems that have only to be tackled and solved, given sufficient time. Thus, most attempts to understand metaphors turn out to be attempts to reduce them to familiar linguistic expressions or familiar concepts. As Jerry L. Morgan has asserted, "The picture of metaphor one often gets is of something to be eliminated as quickly as possible, to get down to the literal meaning that the metaphor covers up."[16] This charge applies to more recent pragmatic as well as semantic treatments of metaphors. Whether reductive solutions are forthcoming, however, will not be the main theme of the following discussion. I think there are good reasons for claiming that the paradox in metaphorical discourse cannot be resolved in principle.[17] However, in this study I wish to explore only how metaphors function verbally and in the nonverbal arts when they exhibit paradox. In turn, we may see also how this function relates metaphorical language, and thus works of art in general, to reality.

These preliminary remarks about the topic of metaphor should indicate my general purpose. There are two tasks to be undertaken, each directed toward a final goal: understanding the arts, both verbal and nonverbal, through a theory of metaphor. One of these tasks is to show how metaphorical structure pervades all creative art. The other is to develop what might be called a *theory* of metaphor but that I think more appropriately should be called an *account* of metaphor. An account avoids the implication of a completed explanation that would include a definition of metaphor and would provide the necessary and sufficient conditions and the principles (or formulas) for constructing and interpreting metaphors. The topic is too problematic to expect such results. I have already confessed that I do not think the underlying issue, which centers on creativity, can be resolved so that the paradox is eliminated. And a theory as I understand it would provide such a resolution. But it does not follow that an explanation in some form is impossible. Thus, I shall propose what I call an account, by which I mean a systematic, critical series of speculations about the functions of metaphorical language, the arts, and reality. I shall provide a picture of how metaphorical expressions function in relation to the world. My intention is to make the picture as appro-

---

[16] Jerry L. Morgan, "Observations on the Pragmatics of Metaphor," in Ortony, ed., *Metaphor and Thought*, pp. 136–47. The quotation is from p. 147.
[17] I have argued this at length in *A Discourse on Novelty and Creation*.

priate and faithful as possible to the phenomena. The discussion will assume a functional approach, that is, an approach that asks how words, sentences, works of art, and things in reality must function in order to provide the experiences we have of them. I shall first propose an interpretation of metaphor that approaches it conceptually, although this is not to abandon the claim that metaphors can be creative in a radical sense. As already suggested, our initial task is to consider what may be called the structure of metaphor: *Structure* refers to a mode of functioning according to which the components of metaphors, their relations, and the metaphors themselves function in larger contexts.

This approach necessarily focuses on the outcome of the creator and the object of attention of the knower. I assume throughout that even though metaphors occur as outcomes of some activity – usually that of human agents who intend to formulate the metaphor – these outcomes provoke responses on the part of those who apprehend them. What provokes responses is a phenomenon that has features that can be distinguished and viewed in relation to one another. In regard to the way that the terms of metaphors function meaningfully, the features of metaphor and their relations are conditions for interpreters' responses. And it is the conditions in the outcome or object, rather than the responses themselves, that will be our focus of attention. It is the ordering of the conditions for such responses that is taken as the structure of metaphor.

In addition to looking at the structure of metaphor, I shall also ask how metaphors are related to reality. In turning to this question, I shall concentrate on the reference rather than the sense or connotative meanings of metaphor. Reference as well as sense and content as well as form are needed to give metaphors their significances or import. This part of the discussion necessarily moves into ontology. My main purpose will be to sketch what an appropriate ontology would need to be and to suggest how it would affect the way that metaphors and, in turn, works of art may be understood.

The second major task of this book is to explore how my approach can be applied to the nonverbal arts, especially how their instances may be understood as metaphors. Accomplishing this purpose is needed because it should show a way to interpret art, and specific works of art as well, while affirming radical novelty. A view of metaphor that leaves room for creative newness is first a view of creativity that makes this puzzling topic as intelligible as is possible.

The first chapter establishes a framework for my account of metaphor. It indicates the assumptions that underlie my conception of metaphor and distinguishes metaphor from other forms of figurative speech. Two fundamentally opposed views of metaphors, the Com-

parison or Substitution Theory and the interaction view, are then outlined and discussed critically. These two views, especially the interaction view as it is generally known, are particularly relevant to my own.
The second chapter reconsiders the interaction view. In this expanded interactionist account, special attention is given to the complexities of interaction that exhibit features to be looked for in the
nonverbal arts. The third chapter develops the interactionist view according to an account of metaphorical reference. The fourth and fifth
chapters extend the account of metaphor to the nonverbal arts. The
fourth is concerned with the application of my view to the formal
characteristics of interacting components in works of art. The fifth
continues the application in terms of the account of reference offered
in the third chapter. The sixth chapter sketches an ontology based on
the idea of metaphorical reference. The appendix discusses how a
part of Charles S. Peirce's semiotics can be developed in support of
this ontology.

This summary of the chapters indicates that my two main concerns
will be addressed in stages. Nevertheless, because of the interrelations
among the relevant issues, my account throughout will need to anticipate, and later to refer back to, discussions of these issues. In other
words, as I proceed, I shall try to make evident the network of ideas
that underly and draw together the strands of the account as they are
introduced successively in each chapter. Let us turn to the initial step
in this effort.

1

A Framework for an Account of Metaphor

Preliminary Considerations

Metaphors and Symbols

Sometimes a literary work as a whole that offers a new insight may be regarded as a metaphor. Such works of art also have been characterized as symbols. For instance, it is common to regard art in medieval culture as symbolic. A Shakespearean tragedy is a symbol of human strengths and weaknesses. And in our own century, Albert Camus's *The Stranger* may be regarded as a symbol of the alienation of individual human beings from their societies. In turn, metaphors that occur in literary works are sometimes called symbols. Whether being metaphorical and being a symbol are equivalent depends, of course, on what is meant by *symbol,* as well as on what is meant by *metaphor.* In order to avoid possible misunderstanding and unnecessary objections on the part of those who take symbols to be the fundamental vehicles of linguistic creativity, I want to point out at the beginning why metaphor will be distinguished from symbol when *symbol* is given a common interpretation.

Although I have not yet described the ways in which metaphors and their components function, it is nevertheless possible at this stage to identify several conditions for distinguishing metaphors from symbols. Of course, there are different conceptions of symbols, and I do not intend to exclude the possibility that someone may use the term *symbol* in a way that is very close if not identical to my use of the term *metaphor.* For example, I think some of Susanne Langer's discussions of symbol suggest this possibility.

Following Langer's terminology, the kind of symbol that should be distinguished most completely from metaphor is the semiotic or conceptual symbol.[1] A semiotic or conceptual symbol is a sign that is humanly constructed and that refers to something independent of itself. A barber pole, for instance, is a symbol of a barber shop. What is referred to can be known apart from the symbol. The barber shop is also referred to by other symbols: by descriptions or by its name, among

---

[1] Susanne K. Langer, *Philosophy in a New Key: A Study in the Symbolism of Reason, Rite, and Art* (Cambridge, Mass.: Harvard University Press, 1942), pp. 53–78.

other things. A semiotic symbol, then, is replaceable. It should be obvious that being replaceable does not apply to metaphors unless we are convinced that paraphrases or explanations can be substituted for metaphors without loss of meaning.

The idea that there are substitute expressions for metaphors is integral to a view of metaphor that is contrary to my account to be developed. Some of the criticisms of this view will be mentioned later. Suffice it to say here that it has been contended that one of the marks of a metaphor is that its peculiar conjoining of terms is integral to its significance. This indispensability of the expression as it is initially articulated must be sustained if the expression is to be regarded as a metaphor. For example, "Man is the dream of a shadow" signifies something that cannot be said otherwise. "Man has no contact with reality" or "Man lives in ignorance of an obscure world" will not do any more than the alternative expression, "Man is a shadow of a dream." If this integral role of the manner of expression, or unique form of exhibiting significance, is lost, the metaphor has become dead or frozen. Thus the significance of the frozen or stereotypical "That is not my cup of tea" is not dependent on keeping the expression itself before one's attention. "Cup of tea" might be used as a symbol for preference or choice of activity, as the significance of "cup of tea," once the expression has been construed as not indicating something we might drink, is stable enough to enable one to use the expression for a single meaning that could be understood as referring to preference. Similar comments could be made about the expression "Achilles' heel." But if some fresh metaphors cannot thus be given one-to-one paraphrases or translations into literal statements, then these metaphors must function differently from semiotic symbols.

Another way to make the point is to note that semiotic symbols are fixed. They lack the multiplicity of meanings that can be generated from many metaphorical expressions. The generation of multiple meanings – the open-endedness, or what Ricoeur calls "plurisignification" – of metaphor must not be taken for ambiguity. Ambiguity is dependent on a condition of undecidability about which of several determinate meanings is appropriate. Open-endedness is a condition of the possibility of additional, accruing meaning. In contrast, once the significance of a semiotic symbol is understood, the symbol no longer is a dynamic source of further meanings.

The power to suggest a plurality of meanings is shared with another sense of *symbol*, proposed by Philip Wheelwright, that is closer to my sense of *metaphor* but that still should be distinguished from it: "A symbol, in general, is a relatively stable and repeatable element of perceptual experience, standing for some larger meaning or set of meanings which cannot be given, or not fully given, in perceptual experience itself."[2] The point of a possible equation of this kind of symbol with a metaphor lies in the condition that the significance of a symbol of the kind that Wheelwright characterizes here "cannot be fully given in perceptual experience." This suggests the openness of metaphors to a multiplicity of significances. Yet there is one difference: the repeatability of the symbol. It has stability even if the symbol is not "altogether exact."[3]

To be sure, metaphors can be repeated. But if they can be repeated with stable significance that is isomorphic in many different contexts, then they must be frozen. Wheelwright goes on to mark off symbols of the plurisignificant kind – which he calls "tensive symbols" and which are most clearly found in literature – from what he calls "stenosymbols," which are used typically in logic. I suspect that his tensive symbols are what I would call frozen metaphors. In any case, this is not the place to discuss Wheelwright's distinction or the implications of his idea of tensive symbols. The only point of considering the latter is to indicate that according to some interpretations of the idea of symbol, one may, and I think wrongly, understand metaphors and symbols – tensive symbols – as the same.

Two other views of symbol should be mentioned. These come just as close, and perhaps closer, to being equatable with metaphor. The two views are those of Carl Jung and, again, Susanne Langer.[4] Both Langer and Jung recognize a distinction between a semiotic symbol and a symbol proper. Yet there is a basic difference. In Langer's view, a symbol proper, or what she calls "the presentational symbol," is what it means, and what it means is internal or immanent to the symbol or the symbolic expression itself. In Jung's view, the apprehension of the meanings of a symbol proper also depends on the formation of the symbol. It cannot be known except through the expression. Yet the meaning is independent of the symbol. And this, I think, differentiates Jung's view from Langer's.

For both Langer and Jung, then, insofar as the symbol is constitutive, the symbol must create its meaning, and this meaning should not be knowable apart from the symbol. With respect to generating their own meanings, Langer's and Jung's symbols seem to be like metaphors. Yet, at least for Jung, this common feature is not sufficient to equate them. For if a symbol is understood, then it and its constituted

[2] Philip Wheelwright, *Metaphor and Reality* (Bloomington: Indiana University Press, 1962), p. 92.
[3] Ibid., p. 94. The symbol and its larger meaning are distinct from each other and are stable.
[4] Susanne K. Langer, *Philosophy in a New Key*, and *Feeling and Form* (New York: Scribner, 1953); Carl Jung, *Psychological Types*, trans. H. Godwin Baynes (London: K. Paul, Trench, Trubner & Co. Ltd. 1923), pp. 601–10. I have discussed these in "Art and Symbol," *The Review of Metaphysics* 15 (1961): 256–70.

meaning will acquire an independence from each other with respect to the context in which the symbol is found. The symbol can be transferred without change from its original context to another context. It takes on a function that enables it to appear in different instances and to denote repeatable unities in experience. For example, the cross is a symbol that denotes various things, for Christians and non-Christians, that can be found in a variety of contexts – in a Gothic cathedral, a Protestant church, or as an emblem on a necklace. Or to use another part of Jung's theory, a symbol can have as its meaning an archetypal factor of the unconscious – a factor that psychoanalytic theory can identify, giving us access to it other than through the symbol alone. In short, for Jung, a symbol can be put into a system.

As already suggested, there is a way in which a metaphor likewise can be transferred and become a participant in a system. But when this happens, it has been frozen and made fit to be an addition to the language or system of symbols – both steno-symbols and tensive symbols, as Wheelwright's terminology puts it. The freezing of a metaphor's significance is illustrated in many words in our language. For example, the words *ruin* and *understand* are now symbols in the more fixed sense. When they were introduced into the language, each was derived from words with meanings different from those they now have. Owen Barfield has offered an extended account of the growth of meaning of the word *ruin,* showing how both ordinary usage and poetry contributed to these changes.[5] In any case, however *ruin, understand* and other terms originated, they now function as signs that are part of the system of our language. It may be that all symbols arise from metaphorical creations. In different forms, this has been proposed by others, for instance, James Edie and Mary Hesse.[6] In any case, if Jung were to grant that symbols in his sense originate in metaphors, and if Langer were to say that her presentational symbols retain unique relations to their meanings, then the only difference at issue here between symbol and metaphor would be verbal.

Metaphors and Analogies

A second preliminary point must be mentioned: Metaphor and analogy should be distinguished. Some of the criticisms to be offered later

[5] For a discussion of the growth of language, including a consideration of *ruin* and other examples, see Owen Barfield, *Poetic Diction: A Study in Meaning* (Middletown, Conn.: Wesleyan University Press, 1973) (first published in 1928).

[6] James Edie, "Expression and Metaphor," *Philosophy and Phenomenological Research* 23 (1963): 538–61; in particular, see Mary Hesse's most recent statement, in *The Construction of Reality,* with Michael A. Arbib (Cambridge, England: Cambridge University Press, 1986), chap. 8.

of theories that treat metaphors as disguised analogies presuppose this distinction, but at this stage I shall not discuss the issue at length. It is necessary only to comment briefly on a feature of analogies, as they are sometimes understood, that, I think, marks them off from metaphors. An analogy depends for its significance wholly on similarities common to antecedent significances. The point of an analogy is to make a comparison. A model of a machine is an analog for the machine because of common features of the two, even if the model were only *like* the machine with respect to its structure or relationships of elements. If analogies attain their significance through their dependence on relations among common features, then they do not introduce new significance into the world. They can be reduced to what was known antecedently.

Another way to put the point is by noting that an analogy can be expressed as a complex simile. Thus if metaphors are implicit analogies, they are elliptical similes. And such a consequence invokes objections that this interpretation "impoverishes the metaphor."[7] By "impoverishes," the objector means more than that a simile has less expressive impact, is less interesting, or is not surprising. Metaphors are impoverished when they are reduced to similes, because similes move toward closing the relationships between meanings put together in metaphor. To say "Life is like a dream" indicates that some one or more characteristics that might be common to lives and dreams are fuzzy experiences, for instance. "Life is a dream," on the other hand, opens up the relationship between life and dreams, because here there is an identity of wholes – life as such and being a dream as such.

On the other hand, similes may have metaphorical roots. As Mary Hesse observes, "A sharp wind is like a knife" does not *just* mean that the wind is like a knife, unless "knife" itself is understood metaphorically.[8] The point is that "sharp" does not apply in the same way to a wind as it does to a knife. "Smiling," in "the flower is like a smiling face," does not apply in the same way to flowers as it does to faces, nor are there any properties that clearly are common as resemblances between faces and flowers. The simile itself depends on a metaphorical application.

As in the case of symbol, I would not insist on the distinction between analogy and metaphor if one were to offer a conception of analogy that did not treat it as merely a comparison. If one means by the concept of analogy a figure of speech that creates a new significance understood not only with the reference to antecedent relations

---

[7] Mary Hesse, "The Cognitive Claims of Metaphor," in J. P. Noppen, ed., *Metaphor and Religion, Theolinguistics 2*, ed. J. Poor (Brussels: Noppen, 1984), p. 30; a revised version of this paper will appear in the *Journal of Speculative Philosophy*.
[8] Ibid.

but also with reference to a special way in which terms foreign to one another are interlocked, then analogy as well as symbol may indeed be fundamentally metaphorical. This would be to regard analogy as having metaphorical roots. Nelson Goodman suggests as much for simile, which explicitly compares things, when like Hesse, he emphasizes that saying that two disparate things are alike depends on a metaphorical relation, a relation not already given as a set of known likenesses. Citing the example of saying a picture is sad, Goodman argues: "What the simile says in effect is that person and picture are alike in being sad, the one literally and the other metaphorically. Instead of a metaphor reducing to a simile, simile reduces to metaphor; or rather, the difference between simile and metaphor is negligible."[9]

This view seems consistent with my attempt to look to metaphors to see how language can function creatively. But other problems arise if analogies do what metaphors do. Surely those who want to reduce similes, analogies, or symbols to creative metaphorical speech would not also want to exclude the possibility that some figures of speech are noncreative or that some figurative expressions are figurative by virtue of the way their components function that is different from the way components of metaphors function. Even if one insists that every instance of figurative language is creative, we nevertheless will need ways to distinguish the various ways that analogies, similes, symbols, and metaphors function in being creative. I do not raise these points in order to reject the view that metaphors are more fundamental than are other figures of speech. But I do want to resist the reduction of all figurative language to metaphorical speech.

Creative and Frozen Metaphors

A third consideration that should be faced at the outset concerns the a restriction on the kind of metaphors to be studied. The examples discussed briefly in the Introduction and the remarks about the distinctions among metaphors, symbols, and analogies should make obvious what will be at issue. But I want to be sure that there is no misunderstanding. I shall examine the clearest cases of the most radical kind of metaphorical expressions. Throughout, my focus will be on metaphors that are creations – creations in exemplifying fundamentally new and valuable significances, which in turn themselves create or generate new significances. The metaphors at issue are those that contribute to and advance a tradition, whether this is the tradition of ordinary language, a literary and a nonverbal art tradition, or the development of scientific theory.

[9] Goodman, *Languages of Art*, pp. 77–8.

Metaphors that are regarded as creations and as creative are frequently thought of as "fresh," "innovative," and "enlightening," in relation to the contexts in which they first appear. Yet not all expressions called metaphors seem to be creations or creative, at least not to the same degree. "Uncreative metaphors," if there are any, are not necessarily so-called dead metaphors, some of which may once have been highly creative. This is why these latter should more properly be called dormant or frozen. As frozen, they can be interpreted analogically, because their fixed significance can be related to other expressions with fixed significance. The point here, however, is that we need only agree that at least some metaphors are, or were, striking creations – as were, for example, root metaphors such as "the world is a machine" or "the world is an organism" or as are some metaphors that appear in poetry, such as the example, "Man is the dream of a shadow."

It should be noted, too, that although my main focus is to be on metaphor in the arts, it will be helpful later to deal briefly with metaphors in science. This turn in the discussion will raise the issue of how creative metaphors relate to the world or to what we consider to be reality. However, I shall waive the issue of how the function of metaphors in the arts may be fundamentally different from their function in the sciences. My only concern in turning to the sciences as well as the arts will be to examine one function, that of providing insight into some aspect of the world that seems to be shared by science and art. The consideration of metaphor in science is appropriate, too, because some of the major theories of metaphor use scientific metaphor as their model and because the issue of how metaphors connect with something "real" is most obvious in science.

Distinguishing Figurative from Literal Expressions

Although the problem of maintaining the distinction between literal and metaphorical expressions has been mentioned and will emerge again later, I emphasize that the distinction may not be hard and fast, especially if one theorizes about the origin of language rather than about what we find here and now. Owen Barfield has raised this possibility, pointing out the difficulties of determining what was once literal and what was once figurative. He discusses how words that sometimes are said to be based on metaphorical transferals from literal meanings can be interpreted instead as literal extensions of what is now taken as metaphorical meaning.[10] For example, *spirit* might just as well have originated in a nonmaterial reference as in a material

---

[10] See "The Meaning of the Word 'Literal'," in *Metaphor and Symbol*.

reference, as *wind,* thought to be its literal forebear, must have come from an immaterial reference. Otherwise, the immaterial meaning of spirit could not have been understood. However, what is necessary as a premise for my discussion is not an interpretation or historical theory of the origin of language. What is necessary is the acknowledgment that the function of some expressions can be distinguished as figurative from others that are not figurative. Those distinguished as nonfigurative approach, if they do not realize, a definite interpretability on the basis of their being traceable to fixed meanings that can be articulated according to accepted grammatical rules, already understood and familiar. Whether literal expressions need to be proved to be true or false through some testing procedure need not be decided. We need only see that some expressions follow established conventions and meanings that are at least relevant to truth and falsity conditions previously assigned to those meanings.

Expressions are used and interpreted literally when they do not seem to require construal or special considerations for their interpretations. This, of course, is not a criterion for deciding when an expression needs to be construed. I doubt that such a criterion can be given. In any case, the meanings or the uses of literal expressions are understood as given directly by the expressions themselves. As Barfield suggests, if we take something literally, then we do not need to understand a tenor or meaning distinct from the meaning of the vehicle of expression.

Whether language originated in literal words and/or sentences that were based on truth conditions or, instead, on what we would now, looking back, construe as figurative conditions (as Giambattista Vico proposed), need not be settled in order to distinguish between present-day literal and nonliteral uses of language. Thus, by *literal expression* I mean an expression that conforms to conventional standards of usage and, where appropriate, to direct testing by standards of truth and falsity. On the other hand, in accordance with such expectations, each metaphorical expression is in some context incongruous with straightforward, literal speech.

As I indicated, Mary Hesse has proposed the thesis that there is a sense in which all language is metaphorical; yet she also insists that we do recognize differences in what we take to be literal from what we take to be figurative applications of terms. For instance, "the point of a pin" is understood as in some sense literal, in contrast with "the point of the argument." If the distinction can be understood in this case, in which *point* in *point of an argument* is a frozen metaphor, certainly the distinction will be all the more forceful in cases in which the metaphor is less frozen – is fresh and so intimately bound up with the way of expression, as in a poetic context, that a translation or paraphrase seems to miss the mark.

One symptom of literal as distinct from metaphorical or creatively figurative expressions is that literal expressions can be paraphrased without loss of significance. It is important, however, to insist that because a paraphrase may not be fully adequate, what resists it is nevertheless meaningful and has cognitive significance, as are so-called literal expressions, though in the case of metaphors, this meaning cannot be expressed in a way equivalent to some previously expressible meanings.

Of course, it can be and has been argued that even so-called literal expressions (assertive and informative) cannot be translated unless they are logical expressions or statements formed for technical purposes in which the uses of the component terms are rigorously restricted.[11] I do not challenge this way of regarding all except logical–technical, literal, expressions, but I do think we should notice that this point indeed recommends a special way of regarding literal expressions. It draws attention away from the common communicative significance of such expressions and toward aspects of expressions that do not fall within standard propositional expectations that concern what is the case or what conforms to conditions of truth and falsity. Thus the advocate of the untranslatability of all nonlogical technical expressions can be asked, What is the function of that part of a literal expression that cannot be translated? If it is rhetorical or emotive enhancement, then what cannot be translated is not what is of cognitive significance. But if what cannot be translated in literal expressions contributes to the cognitive function of those expressions, then presumably, it will perform the same function as do figurative expressions, that is, make them unique. This function may be said to be subordinate and thus not important to the main significance of the literal expression; in which case, we should not care about any cognitive increments that cannot be translated. On the other hand, it might be claimed that this function may contribute in a way that changes the main significance of the literal expression. If the latter is the position affirmed, then it seems that all that is being pointed out is that any literal expression may, if we wish, be construed to function in the way that figurative expressions are supposed to function when they succeed in being cognitively significant, thus showing us something that could not have been shown otherwise. And it is appropriate to ask how they can do this without transforming antecedent meanings, or

[11] See, for example, Israel Scheffler, *Beyond the Letter: A Philosophical Inquiry into Ambiguity, Vagueness and Metaphor in Language* (London: Routledge & Kegan Paul, 1979).

doing what looks like what metaphors do, that is, require the construal of literal expressions so that they do not mean what they obviously would be taken to mean literally. The issue of the paraphrasability of literal expressions will be considered again in the next chapter.

With these preliminary distinctions in mind, I shall now review some of the ways that metaphor has been approached theoretically. The phrase "some of the ways" means that the review will be limited. First, it will be concerned with what may be broadly called philosophical approaches. Second, it will be limited by selecting what I believe are representative views that fall under two fundamental but opposed presuppositions about the nature of explanation appropriate to metaphor. Finally the opposing approaches to metaphor that I have chosen contrast with one another in ways that also bear on the account I shall propose.

A Review of Fundamental Approaches to Metaphor

The task of reviewing the many theories of metaphor proposed even within the past fifteen or twenty years would be enormous. Fortunately, such a review is unnecessary. Others have summarized and criticized the most widely known theories, and I shall rest content knowing that these summaries and criticisms have been made.[12] However, I cannot avoid concentrating on those issues raised by the theories of metaphor that are particularly relevant to my own view. I shall try to bring these issues to light by first mentioning the earliest known accounts that are currently at the basis of a relatively extensive systematic approach to the topic of metaphor. This earliest account is Aristotle's. The reason for starting with Aristotle, it must be emphasized, is not historical but, rather, because Aristotle's view has been so important to determining the main lines of the controversy between the two fundamental conflicting approaches, which, as I shall explain later, may be called the *originativist* and the *reductionist* views. Moreover, whatever one's purpose, it would be an oversight in an account of metaphor to ignore Aristotle's seminal definition.

Aristotle's Seminal View of Metaphor

Probably Aristotle's best-known summary of his definition of metaphor is "A metaphor consists in giving the thing a name that belongs

[12]Cf. J. J. A. Mooij, *A Study of Metaphor, on the Nature of Metaphorical Expressions, with Special References to Their Reference* (Amsterdam: North Holland, 1976), chap. 4. Also, Ricoeur's major work on metaphor includes a vast number of references and frequent brief critiques of the views of those with whom he agrees or disagrees: see *The Rule of Metaphor*.

to something else. . . ."[13] In this definition metaphors substitute names by transferring them from one reference to another. Aristotle then classifies kinds of transference, saying that it may be "either from genus to species, or from species to genus, or from species to species, or on grounds of analogy."[14] The classification, of course, serves as the basis for later distinctions among figures of speech, synecdoche, metonymy, and, as made explicit by Aristotle, analogy. The last type is of particular interest, because as already pointed out, it suggests one of the ways that theorists interpret and try to explain metaphors. Probably the most widespread view is that metaphors are implied analogies or elliptical similes. Although in this definition Aristotle treats analogy as only one kind of metaphor – thus bypassing the issue of whether the transfer that he attributes to metaphor transcends analogy – he does indicate that metaphorical figures of speech are, at bottom, comparisons. He also suggests this idea in another place, where he considers both simile and metaphor and states that metaphors are more powerful than similes because they are more condensed.[15] Furthermore, as Paul Ricoeur points out, in the *Poetics* definition, comparison for Aristotle seems implicit in the notion of transfer, as comparison is what brings two terms together, although this does not imply that a metaphor is an elliptical simile.[16]

I think there are reasons for concluding that Aristotle resisted this inclination to reduce metaphor to antecedently known likenesses. Instead, there is a suggestion that he regarded them as producing something new, new at least in the sense in which a discernment of formerly unrecognized relations or properties might be said to be new. For he does remark that it takes genius, an unteachable ability, to see common characteristics in things considered more different than alike. However, interpreting Aristotle is not the point here. What is the point is the widespread conception of metaphor as implied analogy or comparison and, until relatively recently, only the occasional tendency to resist its reduction to literal expression. In this connection, it may be helpful to see that what was referred to earlier as the two fundamental but opposing approaches to understanding metaphor can be framed in the view that all metaphors are basically comparisons and in the view that denies this. I shall next briefly describe these two approaches.

[13] *Poetics*, 1457b, trans. Ingram Bywater in *The Basic Works of Aristotle,* ed. Richard McKeon (New York: Random House, 1941).
[14] Ibid.
[15] *Rhetoric*, 1406b.
[16] Ricoeur, *The Rule of Metaphor*, p. 24. Ricoeur offers a penetrating discussion of Aristotle's views and their relations to the traditions of poetics and rhetoric that followed him.

Two Poles: Originativism and Reductionism

Whatever the discipline or purpose guiding them, interpretations of metaphor concern a relationship between metaphorical expressions and their contexts. These interpretations can best be understood with reference to two extremes or poles, which I shall call *reductionism* and *originativism*. I acknowledge that the views I shall take as representative of these two extremes do not include Donald Davidson's challenge to interactionism and, for that matter, all views that affirm that there is a cognitive content in metaphors. There is, I think, reason to align Davidson's view with a kind of "seeing-as" view, which regards the prompted effect as a new way of seeing. Without further understanding of whether this newness is irreducible and some account of the relation of the metaphorical expression and its effect – just how can a metaphor which Davidson recommends be taken literally yield something not metaphorical and new? – I see no way to decide with which pole it is more closely associated. In any case, Davidson's view that metaphors are literal and effective not because they have special cognitive content but because they prompt insight rejects the semantic approach to metaphor. A response to his approach would take this study in a different direction.[17]

On the one hand, the reductionist interprets metaphors as cognitive expressions translatable into analogies, similes, or, in general, "literal" language – language that meets antecedently accepted standards of significance. On the other hand, the originativist believes that some metaphors can create unique insights and that these metaphors are irreducible with respect to the antecedents in their contexts. This view assumes at least some metaphors are creations that constitute the things, qualities, or relationships they signify. Metaphors are interpreted as creations of linguistic meanings. In its strongest form, this view also regards metaphors as creating constituents of the world.

It should be obvious that the originativist perspective offers only one view – although I think it takes the most important and certainly the most philosophically extreme form – which resists the idea that metaphors are essentially transferred meanings and comparisons. Certainly, nonreductionism and originativism are not necessarily the

---

[17] I base my comments on Davidson on his "What Metaphors Mean," *Critical Inquiry* 5 (1978):31–47. I should add here that a variety of terms have been used to classify approaches to metaphors, and these share much the same general point of the distinction that I make. However, although I am not happy about introducing still another set of terms, it is probably more efficient, if not more accurate, to adopt the terms most useful for the account of metaphor I shall propose. The term *originativism* might seem unnecessary and awkward. I admit that it is awkward. But it, or some other term that probably would be equally awkward, is necessary to highlight what is at stake in the opposition between the position it names and reductionism.

same. A nonreductionist, for instance, might hold an emotivist view, which claims that metaphorical expressions are simply nonsensical; only with respect to their emotional effect do they make sense. The emotivist view must be considered further later, once the main opposing views have been better distinguished.

In attacking the issues that are of special concern in this study, it will be helpful to select several fairly recent views that contrast with one another most explicitly on the question whether metaphors are creative. I shall focus on what has been called *interactionism*, taking this as the prime example of originativism. As the model for interactionism, I shall use Max Black's widely discussed version of interactionism, and for the opposing approach, I shall take John Searle's recent criticism of interactionism.[18] In addition, I shall later refer briefly to still another approach which has been called *extensionalism* and which introduces philosophical nominalism to the issues. A brief sketch of the various positions that fall under the two fundamental approaches will provide a framework within which to concentrate on the key writers. In addition, special attention will be given to the origin of interactionism, at least as it arose in the Anglo-American tradition.

Beardsley's Classification of Theories

Monroe Beardsley has classified and discussed the major approaches to understanding metaphor.[19] Because Beardsley's classification is relatively well known and available and because it outlines the views so clearly, it will be convenient to use it and relate it to the originativist and reductionist positions. According to Beardsley, there are four systematic views: the Emotive Theory, the Comparison Theory, the Iconic Signification Theory, which he says has grown out of the second, and finally, the Verbal-opposition Theory, the last of which is the basis of his own view of metaphor. It is interesting that he omits any reference to what has been identified as interactionism. This omission could be explained as the result of a different use of terminology. Thus, interactionism might fall under the Verbal-opposition Theory. However,

---

[18] Black, "More about Metaphor," and in his initial discussion of the topic, "Metaphor," *Proceedings of the Aristotelean Society*, N. S. 55 (1954–5): 273–94, which also appears in *Models and Metaphor: Studies in Language and Philosophy* (Ithaca, N.Y.: Cornell University Press, 1962). When referring to the early statement, I shall use the pagination in *Models and Metaphor.* John Searle, "Metaphor," in *Expression and Meaning* (Cambridge, England: Cambridge University Press, 1979), pp. 76–116. Reprinted in Ortony, ed., *Metaphor and Thought*, pp. 92–123; and in Mark Johnson, ed., *Philosophical Perspectives on Metaphor* (Minneapolis: University of Minnesota Press, 1981). I shall use the pagination in *Metaphor and Thought.*

[19] Monroe Beardsley, "Metaphor," in Paul Edwards, ed., *The Encyclopedia of Philosophy* (New York: Macmillan, 1972), vol. 5, pp. 284–9.

this conclusion is questionable, as Beardsley identifies his own view with the Verbal-opposition Theory, and elsewhere he suggests that he is not an interactionist. Despite this question about where Beardsley would put interactionism in relation to his classification, I shall assume that it is a species of the Verbal-opposition Theory. Beardsley's own theory, as he sees it, then, would be another species.

The Emotive Theory, already alluded to in the preceding comments on nonreductionism, sees metaphors as meaningful in nonliteral ways only in the sense that they are interesting and sometimes powerful because of their emotional expressiveness. They are at least entertaining in their nonsensical way of saying something. The Comparison Theory has been referred to in regard to views that construe metaphors as implied analogies or as expressions that assert antecedent relations. Aristotle's example "the empty cup of Ares" illustrates an expression that a comparison theorist would regard as based on a resemblance between Dionysus' possessing a filled cup, which serves as a kind of emblem of Dionysus, and Ares' possessing a shield. The Iconic Signification Theory sees metaphors as bringing together, through reference to iconic signs, expressions that refer to differing things in differing domains but that, although drawn from different domains, nevertheless have similarities. To use Beardsley's example, we can say that "time is a river" refers to two things that in some respects are similar, for example, one-dimensional directionality. The fourth class of theories is the Verbal-opposition Theory. This theory, which is essentially Beardsley's own, distinguishes marginal meanings (or suggested connotations) from central meanings (the connotations of dictionary meanings). Metaphors play on the transfer of some marginal meanings of one term in a metaphor to the central meaning of the other term. This view will be taken up later. Beardsley's swiftly made criticisms of the first three of the four views center on the failure of each to do justice to two features of metaphor. The first is the tension generated by the linking of terms or expressions that belong to different domains and that therefore are not in harmony with established ways of understanding. The second feature is the meaningfulness or intelligibility of metaphors. Let me quickly reinforce and extend, in my own terms, Beardsley's reasons for objecting to the first three theories.[20]

The Emotive Theory. Beardsley rejects the Emotive Theory chiefly because it does not grant that there is cognitive meaning in metaphors, at least with respect to what is metaphorical when two disparate mean-

---

[20] Beardsley offers more extended criticism in *Aesthetics: Problems in the Philosophy of Criticism* (New York: Harcourt, Brace, 1958).

ings are brought together. Beardsley insists (and I think rightly) that metaphors differ cognitively from expressions of nonsense. But is there a reason we could offer to the emotivist for insisting that there is cognitive significance in the apparent nonsense of at least some metaphors? Let us go beyond Beardsley and pursue this question about emotivism for a moment, as emotivism offers a fundamental challenge to the interactionist account of metaphor: that metaphors have their own special, new, cognitive significance.

In the final analysis, there is no way to demonstrate meaningfulness if one does not recognize it. For a stubborn skeptic, this would be true of even the most obvious example of clarity, such as the intelligibility of a deductive demonstration, if the skeptic denies the law of noncontradiction. The one who insists on intelligibility, however, can try to find ways in which the skeptic – in this case, the emotivist – inadvertently admits intelligibility. I think emotivists at least come close to such an admission, because they must presuppose that something intelligible is associated with the emotional expressiveness of metaphors. They must at least trivially, because to recognize unintelligibility is to recognize intelligibility contradicted. But more important, intelligibility is also acknowledged whenever it is recognized that there is incoherence or incongruence of some kind in the literal interpretation of metaphors, and at the same time, it is recognized that different metaphors are differently exciting in accordance with the ways they conflict with intelligibility. If something intelligible were not discerned, the difference in unintelligibility and consequent emotional expressiveness would not be recognized. All metaphors would be the same in the way they affect us. For instance, the expressions "liquid chains" and "colorless orange" are not unintelligible in the same way but, rather, in intelligibly different ways. To be sure, this point does not yield a positive reason for seeing significance in metaphors. It gives no criterion for explaining and explicating significance. But it does, I think, indicate that something more than emotional expressiveness is recognized when the "nonsense" of a metaphor is encountered.

Moreover, as Paul Ricoeur has pointed out, there is reason to regard emotional expressiveness as itself containing cognitive significance. Emotion is linked to objects. Mikel Dufrenne has argued that we can locate cognitive significance in emotional qualities perceived as objectively present for aesthetic attention – serenity, agitation, and despair, exhibited as qualifying aspects of colors, lines, shapes, and textures in works of art.[21] Emotivism does not see that its own way of

---

[21] Ricoeur, *The Rule of Metaphor*, pp. 227–28; "The Metaphorical Process as Cognition, Imagination, and Feeling," *Critical Inquiry* 5 (1978) 143–59; Mikel Dufrenne, *Phenomenology of Aesthetic Experience*, trans. Edward S. Casey (Evanston, Ill.: Northwestern University Press, 1973).

interpreting metaphors, carried a step further, would give back significance — significance gained out of both the force and the kind of impact that come from what is apparently nonsensical.

The Comparison Theory. The Comparison Theory and its derivative, the Iconic Signification Theory, attribute intelligibility to metaphor. However, as Beardsley points out, they cannot explain the tension in metaphor. In interpreting metaphors as implicit or elliptical similes, the Comparison Theory claims that metaphors suppress the *like* as *as* that makes explicit a comparison between subject term and modifier. Similarly, the Iconic Signification Theory regards some one, or a set of, resembling characteristics as common to referents of the metaphor's main terms. In both cases, metaphors are construed so that they lose the tension that initially provoked attention. Beardsley argues that if metaphors are explained by interpreting them as comparisons, they will not be special in relation to nonmetaphorical language. What Beardsley does not go on to say, however, is that in denying that metaphors are special, these two theories deny novelty. If familiar literal expressions can be substituted for metaphors, then metaphors will reduce to what was antecedently known.

It is interesting that Beardsley does not formulate his criticism in terms of this implied reductionism. Perhaps his passing over the point is an indication that he too may be a reductionist, in the final analysis. That he may be can be seen in a later article.[22] Although he claims that his theory, which is a form of the Verbal-opposition Theory, accounts for the creative aspect of metaphors, his account falls back on an appeal to antecedent "marginal" meanings. I shall return to this point later. But first it is necessary to describe further Beardsley's classification and critiques of theories in order to use them as a larger framework within which to fit reductionism and creationism.

As we observed, the Comparison Theory and the Iconic Signification Theory imply that each metaphor can be translated into one or more other expressions without loss of significance. Thus, these views of metaphors can be said to fall under what Max Black calls the "substitution view."[23] A metaphor has a substitute: The substitute is a literal statement, expressible as an analogy, a simile, or a paraphrase, and in the last case, the substitution is a series of literal statements proposed to explain the full cognitive meaning or significance of the metaphor.

---

[22] Monroe Beardsley, "The Metaphorical Twist," in *Philosophy and Phenomenological Research* 22 (1962): 293–307.

[23] Black uses this term in "More about Metaphor," in *Metaphor and Thought*, and in his initial discussion of the topic, "Metaphor," in *Models and Metaphor*, p. 31.

This way of subsuming the Comparison Theory under the substitution view is introduced for two reasons. It indicates the way that comparison may be thought to ground metaphor. And it emphasizes the point that whatever the translation – into similes, analogies, or paraphrases – metaphors are construed in terms of the reductionist view. Metaphors can be reduced just to the extent that a substitution for them can be given. And to view metaphors as being significant because they reveal comparisons is to construe them so that they lose their force as metaphorical. They are dispensable. This way of putting the point does not add substantively to what was said earlier about reductionism. But it does call attention to one of the principles of the originativist view, namely, that no paraphrase, and likewise no simile or analogy, can adequately disclose the significance of a creative metaphor.

There is a tradition of interpretation that rejects the claim that metaphors and, more generally, works of art can be explicated without loss of significance, whether by paraphrase or analysis. As we shall notice later and as already indicated, Max Black is within this tradition. For the moment, however, let me cite Stanley Cavell's argument against the adequacy of paraphrase, although I should point out that in citing Cavell, I do not mean to suggest that he would agree with my claim that there is cognitive content in what cannot be paraphrased. Taking an example from Shakespeare's *Romeo and Juliet*, Cavell argues that the meaning of Romeo's "Juliet is the sun" cannot be explained or formulated by any finite series of paraphrases. One may say that it means "Juliet is the warmth of his world," "his day begins with her," or "only in her nourishment can he grow."[24] But these meanings cannot substitute for the original. They are not enough. Every summary of sentences intended to give a paraphrase is recognized as needing an "and so on." In short, the metaphor in its initial formulation is indispensable.

Considering one of the examples offered in the Introduction, "The world is an unweeded garden," it should be noted, too, that any attempt to translate its meaning encounters two crucial problems. First, in this case, the expression is context bound, and so any so-called explication would be inadequate without taking into account the surrounding aesthetic environment. But more important, even if we look for meaning in the expression taken out of context, the terms will be drawn from domains that are (or were) radically different from one another. The metaphor depends not simply on similarities but also on dissimilarities. As suggested, Aristotle did not so clearly support a

[24] Stanley Cavell, "Aesthetic Problems of Modern Philosophy" in Max Black, ed., *Philosophy in America* (Ithaca, N.Y.: Cornell University Press, 1967), chap. 4, pp. 74–97.

comparison theory, as is usually thought, at least in any simple form. He called attention to the role of dissimilarities and added that one cannot learn a technique for constructing metaphors – for seeing similarity in dissimilars – but instead must have intuitive perception. The command of metaphor is a gift and cannot be taught.

Aristotle's insight reappears in another form in Black's criticism of the comparison view. Black observes that in comparisons of items (i.e., in the case of metaphors rather than in formal or scientific statements) a likeness is imprecise and may not even be present until the metaphor is formed.[25] In the final analysis, however, the issue between the substitution, or reductionist, view and the originativist view (which sees the original and specific formulation of creative metaphors as indispensable) turns on the question whether language can grow qualitatively. Can language evolve in the sense that meanings and references not present implicitly or explicitly in the language at one time are introduced into it for the first time? Or is language preformed so that the first spoken words imply all the significance found in each language in the present and in the future? Such an alternative presupposes a commitment to a complete determinism. I shall not argue against this view here. Suffice it to say that determinism cannot be demonstrated and requires a self-sufficient, predetermined origin that is no more explicable than is a view that affirms the introduction of real (irreducible) novelty in at least some cases of change. If language can evolve in a way that is more than a process of making explicit what was already there, then some instances of linguistic expression must function in the way that the creationist says metaphors function.

Let us now turn to one of the main theories of metaphor, interactionism, which in its extreme form clearly belongs to the originativist view. As an entry into interactionism, the ideas of I. A. Richards, who laid the groundwork for it, should be considered. We then will be able to see what Beardsley's Verbal-opposition Theory shares with interactionism. Once this is understood, Max Black's interactionism can be dealt with as a primary representative of orginativism, which has as its direct opponent a thesis by John Searle.[26]

Interactionism

Origins in I. A. Richards's Theory. I. A. Richards is the chief forerunner of interactionism in the Anglo-American tradition. In fact, Max Black

[25] Black, "Metaphor," p. 37.
[26] Searle, "Metaphor."

regards his own interactionism as "a development and modification of I. A. Richards's valuable insights."[27] Richards refers to "the inter-animation of words" to cover the way that words depend on one another when they function in metaphorical sentences. The degree of interdependence varies. Scientific and technical contexts use words that have independent meanings because such words have fixed definitions. For example, "Water boils at 212 degrees" uses terms that have fixed meanings so that they can be repeated in other contexts without loss of meaning. And they and the sentence can be replaced with expressions that refer to the same fact. By contrast, in poetry, words are most dependent on one another. "The world is an un-weeded garden," for example, uses words that lose much of whatever prior precision they had. These intimate relations among words are particularly strong in metaphors. Thus the terms of metaphors, the key terms, which Richards calls "tenor" and "vehicle" and which initially stand in tension, interact with one another. And this interaction is the condition for a meaning not carried by any of the terms as they function independently of the metaphorical context.

We should note that Richards lapses at least once into what looks like a comparison view, because he wants a ground for metaphor, and this seems to lie in something in common that is referred to by the terms.[28] It seems that a rationalist motive to find connections even for metaphors has infected Richards's view.[29] Yet Richards resists reductionism, I think, when he acknowledges that in the final analysis we may not be able to say how metaphors work. Thus the terms of metaphors generate meaning through internal but dynamic relations. The terms are "copresent" with one another and result in a meaning "not attainable without their interaction." The key terms influence and change one another. For example, *under* and *stand* were mutually influential when they first came together to form the word *understand*. *Blue* and *mood* affected each other when joined in *blue mood: Blue* no longer refers just to a color, and *mood* no longer refers to an emotional state that is devoid of the qualitiative enrichment contributed by its reference to a color.

It is important to observe that Richards clearly repudiates the idea that the terms of metaphors are related only through common meanings or resemblances. Interaction is not confined to the resemblance among things referred to by the key words in metaphors. To illustrate this, he explains: "When Hamlet uses the word *crawling* [speaking to Polonius] its force comes not only from whatever resemblances to ver-

[27] Black, "More About Metaphor," p. 27; Richards, *The Philosophy of Rhetoric.*
[28] Max Black also calls attention to this lapse in "Metaphor," p. 39.
[29] See Richards, *The Philosophy of Rhetoric,* p. 117.

min it brings in but at least equally from the differences that resist
and control the influences of their resemblances."[30] Disparities are as
operative as similarities are. And the role of disparities opens the significance of metaphors so that they can act to bring out resultant
meanings not given in the meanings of the terms they bring together.
Describing the functions of differences and similarities in metaphors
will be part of the first major task of this book.

An interaction view should be expected to include some consideration of the distinctions among the kinds of terms, or, more accurately,
the kinds of functions of terms, that can be identified in metaphors.
As indicated, Richards's view explores interaction with reference to
the distinction between tenor and vehicle. This distinction, which is
fairly well known, is not as clear as it is sometimes taken to be, but I
shall not attempt to clarify Richards's meaning. It is difficult, however, to see how the distinction between tenor and vehicle is to be
applied consistently to examples. Further, as it is formulated by Richards, the distinction is not required for an explanation of my own
view. Black himself employs a different way of distinguishing the
functions of terms, and I think his terminology is more helpful. Let
us then move on to Black's version of interactionism, though not before glancing at Beardsley's Verbal-opposition Theory, which in some
important ways overlaps interactionism.

Monroe Beardsley's Verbal-opposition Theory. Beardsley's own theory resembles Richards's interactionism in calling attention to the tension
attributable to the relations of the main terms in metaphorical expressions as well as in recognizing a second level of meaning to which
construal is forced on the hearer or reader because of this tension.
An expression taken to be metaphorical is regarded as differentiating
between two sets of properties in the intension or signification of its
major terms.[31] These two clashing sets of properties are what Beardsley
calls the "central" meanings (dictionary or accepted meanings) as distinct from its "marginal" meanings (remotely associated meanings).
When a term is combined with others, there is a logical opposition
between the central meaning of one term and the central meaning of
the other terms. This opposition alerts us to the possibility that an
expression may be a metaphor and that we need to shift from its central to its marginal meaning. For example, the expression "spiteful

---

[30] Ibid., p. 127.
[31] I rely here on Beardsley's summary of his view in "The Metaphorical Twist." The
more extensive explanation of the theory is given in his *Aesthetics.*

sun" alerts us because the properties and behavior of the sun do not include or presuppose (or have not included and presupposed) properties and behavior attributed to spiteful people. The modifier "spiteful" must be given a "metaphorical twist." The interpreter of a metaphor, then, must look for connotations or marginal meanings that can be attributed without contradiction or falsity of application to what the central meaning of the other term conveys. In his earliest formulation in which he refers to his own view as the "Controversion Theory," Beardsley states: The astute reader (or listener) "must look about for another possible meaning. If he can find it among the connotations of the modifier, he can give meaning to the whole expression."[32]

If this last point is taken as it stands, Beardsley's view looks like a version of the Comparison Theory in the sense that one should be able to say what a metaphor means by translating it into a comparison of the subject and the modifier with respect to the connotations that the astute interpreter finds. However, Beardsley does address the question whether he should grant more – more in the sense that opens his theory to the acknowledgment that metaphors create meaning. In the earlier version, he observes: "The Controversion Theory explains one of the most puzzling and important features of metaphor, its capacity to create new contextual meaning."[33] But a few lines later he adds, "The metaphor does not create the connotations, but brings them to life."[34] To say that the metaphor "brings connotations to life" suggests that the connotations were antecedent and actual, or potential and ready to be actualized. And this is to deny that they are created in a radical sense; they must have been present in some sense before the metaphor was expressed. To that extent at least, in his earlier version of his view, Beardsley is not an originativist, and he even seems to fall back on some form of reductionism.

In "The Metaphorical Twist," however, Beardsley returns to the issue and claims to answer some of his critics who said he did not do justice to the creativity of metaphor. Thus he affirms his intention to show why a metaphor may have an "element of novelty" in its meaning. He says that his Verbal-opposition Theory "allows for novelty, for change of meaning, even for radical change." Yet his explanation does not make clear just what is novel. According to the theory, remote properties (those not understood as standard parts of the cluster of connotations commonly accepted as relevant to a term) shift when selected and attributed to the referent of another term in the metaphor.

In the metaphor "inconstant moon," for instance, some of the con-

---

[32] Beardsley, *Aesthetics*, p. 139.
[33] Ibid., p. 143
[34] Ibid.

tingent properties of inconstant people are brought into prominence and attributed to the moon. These properties may then be given a "new status as elements of verbal meaning" and "become part of the meaning of 'inconstant,' though previously they were only properties of those people." When this happens, Beardsley explains, "The metaphor transforms a *property* (actual or attributed) into a *sense*."[35] But what exactly is created? The selection of properties does not seem to be a creation. Instead, it is simply a rearrangement of antecedent properties as these are identified for inclusion in that to which the term's connotation refers. The interpreter must find antecedent non-standardized, secondary, or peripheral properties that have been rearranged.[36] But this rearrangement somehow becomes a sense. What is new, then, is the "sense," and presumably this depends on the "new status" of the relevant, "eligible" properties. And if novelty is present, it must be found in the way that the new status of properties shows them to be transformed and to yield something unprecedented.[37] Beardsley does not explain how a property that belongs to things can be transformed into a linguistic item. Nor does he explain why a sense should be new, although it may have a status (ontological?) different from that of the properties.

Let me suggest that Beardsley's senses into which properties may be transformed could be gestaltlike characters or ordered identities of clusters that cannot be reduced to the elements of the clusters, that is, cannot be reduced to the complex of meanings in the connotations denoting the properties that are made relevant to the terms spoken of metaphorically. (This is not inconsistent with understanding Beardsley's "sense," as like Gottlob Frege's "sense" as distinct from "reference" – which may be Beardsley's conception of sense.) If Beardsley means this, then his sense into which properties are transformed may be new. Yet Beardsley resists aligning his own theory with interactionism, which purports to affirm a more radical newness.

Max Black's Interactionism. Let us then turn to Black, who identifies his own view as interactionist and who explicitly proposes that there is reason to affirm creativity in some metaphors. As pointed out in the opening remarks in the Introduction to this book, Black says that it is reasonable to suggest that metaphors sometimes create similarities rather than formulate antecedent resemblances. In order to move quickly to the heart of the issues that this suggestion raises and thus lay a basis for a new look at interactionism, I shall quote, at some length, part of Black's own summary of his position:[38]

---

[35] Ibid., p. 302.
[36] Ibid., pp. 301–5.
[37] Ibid., p. 302.
[38] Black, "More About Metaphor," pp. 28–9.

1. A metaphorical statement has two distinct subjects, to be identified as the "primary" subject and the "secondary" one. . . . The duality of reference is marked by the contrast between the metaphorical statement's *focus* (the word or words used nonliterally) and the surrounding literal *frame*.

2. The secondary subject is to be regarded as a system rather than an individual thing. . . . In retrospect, the intended emphasis upon "systems," rather than upon "things" or "ideas," (as in Richards) looks like one of the chief novelties in the earlier study [the original discussion in *Proceedings of the Aristotelean Society*].

3. The metaphorical utterance works by "projecting upon" the primary subject a set of "associated implications," comprised in the implicative complex, that are predictable of the secondary subject. . . . In the earlier study, I spoke of a "system of associated commonplaces" (which later provoked some pointed criticisms by Paul Ricoeur). My notion was that the secondary subject, in a way partly depending upon the context of metaphorical use, determines a set of what Aristotle called *endoxa*, current opinions shared by members of a certain speech community. But I also emphasized, as I should certainly wish to do so now, that a metaphor producer may introduce a novel and non-platitudinous "implication-complex."

4. The maker of a metaphorical statement selects, emphasizes, suppresses, and organizes features of the primary subject by applying to it statements isomorphic with the members of the secondary subject's implicative complex. . . .

5. In the context of a particular metaphorical statement, the two subjects "interact" in the following ways: (a) the presence of the primary subject incites the hearer to select some of the secondary subject's properties; and (b) invites him to construct a parallel implication-complex that can fit the primary subject; and (c) reciprocally induces parallel changes in the secondary subject. This may be considered a crux for the interaction view (an attempted explication of Richards's striking image of the "interanimation of words").

It is noteworthy that Black excludes the role of tension in metaphors. Indeed, before summarizing his interactionism, he makes a point of objecting to Beardsley's notion that tension in the form of falsity or logical absurdity is a necessary condition of a metaphor. Nevertheless, I think Black's rejection of the idea that metaphors manifest logically conflicting terms is not as thorough as he believes it to be, for he does grant this much: An expression or statement may be interpreted metaphorically not when it shows falsity or incoherence but instead when it shows "the banality of that [literal] reading's truth, its pointlessness, or its lack of congruence with the surrounding text and non-verbal setting."[39] But banality, pointlessness, and lack of congruence in context all serve at least as negative conditions. If such conditions are not instances of tension as *tension* is ordinarily used, they are instances of the absence of "fit" in the context.

Moreover, if Black could accept Beardsley's distinction between two classes of metaphors, I think he would grant that the second, the "fresh and novel," shows tension. Even if banal metaphors do not, surely

[39] Black, "More about Metaphor," p. 36.

creative ones do. If Black or anyone else is willing to regard some metaphors as creative, then those metaphors will need to meet this minimal condition. And Black does seem willing to grant this and perhaps more, as he admits that if tension is not understood as a "diagnostic criterion" but as "essential to a metaphor's *being* a metaphor," then he will accept the relevance of tension. But what he wishes to emphasize is that *tension* for him is less suggestive than is his preferred term, *interaction*. In any case, with this interaction view as his base, he rejects the comparison view and, as we have seen, affirms the view that some metaphors are creative.

What does Black mean by *creative*? The answer to this question is suggested in several statements found in his summary. First, he says that "a metaphor producer may introduce a novel and nonplatitudinous 'implication-complex.'" An "implication-complex" (which is the outcome of the interaction of implicative complexes) is related to what he had earlier called a "system of associated commonplaces," or shared opinions. An implication-complex apparently includes but is more than what, in the later version, he calls "associated implications." Thus, in this later formulation, an implication-complex seems to be a system that is not restricted to a prior system of opinions. Black makes a point of saying that it can be novel. This, of course, is consistent not only with his rejection of the comparison theory but also with what he affirms in other places: "Yet the meaning of an interesting metaphor is typically new or 'creative,' not inferable from the standard lexicon."[40] Black also believes that "a metaphorical statement can sometimes generate new knowledge and insight by *changing* relationships between the things designated (the primary and secondary subjects)."[41] And perhaps most dramatic is the statement quoted in the introduction to this book, ". . . it would be more illuminating in some of these cases [i.e., of metaphors imparting similarities difficult to discern otherwise] to say that the metaphor creates the similarity than to say that it formulates some similarity antecedently existing. . . ."[42]

When Black turns to a defense of his earlier proposal that metaphors may create, he argues that objections to the contention that a similarity can be created rest on assuming that similarity must be an objective relation independent of a subjective perspective. But, he argues, similarities have subjective as well as objective aspects, and each can contribute to the other. This explanation, of course, is crucial and will be discussed later. But we should observe first that the upshot of his discussion is that metaphors can, as he puts it, create in the way that a new slow-motion appearance or "view" of a galloping horse is a

---

[40] Ibid., p. 36.
[41] Ibid., p. 23.
[42] Ibid., p. 37.

creation. Just as the movie projector is an instrument that makes this new view possible, so metaphors are "cognitive instruments" necessary for perceiving connections that are "present," once perceived. Metaphors help constitute aspects of reality. Thus, what Black seems to mean in saying that similarities have both subjective and objective aspects is that similarities are objects of attention and are given their character by means of the kind of attention directed to them. His account of why it is reasonable to say that metaphors may create similarities, then, is that this claim "is no longer surprising if one believes that the world is necessarily a world *under a certain description* – or a world seen from a certain perspective. Some metaphors can create such a perspective."[43]

Black's account of the sense in which metaphors can be creations raises many issues, one of which should be considered immediately. The others are of particular importance to later developments of my own interactionism and so will be treated later.

Of immediate concern is whether Black does not weaken, if not abandon, his originativist proposal that metaphors create what was not already available to be discovered. There are statements in his explanation of how metaphors function that suggest that he lapses in just the way he says Richards does, that is, by saying that the change of meaning is based on a "ground" found in the "common characteristics" of the two terms. Black's ground for interaction is an isomorphism between subjects. As is seen in the fourth point of his summary, the outcome of interaction between the systems of implicative complexes of the secondary and primary subjects results from "applying to it [the primary subject] statements isomorphic with the members of the secondary implicative complex." Again, in summarizing his position at the end of his article, Black states:[44]

I have been presenting in this essay a conception of metaphors which postulates interactions between two systems, grounded in analogies of structure (partly created, partly discovered). The imputed isomorphisms can, as we have seen, be rendered explicit and are then proper subjects for the determination of appropriateness, faithfulness, partiality, superficiality, and the like.

If metaphors offer insights that reveal analogies of structure or isomorphic connections between subjects, then they seem, after all, to be compressed analogies, if not elliptical similes. This seems prima facie contrary to the preceding claim that metaphors may create similarities rather than formulate "some similarity antecedently existing." The similarity for which the metaphor is responsible seems to be a for-

---

[43] Ibid.
[44] Ibid., p. 41.

merly unrecognized relation – and such a relation presumably would need to be "antecedently existing." This apparent lapse into interpreting the meaning of metaphors by finding antecedently established significance is also suggested by Black's interesting image of the way that a secondary subject acts like a filter. Thus, something is viewed as something else, and each of these things is antecedently established. But if a new insight results, then both the secondary subject's filter and what it views will need to be different from their initial characters. And a third relation, perhaps an unprecedented lens, will need to emerge. Perhaps Black would grant this. In the earlier article, he does say that the filter may be affected by the principal subject. He explicitly denies reductionist interpretations. And he goes to some length to argue against them, even calling attention to Richards's lapse into a kind of reductionism. I should like to propose, then, how the originativism suggested in his view can be preserved if the two words, *partly created,* in the last quotation are given more weight than are his references to isomorphisms and analogies.

That the created dimension deserves more weight may be reinforced by a closer examination of what Black says about the statements that are isomorphic and that connect the implicative complexes of primary and secondary subjects. In describing the way subjects interact, he observes that the hearer of a metaphor is invited to construct a parallel implication-complex that can fit the primary subject and reciprocally induce parallel changes in the secondary subject. This statement raises the question of the meaning of *parallel* in this context. Are parallel changes in one complex strictly identical with changes in the other? I think not. I believe Black's explanation indicates that the isomorphism is not one of strict identity and that it permits the two implicative complexes of primary and secondary subjects to be fundamentally different from each other. The isomorphic connection is not sufficient to make the meaning of the metaphor fully cognitively significant.

Black, I think, implies, if not intends, this is his treatment of his example of how metaphors work. He says of "Marriage is a zero-sum game" that some connections between the two subjects are brought together by similarity rather than strict identity and that some relations might be called "metaphorical coupling." It seems to me that these statements tell us that what is related by parallelisms is neither strictly identical nor connected by a relation of strict identity but, rather, is held apart, while being similar in a sense that is inseparable from the function of dissimilarities.

What remains parallel does not converge. Black's specific example of the statements is the primary subject's implicative complex said to correspond to a statement in the complex of the secondary subject bears this out. The two statements are "Marriage is a struggle between two contestants" and "A game is a contest between two opponents." Their correspondence depends on the interpretation of "contest," "opponents," and "winning" – which is also included in the complex of the secondary subject, "a zero-sum game."

Further, there is what Black calls "an ambience" which accompanies the secondary subject and affects its interpretation as it relates to the primary subject. If I am correct in inferring that the parallel relation to which Black refers is one in which the implicative complexes of two subjects can be integrated as neither strictly identical nor exhaustively cognitively significant by reduction to an isomorphism of strict identity, then I believe the creativity of metaphors is maintained and cannot, by implication, be reduced to antecedent isomorphisms. The outcome of a metaphor such as "Marriage is a zero-sum game" is a novel nonplatitudinous (to use Black's own criteria for creative metaphors) implication-complex. This complex is that of neither the primary nor the secondary subject. As novel, it can be articulated only by the metaphor – it offers, as Black puts it – an insight not expressible in any other way. It is the marriage game that the metaphor's two subjects create and reveal to the interpreter. Whether Black would agree to this rendition of his interactionism is questionable. Yet I think what he says suggests what I have proposed, and I would like to keep in mind what I have said about the outcome construed as a peculiar dual subject with its new and irreducible meaning complex – its new implication-complex – when I propose a development of the interaction view later in this book.

Interactionism and Paradox. The tension referred to in this account of metaphor between creation and discovery, novelty and antecedent ground, and variations of these polarities is, as I asserted earlier, inevitable. The tension is greatest, however, when the sense in which metaphors can be said to offer creative insight is considered more closely. This consideration, of course, touches on the sense in which metaphors express truths, a topic to be treated in the third chapter.

What has been said about the tension generated according to Black's view of how the components of metaphors function suggests the paradox referred to at the outset and to be addressed later in the discussion of the sense in which metaphors articulate new meanings that may be related to assertions about the world.

It is important here to emphasize that in referring to tension and paradox, I want to call attention to the peculiarities of creative metaphors in both creating, in the sense of constituting something not antecedently available to interpreters, and discovering, in the sense of articulating meanings that are not arbitrary or are constrained by something independent of them. The source of these constraints and the sense in which a source can constrain the very act of constituting it will be discussed later. The grounding of metaphorical creations so that they offer insights should be seen as relevant both to metaphors that introduce new values into our understanding and to those that seem only to change our habits of thinking and perceiving in value-neutral ways. I do not think that habitual changes of the latter sort are completely value neutral. Even simple perceptions seem to require evaluative factors of selection, interpretation, and presupposed criteria of intelligibility with respect to unifying data. But when such evaluative factors do enter perception and thinking, as in the case of the selecting for some purpose a slow-motion picture of a galloping horse, to use Black's example, the change in the process of perception is not arbitrary but is under the guidance of certain constraints that prompt the creator and interpreter to regard the instrument of change as insightful, rather than as uninteresting or trivial, as well as creative.

In any case, what I am suggesting is not so much a repudiation of Black's view that isomorphisms play a role in interacting systems as it is a plea for acknowledgment of the problem – which I claim is a paradox – that arises when we want to maintain both creativity and nonarbitrariness for the creator and interpreter of what is created. Put in another way, my point is that if the idea of creativity is taken to mean more than that creating is discovering something already determinate and potential, then one should not construct a view for which what is said to be new is (or was) "implicit," or present as a ground for relating the creation's key terms.

If creating is making explicit what is implicit, creating is not generating but, rather, is discovering what is made explicit and identified as an isomorphism. Unrecognized similarities may be discovered and play a role in interpreting metaphors, but more than these will be involved if the metaphor creates. If this were not so, then we would have once more a kind of the comparison view and an implied determinism by which metamorphical insight is predictable in principle, or deducible in a system that contains the connections among similarities known and becoming known as the system is worked out.

Before proceeding to further considerations of interactionism, however, Searle's reductive criticism must be addressed. Consideration of Searle's essay should help in describing the contrast between the reductionist and the originativist views.[45] And looking further at this contrast should help sharpen the idea that metaphors may be creative.

[45] Searle, *"Metaphor."*

John Searle's Objection to Interactionism

Searle's objection to interactionism presupposes the kind of rationalism that undergirds most studies of creativity and of metaphor. This rationalism opposes any view that seems to imply that something can remain intelligible and that, at the same time, cannot, and need not, be correlated with something familiar, antecedently known, or at least antecedently operative and discoverable. Such reductionism is typical of the comparison theory.

Searle opposes the idea that metaphors are comparisons, but he does not oppose the view that knowledge of what we are familiar with provides the meanings of metaphors. And he opposes interactionism. His attack on interactionism, as he sees it, does not commit him to the view of its usual opponent, the comparison view. Searle thinks that the problem of metaphor concerns the relations between word and sentence meaning on the one hand, and speaker's meaning, or utterance meaning, on the other. Accordingly, there are two meanings, each located in a distinct expression, the explicit (literal) word or sentence and the speaker's (metaphorical) utterance. Metaphorical meaning is to be found in what the speaker utters that departs from what the word, expression, or sentence literally means. In other words, we want to know how the hearer (or reader) comes to understand or "comprehend" the utterance meaning when the hearer is presented with only the sentence meaning.

For example, "Sam is a pig" is a "defective" sentence if taken literally and if Sam is a human being. Thus, if the sentence is not to be rejected as nonsensical, the hearer must search for something the speaker or writer utters that is not expressed when the sentence is interpreted literally. What is uttered is an attribution of some features of pigs to Sam – gluttony and sloppiness, among other possible features. The second assertion means something literally and is a paraphrase of the first expression. Searle grants that we often feel that the paraphrases of metaphorical sentences are inadequate. But the inadequacy is psychologically explained: It is felt because in itself the paraphrase does "not reproduce the semantic content which occurred in the hearer's comprehension of the utterance."[46]

Searle finds theories that treat metaphors as comparisons (implied similies), as well as interaction theories, to be inadequate. Comparison theorists do not recognize that comparisons are steps in, rather than the results of, finding the metaphorical meanings of sentences. Sam and pigs, for instance, are in part compared as the features to be attributed to Sam are found.

[46] Ibid., p. 123.

Similarity statements (Sam is like a pig) are not, however, the same as the metaphorical statements, which they allegedly explain. "Sally is a dragon" does not entail an existing dragon, and therefore the sentence does not assert a similarity between Sally and a dragon, although Searle thinks it is true that a similarity may play a role in understanding the metaphor. On the other hand, interaction theorists do not see that there are exceptions to what Searle believes is their assumption that one of the terms or expressions in a sentence interpreted metaphorically must be taken literally. But more important, they do not adequately explain how the meanings (senses and beliefs) associated with references interact and change meanings creatively. It is this latter objection that is of primary concern. Accordingly, I shall bypass the issue of whether one must consult speakers' intentions in order to recognize that an expression is figurative. Even if Searle is correct in saying that interactionists assume that "all metaphorical uses of expressions must occur in sentences containing literal uses of expressions" – an assumption that seems to Searle "plainly false" – the issue with which we are concerned is whether interaction in metaphors can be creative, which is to change meanings.

Searle agrees with the interactionists that the components of metaphors are related so that both the subject and predicate terms must be taken into account if utterance meaning is to be determined. Each subject term restricts the range of meanings that can be recognized in the metaphorical sentence and the speaker's utterance. Attention to these restrictions enables the hearer or reader to understand the metaphor's utterance meaning, which makes sense of the original sentence, or the metaphor. A set of characteristics, then, connects the subject and predicate in the metaphor. "Sam is a pig" is understandable in terms of these characteristics, such as gluttony and sloppiness. What "Sam" applies to has these characteristics, characteristics that pigs have. Searle's principles for understanding metaphors indicate how such characteristics are understood in connection with both the subject and the predicate. Thus, Searle's view is consistent with the point that the metaphor's major components make differences to one another. However, Searle does not think that this shows that anything is created. Obviously here he challenges Black's suggestion that some metaphors create new similarities. Some of Searle's reasons for doubting this possibility are offered in a brief analysis of examples.

This analysis pertains to the possibility of showing that an "association" (which did not previously exist) between the predicate term of the speaker's utterance (the metaphorical meaning) and the predicate term of the original sentence can be created by the relation of subject to predicate in the original sentence. Searle insists that the different predicate R is the result of the restrictions imposed by the subject terms. The metaphorical sentence "Kant's second argument for the transcendental deduction is so much mud/gravel/sandpaper" gives metaphorical meanings that are different from "Sam's voice is gravel," because of the difference between "Kant's argument" and "Sam's voice."[47] Consequently, the predicate *gravel* has different meanings in each sentence. Searle does not say what these different meanings are. But whatever they are, he claims that his own theory, rather than the interactionist's, provides what he calls a "plausible" explanation for the distinct meanings: They are not based on the fact that the different combination of S and P (subject terms and predicate terms of the metaphorical sentence) create new R's (the predicates of the utterance meaning) but on the fact that we have a specific set of associations with the P terms, *mud, gravel,* and *sandpaper.* According to a set of principles that Searle set forth earlier, the "different S terms [Kant and Sam] restrict the values of R differently." He says that the R's that can be true of a voice are different from the predicates true of arguments for transcendental deductions. Thus Searle asks, "Where is the interaction?"[48] Again, Searle does not say what these different R's are, nor does he go into detail about how different subject terms restrict differently so that different predicates in the utterance meaning can be identified. Presumably, he thinks that his account of the principles for metaphorical meanings shows this. The point, however, is that what happens is not interaction. And most important is his rejection of the suggestion that the distinct meanings of the Kant and Sam metaphors are created meanings. He opposes the idea that there is a new meaning in, or emergent from, the predicate terms of either sentence or utterance meanings. What are his reasons for rejecting this?

Interactionism, Searle explained earlier, cannot show that interaction takes place in any literal sense of interaction. However, no interactionist whom I know claims that nonliteral terms can be avoided in an account of metaphor. Further, Searle does not show that Black's discussion of how selections of implicatures that form systems of meanings understood through subject terms of metaphors does not explain the term *interaction.* He claims only, in a footnote, that this account is insufficient. One might ask, too, whether Searle's own admission that one must "go through" one semantic content to another to "figure out" metaphorical meaning can be understood in as literal a way as he seems to expect of the term *interaction.*

More important to my purpose, however, is Searle's insistence that the creation of meaning as an explanation of the way that a predicate applied to different subjects can generate different meanings seems

[47] Ibid., p. 119.
[48] Ibid.

"implausible," and "the more plausible explanation" is his own. Asserting that a view is not plausible and claiming his own is more plausible hinges, of course, on assumptions about what is acceptable as plausible. I think Searle's notion of plausibility is based on a rationalism that requires that an explanation relate what is to be explained to something familiar or something antecedent. Certainly this is what his own theory does. But if this assumption governs what is plausible, then, of course, no originativist view has a chance. Created newness is closed off from the start.

However, if this rationalist assumption is rejected or at least held in abeyance, then we may look further for reasons that what Searle calls the metaphorical or utterance meaning might be created. Considering Searle's example once more, one might argue that surely the association or the relation of mud or gravel or sandpaper with Kant's transcendental deduction is (or was) new. The relation may not be a creation in the most demanding sense – to be something insightful or newly intelligible and valuable in itself and as a contribution to future understanding. Nevertheless, it is a new relation insofar as it brings about an unprecedented relevance of meaning to the sentence subject, Kant's deduction, a meaning for Kant's deduction that did not, before its utterance, exist as something that made things intelligible. After all, Black, whom Searle opposes on the question of created similarities through interaction, suggests not that some isolated quality or meaning may be created but that a similarity understood within the context of a system of associated or implicated meanings may be created. Meanings not already recognized may then play a role in giving the world intelligibility, because their identities are made possible through a new system, or a new ordered relation of meanings, that can be discovered through the metaphors.

Views such as Searle's, however, must exclude suggestions of this kind because they – as may Beardsley's when examined closely – presuppose that explaining requires referring explananda to antecedent items. Thus Searle probably would object to what I have said about what is created on the ground that the so-called new relation or similarity said to be given in a system still has not been identified. But of course, it cannot have been identified if we refuse to acknowledge that the system's identity or unity is discerned only in and through the metaphorical sentence, that is, the literal sentence meaning in Searle's scheme. If it is unique, it cannot be identified with reference to other cognitively equivalent utterances. The identity or unity is unprecedented.

As I shall try to show, what is new is a gestaltlike family resemblance. Thus this study must focus on how terms in metaphors function so that this gestaltlike resemblance is possible. With respect to this consideration, the task is like Black's. However, the direction must be different, as the idea of a gestaltlike outcome departs from Black's view because the outcome is more than a perspective. I shall argue that metaphors create integrated wholes that generate more than linguistic items and are something more than conceptual perspectives.

Although the review of approaches in this chapter is far from exhaustive, it does outline some of the most widely known discussions of metaphor. And these discussions, I think, do clarify the opposing attempts to describe and, insofar as possible, account for the puzzling way in which metaphors function as meaningful linguistic expressions. These poles of interpretation of metaphors should provide a framework, as well as help indicate the reason, for the reconsideration of interactionism, which is the topic of the next chapter.

2

A Reconsideration of Interactionism

Despite the variations among the theories of metaphor considered in the previous chapter, there is one point that these interpreters hold in common: They all recognize that the major terms or components of metaphorical expressions – at least in light of their larger, if not immediate, contexts – somehow function in a way that is different from the way they function in literal expressions. Each writer's account of the way that a literal interpretation of an expression is related to the metaphorical construal differentiates each theory from the others. As we have seen, both Richards's and Black's conceptions of how a metaphor's terms function literally and metaphorically have been characterized as interactionism, a view that affirms that some metaphors may be creative and constitute insight. It is interactionism that is to be reconsidered with the aim of showing how terms function in relation to those metaphorical outcomes that are both creations and insightful.

Terminology and Assumptions

Significance

With respect to terminology, it will be helpful to use the term *meaning unit* as an alternative to *terms* and *constituents* which are said to function within metaphors. The expression meaning unit is proposed in order to suggest that whole sentences as well as single words and phrases can be components of metaphors. Meaning unit applies to any articulation or determination of an expressive medium that can function in a verbal and/or extraverbal context so that the articulation or determination is significant. If an articulation is significant, it must be intelligible. Thus, I assume that at least one term or concept in a meaningful utterance must exhibit intelligibility. I shall not try to define *intelligibility*, because such an attempt would either flounder or lead in a circle, given the broad and fundamental function of the term; it may well be that the term is primitive. However, it is necessary to indicate the basic conditions under which a thing can be said to be intelligible.

If something is intelligible, it is understandable or knowable. But what do *understandable* and *knowable* mean? One answer that partially specifies these terms and, in turn, intelligibility is that whenever any of these terms is applied to something, that thing is regarded as a presence, as something noticed and thus as something that may be or become a term in a relation. The relation may be triadic, the only kind of relation that, for C. S. Peirce, can be fully meaningful. Or the relation may be more complex. If it is a triad or is more complex, it is itself either a system or part of a system. Intelligibility, then, is the condition of apprehending something as actually or possibly part of a system. Another way of saying this is to describe intelligibility as the condition that what is intelligible must be or be part of some kind of structure, or it must be an actual or possible component of a structure in terms of which the intelligible thing functions in some way.

There are, however, two reasons that this description of intelligibility raises problems. First, if we were to pursue the attempt to make intelligibility intelligible by means of a determinate description, we would need to ask for the condition under which something can be said to be structured or systematic or, most simply, in relation. Further, we may ask, are all structures or systems intelligible? If so, is there anything intelligible that is not systematic? What shows something to be structured or systematic rather than simply an aggregate or series of items? A full treatment of this will not be attempted here. But a thing is in relation if an attribute that is predicated of it is a condition for another (or the same) attribute's being attributable to something else. If being-to-the-left-of an object (one) is attributable to an object (two), then being-to-the-right-of will be attributable to object (one). If being a perspective is attributable to a metaphor, then being an object or referent will be attributable to something other than the metaphor. The intelligibility of monadic relations, of course, poses a problem. This issue will be addressed briefly in a moment, when I shall suggest that self-identity is a fundamental kind of intelligibility. In any case, I shall take for granted that we do know when we apprehend things in relation.

The second reason that my description of intelligibility raises problems is that requiring relations seems to preclude intelligibility from phenomena that resist being connected with anything else. I do not, however, wish to withhold the application of the condition of intelligibility from things that do not appear to stand in relations. There is a sense, I think, in which intelligibility can be attributed to monadic relations, or single, unconnected items. Thus, another sense of intelligibility, which must be added to the idea of being systematic or structured, applies to the condition for noticing and attending to something in terms of the respect in which it is autonomous, that is, for attending to the respect in which something has no immediately rec-

ognized positive connections with anything else. When Cézanne sur-
passed his tradition by breaking his color palette (as did the impres-
sionists), but in a way that made shapes solid and stable, he presented
a new respect in which painting can be effected. This respect in which
he painted was different from anything preceding it. This is not to
say that it had no relations whatsoever to anything else. But it is to say
that his way of painting was, in a crucial respect that affected the
tradition after him, disconnected from his past. Moreover, attending
to something different and in terms of this respect is discriminating it
and thus recognizing it as distinct from other things in its context.
And insofar as it is autonomous, then, it must participate in at least
one relation, namely, difference.

The form of intelligibility at issue here may be called *autonomous
intelligibility*. An object of attention is intelligible in this sense if it can
be discriminated and apprehended as something present that com-
pels attention, regardless of any other noticeable thing on which it
may depend for some purpose and regardless of any properties or
similarities that might be referred to in order to describe it. It just is
what it is, and if it is intelligible in this way, it cannot be described
(which requires predications that presuppose resemblances and thus
other identities). Autonomous intelligibility may belong to new relations as well as new relata. The innovations of the impressionist painters, for instance, introduced both new relata, in the form of unprecedented differences in the way color areas are broken on the picture
surface, and new relations, in the ways their impressionist styles dif-
fered from those of previous landscape painters. But a relation – in
this case, a complex relation – is thus new by virtue of its initial difference from other relations and relata. It is a new type that is introduced by its token – the token here being an individual painting that
exhibits a complex of qualities that at the same time exemplify the
new type, that is, the visual meaning given to its interpretation. In this
sense, its intelligibility is autonomous. As new, it is instanced for the
first time and must be distinguished on its own terms. Such intelligibility must be granted if we are willing to grant novelty. If there are
occasionally new things that evolve (physically, biologically, ideation-
ally, linguistically, and so on), then the new things must be recognized, discriminated, and identified initially for what they are, before
they are understood in their contributions to their traditions or, more
generally, before they are understood as related to anything. They
are shocking in being disconnected, but they are not rejected, in the
long run, at least, although innovations are often belittled and rejected when they first appear.

Autonomous intelligibility is a problem for a view that demands
that what is cognitive must be intelligible by virtue of mediation or by

means of a triadic relation. That is, if we say that nothing is meaning-ful and thus intelligible unless it is something related to an interpreter and something else to which the interpreter is led to recognize (an object or referent), then we will reject autonomous intelligibility, at least as something given at any finite time for a finite intelligence. Yet I think it is undeniable that sometimes things are discriminated and noticed for their own sakes, apart from other things and relations. Let me approach this point from a slightly different perspective in order to indicate why I think we can include autonomous intelligibil-ity without abandoning the position that intelligibility requires media-tion.

I stated that something attended to as a presence is an initial con-dition of intelligibility. A presence attended to is displayed. It spreads out, initially as a manifold of indiscriminate points or moments. It appears as indeterminate. In the case of an instance of created new-ness, such a presence, if it is at once autonomous and intelligible, is attended to as something that is not fortuitous. It bears its own neces-sity, and it appears as responsible – responsible to itself but also as ready to be responsible for something else. Thus it also manifests an incipient familiarity as well as an explicit unfamiliarity. This is not to say that it appears to be ready to disclose something underlying or implicit within it. It may later be understood as disclosing something. But what it then discloses is not exclusively some implicit, antecedent knowable item. Rather, what it discloses is something that is not un-covered or brought forth from what had not been recognized. It is something that comes into being, something that is originated. Thus it originates relations to be discovered. Its emergence appears as an intrusion into what was familiar and what will be familiar. But insofar as it is an intrusion, it is disconnected and monadic.

Consequently, when such things catch our attention (and when at-tending is not describing), they appear as relatable. They force them-selves on our attention not only because of invoked anticipations that they might be seen to fit into systems or into an advancing tradition. They appear as exemplary or as new rules, new dispositions, to con-trol aspects of the future. But as new and unfamiliar, they are auton-omous. Of course, something attended to as autonomous in this way may force itself on only a few observers, as was the case for impres-sionism when it was first introduced into nineteenth-century painting. But it did this, even though for only a few critics initially, because those critics were able to see that it was exemplary for constituting changes in the system or tradition of oil painting at that time.

The future system, or the subsequent changes in the tradition, is, of course, neither given nor known at the time. Indeed, the system to be generated in the future is something that the autonomously intel-

ligible thing helps constitute — if that thing is a creation. It is the expectation of such future development that impresses us with the thing's
intelligibility. With this qualification, then, I shall propose that to say
that something is intelligible is to say either that it is structured and
functioning as a participant in a complex of relations that make up at
least a partial system or that it is immediate but exhibits a readiness to
be mediated.

To return to the expression *meaning unit,* it can be said that a meaning unit is what has significance, which, in turn, is to be intelligible.
And this is to be encountered as an identity, whether the identity is a
relation between two or more items in experience — as a word that
relates to an object by calling attention to that object — or is an item
that is recognizable in itself, prior to its being defined through connections with other things — such as a new coherence in a painting or
musical composition that is the outcome of a creative act.

The term meaning unit, however, is not identical with *unit of significance. Meaning unit* will be understood primarily to refer to senses,
that is, connotations and/or intensions. But meaning units may also
function so as to include references, and in those cases, meaning gains
significance or import. Connotations and intensions form meaning.
They indicate what a thing is. In verbal language, they are expressed
in the words and phrases by which we make sense of what we want to
say. Properties and qualities are the objective conditions for the intensions. References are the relations of words and phrases to the condition of relevance for properties and qualities. The two sets of terms
the morning star and *the evening star* have different connotations and
intensions, but they both have the same referent, otherwise known as
Venus.

Roman Ingarden uses the expression *meaning unit* in his account of
the components of a work of literature.[1] His use of the expression is
fairly rigorous, as the term is intended to be correlated with a specific
level or stratum of the structure of a literary work. My use of the term
is intended to cut across all levels of such structures. Occasionally, I
shall also use *meaning focus* as an alternative, in order to emphasize
that a meaning unit need not be a completely delineated, determinate, fixed item. As I suggested, a meaning unit need only have sufficient identity to be recognizable as intelligible in the minimal sense
that it be seen as being a possible component in a larger meaningful
unit. This broad use of *meaning unit,* of course, includes connectives,
articles, and the like, as well as nouns, verbs, and adjectives.

For a moment, I shall waive the issue of the relationship between

---

[1] Roman Ingarden, *The Literary Work of Art,* trans. George G. Grabowicz (Evanston, Ill.:
Northwestern University Press, 1973), p. 18.

specific words or specific linguistic expressions regarded as physical or perceptual things (i.e., as what have been called *tokens*) and their meanings (i.e., what have been called *types*). I shall take meaning units to be types rather than tokens. That is, a meaning unit is what is understood as the basis for recognizing and identifying different groupings of perceptual qualities (tokens), such as marks on paper and sounds emitted from vocal chords, as instances of the same meaning (type). Meanings as types must be discernible in order to identify words or expressions as the same amidst numerous instances or tokens. Later we shall consider the possibility that perceptual presence (the token aspect of meaning) may modify significance or import. The larger task, however, is to see how meaning units identifiable from one instance to another interact as constituents of metaphors.

Context

A metaphor must either take the form of a whole declarative sentence or depend for its metaphorical function on one or more implied sentences. Further, metaphorical expressions occur in contexts in which larger units of expressions are at least implied. Paul Ricoeur's entire theory of metaphor is based on his contention that a sentence context is essential to metaphor. And a similar, though more general, point is made by Donald Davidson, for much different purposes, when he says that words have no function "save as they play a role in sentences: their semantic features are abstracted from the semantic features of sentences, just as the semantic features of sentences are abstracted from *their* part in helping people achieve or realize intentions."[2] Uttering a single word, then, may have a metaphorical function, depending on the context. If someone simply said "Colorful" or "Brilliant!" neither term would be metaphorical or significant unless there were a context, for instance, a musical performance to which the utterer were listening. In that case, the expression *colorful* or *brilliant* would presumably be interacting with implied terms in a sentence applying to the performance, such as "That was a brilliant performance." If someone sitting by a river bank, looking at a stream of bubbling, gleaming, and flowing water, were to say "It is life," the meaning context that relates metaphorically to what is said would be implicit. Within the speaker's setting, what is said has a context that is intelligible, but intelligible metaphorically, if interpreted in terms of some aspects of the context, that is, among other things, the speaker's

---

[2] Ricoeur, *The Rule of Metaphor;* Donald Davidson, "Reality Without Reference," in Mark Platts, ed., *Reference, Truth and Reality: Essays in the Philosophy of Language* (London: Routledge & Kegan Paul, 1980), p. 135.

staring at the water. "It" presumably refers to something the speaker is thinking about that may have nothing to do with the setting (unless the speaker refers unconsciously). Assuming the relevance of the river, the speaker's statement could be translated as the metaphor "The river (or the flow of the river) is life" or "Life is a river."

Sentence Form

The main point, however, is not whether all the meanings that make an expression a metaphor must be made explicit but, rather, how the meanings that are explicit are presented. As Aristotle's description implies, meanings in a metaphor depend on negation, the assignment of a name to something to which the name does not belong. A metaphor expresses something contrary to what is accepted as literal or correct with respect to the way that meanings are normally related to one another in the language (and context) in a sentence form appropriate to the metaphorical function. Metaphors do not always appear in sentences that connect subjects and predicates with the verb *to be*. "Sadness spread slowly over his face" or "Repressed unconscious desires drove him to surpass his brothers," for instance, are not in the forms of statements that designate identities, such as "Man is the dream of a shadow" or "Richard is lionhearted," which use a form of *to be*. If the proposal I shall introduce later is to have value for understanding how creative metaphors in general function, the suggestion should not be limited to explicit identity statements using a form of the copula *to be*. What has been said about the relevance of context applies here, too. Those metaphorical expressions that do not take the form of explicit identifications are nevertheless significant because they presuppose contexts that do include such identities. "Time flies" presupposes identifying what *time* refers to with something that flies. "Drop that idea at once" is a command, but the metaphorical function of "drop that idea" presupposes an identity of idea with something that can be dropped.

Interaction in Metaphorical and Literal Expression

Literal and Metaphorical Interaction

The problem of distinguishing literal from figurative expressions was broached in the Introduction. To begin our reconsideration of interactionism, we must examine this problem further. The claim that the terms in metaphorical expressions function in ways that differ from the ways that terms in nonfigurative expressions function may be challenged. The challenge might be made on the grounds referred to earlier, that there is a sense in which every phrase or sentence, that is, any meaningful literal or figurative verbal expression that includes more than one meaning unit articulates its meaning in special ways so that the sentences articulated cannot be paraphrased. This challenge may be expanded by arguing that both literal and figurative statements articulate meanings through the interaction of meaning units. To cite an example from Roman Ingarden, "the smooth red sphere" is an expression in which each term affects the other.[3] I am not concerned with all that Ingarden intends in discussing this example; however, for our purposes, what is important is that both what he calls "functional words" – such as *besides, that, red* – and nominal words – *sphere, chair* – act on each other when given places in nonfigurative and figurative sentences. Functional words may contribute to specifying a referent, and nominal words may, with the functional words, contribute to the function of the sentence as a whole. Both kinds of words specify the way their contexts, that is, their sentences, refer to objects. In the example just cited, changes occur in the isolated meanings of *red* and *smooth*. As Ingarden says, "The moment they become components of the compound expressions, they perform entirely determinate functions with respect to their object."[4] Their meanings are stabilized by focusing on a specified object denoted by *sphere*, and a convergence of meaning narrows the range of objects that the sentence might denote. Should Ingarden's discussion be understood as implying the preceding suggestion that metaphorical interaction is at the root of all linguistic expression? Let it be conceded that although a hard and fast distinction between literal and metaphorical expressions is not always obvious, there are contrasts evident when a fresh metaphor stands out from the midst of otherwise conventionally used literal discourse. How, then, do literal and metaphorical expressions differ with respect to interaction?

In general, there is a more complex and subtle interaction in metaphors. And most important, in a metaphor the interaction is a condition for new significance. The interaction within a literal expression specifies its meaning directly and with predictable semantic combinations. Its terms mutually limit one another in rule-bound ways so that its components can be identified, conceptualized, and understood with reference to terms and sentences other than those with which the interpreter started. Once the meaning of "the smooth red sphere" is uttered and interpreted within a context, the sentence can be translated without loss of reference into sentences that could have expressed the significance of the literal sentence before its utterance.

[3] Ingarden, *The Literary Work of Art*, pp. 72–3.
[4] Ibid.

Definitions appropriate to the terms *smooth, red,* and *sphere* are joined and conceived with reference to a thing identifiable by spatial coordinates, pointing, or other descriptive operations. It may be said, then, that the literal statement has a stable meaning, that is, in its meaningful context, it is *closed.* In a metaphor — that is, one that is fresh and creative rather than hackneyed or frozen — no such identification is readily available and may never be available. The function of its interacting terms is not to narrow a range of given, established, and fixed meanings so that something already given as a referent by the subject of the expression can be characterized. In a metaphor, the so-called functional terms do not interact simply to delimit the subject. Instead, they interact to delimit themselves, to transform themselves, and thus to deliver a specific significance to the subject that is not already given, ready to be formulated. In the literal statement, *red* and *smooth* narrow the determination of the subject, the sphere. They do not change the significances of the words. They affect our understanding of the subject; it does not affect our understanding of them. In a metaphor, on the contrary, in "Man is the dream of a shadow," for instance, the systems of meanings presupposed by dream and shadow make differences to one another, so that being a dream and being a shadow are not the same when simultaneously applied to the subject. And they are transformed further by the system of meanings associated with the subject, man. The dream here becomes thin and dark; the shadow becomes unreal; man loses substantiality; and the dream and the shadow are humanized. The interaction or determination of terms in metaphors is multidirectional.

Unparaphrasability

The interdependence of meaning units in a metaphor is one of the conditions for the unparaphrasability of metaphorical expressions. This does not mean that analysis, explanation, and interpretation are irrelevant. The examination of the literal meanings of terms and the comparisons of their connotations or systems of implications are a step in understanding them. Suggesting what the new significance is that arises can be prompted, though not exhausted, by interpretations that include comparisons.[5] However, if an interpretation proposed as a paraphrase is offered as an equivalent, it will fail, as the meanings of metaphors are bound to their terms as they work together uniquely.

---

[5] Several authors have made this point. Searle's analysis, though anti-interactionist, brings out the initial need for comparison in understanding metaphors. See also Roger Tourangeau, "Metaphor and Cognitive Structure," in David S. Miall, ed., *Metaphor: Problems and Perspectives* (Atlantic Highlands, N.J.: Humanities Press, and Sussex, England: Harvester Press, 1982), pp. 14–35.

We cannot expect to understand the significance of a metaphor by systematically eliminating all but previously recognized common features in the systems of meanings that its terms bring together.

The possibility that metaphors can, after all, be paraphrased, was mentioned in the first chapter. The comparison view treats metaphors as replaceable by comparison statements that are taken literally. Further, Searle's argument against interactionism concluded that there are not special (new) senses resulting from metaphors and that there are rules for translating metaphorical expressions. In opposition, the interaction view as represented by both Richards and Black (insofar as they do not inadvertently lapse into the comparison view), maintains that metaphors cannot be paraphrased, because their cognitive meanings are not exhausted by translation into one or more comparison statements. Stanley Cavell's rejection of the hope of finding paraphrases as equivalents of metaphors has already been mentioned. Recall that he says that when we try to state just what, for example, "Juliet is the sun" means, we never completely satisfy the demand for meaning; we inevitably add an "and so on" to the list of expressions purportedly paraphrasing the metaphor. Cavell interprets the "and so on" as the expression of an expectation for more senses or meanings.[6] Later, I shall suggest an alternative to the view that this expectation is for something more than future senses. However, whatever the condition for the "and so on," the recognition of inadequacy is there.

Max Black also denies the adequacy of paraphrase, but on the ground that the paraphrase says too much with the wrong emphasis. Although his words are "too much" rather than "not enough," the point is, I think, the same. Black is especially concerned with the condensed focus of the metaphor that says what it means in one stroke, without the baggage of the ever-incomplete literal statements of the paraphrase.

However, it is appropriate to return for a moment to the objection, already mentioned, to this claim of unparaphrasability, namely, that no statement can be fully paraphrased. A version of this objection was made by Israel Scheffler. Scheffler argues that the standard of translation expected for a paraphrase, that is, the equivalence of insight, is so strong that it is "vacuous."[7] He contends that this standard cannot be met by any translation, whether it be literal or figurative. Thus, he claims, "no statement . . . is expendable."[8]

It is difficult to determine just what the defenders of paraphrase want to defend if they argue that all expressions, nonfigurative as well

---

[6] Cavell, "Aesthetic Problems," chap. 4, pp. 79–80.
[7] Scheffler, *Beyond the Letter*, p. 113.
[8] Ibid.

as figurative, elude exhaustive paraphrasing. Do they wish to maintain that every instance of speech is creative in articulating a new intelligibility or meaning? This consequence of the objection to unparaphrasability is suggested by Scheffler at the end of his book when he says that literal (theoretical) statements are not different from metaphors that, if creative, gain refinements through further investigation that are prompted after they have been uttered. But surely we need to distinguish at least degrees of such enrichment of language. "Cats have four legs" may not be fully paraphrasable if complete specificity is demanded – a specificity that would be irrelevant for purposes of information that are normally served by such statements – but it is hard to see how the expression creates new meaning. Like "the smooth red sphere," the ordinary conceptual purposes assumed in interpreting it permit – indeed, require – us to be able to translate it. No special significance of the term *red* needs to be recognized to apply the term to the sphere, as is required when *smiling* is applied to a flower.

On the other hand, if those objecting to unparaphrasability want to deny that new significance accrues to any instance of language, metaphorical and literal, they seem to be invoking emotivism in some form. Insight or cognitive significance is denied to what is claimed to be an inexhaustible aspect of meaning. What else could this aspect be except either emotional tone or ornamentation?

Perceptual–Qualitative Conditions

It was suggested earlier that perceptual conditions might be thought to affect meaning and consequently the cognitive insights of creative metaphors. Thus we may ask whether the internally related meanings of metaphors include, or are at least affected by, what, for literal expressions, frequently are thought of as extraneous factors such as sound quality, feeling tone, and even the visual shape of words and lines. The view that such factors operate in metaphorical expressions, particularly as metaphors constitute poems, might be associated with those interpretations of metaphor that distinguish it by its noncognitive function. If such factors do contribute to the effect of the poem or metaphor, without thereby helping constitute the meaning, then we might say that the key difference between metaphorical and literal or discursive expressions that are considered false or incongruous in context is the prominence in the former and the inconspicuousness in the latter of the so-called meaninglessness conditions of sounds and visual qualities. In this view, these perceptual–qualitative conditions lack meaning in that they do not seem to signify anything about the world, at least directly. They do not give us insight. Yet they may enhance or reinforce the impact of those elements that have such a function – the excitement or enthusiasm, for instance, with which the meaning is understood.[9]

I think this view is correct insofar as it recognizes the role of non-cognitive conditions in cooperating with cognitive meanings. Certainly in poetry perceptual qualities are relevant to the poet's or speaker's choice of words, which in turn present specific meanings. Alliteration, rhythm, loose or strict rhyming, suggested visual qualities, or imagery and feeling tone are integral to the total effect of many or most poems. To what extent, if any, these conditions make their contribution because they constitute or are integral to what is intrinsic to the cognitive meanings is an important issue. If there are nonverbal metaphors, as I shall try to show later, these conditions will be essential to meaning. And for verbal metaphor, surely it is a mistake to separate or dissociate completely the intelligibility of the metaphorical expression from its qualitative aspects. In metaphorical interaction, these may contribute to what is regarded as intelligible, even if these factors are not in themselves, separately, cognitively intelligible.

The idea that qualitative aspects contribute to the way that meaning units function in metaphors is consistent with the views according to which icons serve as the basis for metaphorical meanings. This view, at least as it was formulated by Paul Henle, is most closely related to the Comparison Theory (Beardsley calls it a species of the Comparison Theory) because the icon or image said to be suggested by a metaphor relates the meanings of the metaphor's terms through a similarity, a similarity presented by the (described) icon. Iconic factors, then, seem to be taken in themselves as intelligible. What I am proposing, however, is not that icons are the keys to metaphorical meaning, although icons surely may be suggested by metaphors. Rather, what I am suggesting is that qualitative aspects that may include iconic signs and also other factors such as suggested sounds, colors, and feeling tones affect the way that meaning units are interpreted. For instance, the meaning units in "time flies" are understood in the light of the sense of swiftness and movement, increments in sequence, the repetition of relatively high pitch, as the i sounds in both words, which heighten the sense of movement. If I am correct about the interrelation of such qualitative factors and verbal meanings, then qualitative aspects will certainly be intrinsic to the intelligibility of what is understood as a whole in metaphors.

It may also be claimed, as suggested in the previous chapter, that feelings have their own cognitive structure. Consider, for example,

---

[9] See Ruth Hershberger, "The Structure of Metaphor," *Kenyon Review* 5 (1943).

how music affects feeling tones. I do not mean that music evokes associations that in turn invoke feelings in hearers. It may do this, but that is not its musical function. Rather, I have in mind the way that the organization of sounds exhibits intrinsic qualitative interaction and the way that some of the qualities of tones exhibit certain structures that are isomorphic with the structures of feeling responses. Susanne Langer has made an excellent case for this.[10] But if music – which has as a necessary condition calculable pitches, meter, line and harmony, and patterns of sounds that are subject to quasi-mathematical analysis – has structural, emotive import for listeners, then it does not seem unreasonable to view musical sounds as intrinsically cognitive or intelligible. They are identities contributing to systems, systems that are not directly verbally conceptual but that are conceptual according to shared structures, for instance, ordered types of pitch relations or keys as well as specific formal organizations, such as sonata-allegro and rondo. Qualitative conditions can contribute to cognitive meaning at least in the sense of what is autonomously intelligible, as discussed.

Paul Ricoeur has argued that feeling is a necessary component in the ways that metaphors function.[11] And he insists that feelings are congitive. When a metaphor is apprehended, its new import is felt as well as understood. His conception of feeling, which lies at the basis of his thesis, requires first distinguishing feelings from emotions, which are internally and bodily directed, and then proposing that feelings are intentional and outwardly directed. Thus he claims that feelings are "interiorized thoughts." Although he does not develop this proposal beyond the stage of a relatively brief suggestion, Ricoeur does point to a dimension of metaphorical processes – at least of those that are interpretive, and of cognitive experience in general – that has been overlooked or minimized by the most frequently cited discussions. In any case, it seems appropriate to acknowledge the function of qualitative considerations in affecting metaphorical meaning. As I shall propose later, the metaphor's intelligibility is related to its components as something like a family resemblance functioning as a gestalt in relation to its parts. And because the metaphor's components include qualitative aspects of the terms recognized as articulating the meaning, these may enter the community that makes up the family of a metaphor's components. This kind of interaction is important to the metaphorical structure to be discussed later.

[10] Langer, *Feeling and Form.*
[11] The place in Ricoeur's writing to which I refer is more recent than *The Rule of Metaphor.* His proposal regarding feeling and metaphor is in "The Metaphorical Process as Cognition, Imagination, and Feeling," *Critical Inquiry* 5 (1978): 143–59.

Three Key Features of Metaphors

Let us now return to the way that meaning units interact cognitively, considering three key features that can be attributed to the structure of metaphors, that is, to the connections among the ways their constituents function internally and externally. These features depend on the characteristic ways in which the meaning units interact: (1) tension, (2) the presence of two "subjects" or "anchoring" meaning units, and (3) the interrelation of meaning units in an integration or family resemblance that functions like a community.

Tension

The first characteristic, tension, is associated with both Beardsley's and Richards's theories of metaphor.[12] A metaphor expresses its meaning through a tension, through some form of opposition, strain, or conflict of meaning with themselves or their context. It should be emphasized that as used here, tension does not specifically refer to a psychological condition. Although the condition of tension might be felt, the feeling is not the condition. What is important is the negative dimension, or the incongruity attributable to metaphor, which is a structural condition. Until recently, this negative aspect of metaphors has been overlooked or at least minimized by the dominant theories of metaphor – it is probably Beardsley who is most responsible, although Richards had already called attention to tension.

As already suggested, if we reflect on what Aristotle said, we can see that he was not unaware of the negativity on which metaphor depends, although he did not pursue the point. Yet most interpretations based on Aristotle ignore this aspect of metaphor in the attempt to find some "ground" or explanatory relationship on which metaphors depend. Even Richards, who notices the importance of the negative when he says that unlikenesses are more at work than likenesses are, slips into the view that there is a ground for each metaphor, even though we may not be able to say what it is.[13] And Beardsley, even though he makes much of the tension as part of his controversion or Verbal-opposition Theory, accounts for metaphors by implied asso-

---

[12] The importance of metaphorical tension has been discussed by William Wimsatt, Jr. in *The Verbal Icon: Studies in the Meaning of Poetry* (Lexington: University of Kentucky Press, 1954). It was also the focus of my attempt, in *A Discourse on Novelty and Creations*, to explore how metaphors exhibit certain essential characteristics of created objects.

[13] Richards, *The Philosophy of Rhetoric*, pp. 117–18.

ciations and remote or subsidiary connotations and thus reverts to a search for what is not in tension and what must be antecedent to the creation of the metaphor that is said to work by virtue of these meanings. This is to look beyond the importance of the tension that is presented by a metaphor. However, even though they look for explanations that assuage the tension that they admit, both Beardsley and Richards do consider tension as an initiating condition of the interpretation of an expression as metaphorical. It is necessary to examine more closely the conflict at the basis of this tension.

Before we continue, an objection to attributing tension to metaphors should be acknowledged. Consideration of this objection will serve as a way of looking again at the importance of context in the recognition of tension. We have noted that although Black is an interactionist, he is critical of Beardsley's conception of metaphorical tension. The point of Black's criticism is that tension is not a defining feature of metaphors. It may, he says, be present in nonmetaphors. Moreover, some metaphors lack tension. Yet recall that Black himself says that something uncommon must be noticed – its "banality" or "pointlessness, or its lack of congruence with the surrounding text and non-verbal setting."[14] And he concedes that tension may be one of the features of metaphorical language.

Recognition of tension depends not only on seeing incompatible relations among an expression's meaning units but also on recognizing the context in which the expression occurs. Thus, if they are taken literally, terms in metaphors will not connect intelligibly with a literal (i.e., a standardized) meaning context of other explicit or presupposed sentences. For instance, the expression "Man is an animal" does not, in classificatory contexts, exhibit an internal clash. It is literally true and would in fact be taken that way if uttered in a biology class. But if uttered by a victim of a crime, it would be incongruent with a literal reading. The meaning context, then, is not simply internal. It is not simply the conjoined systems of associations and presupposed intensions or senses of each internal meaning unit. Each of the terms *man, dream,* and *shadow* in "Man is the dream of a shadow" has its own "standard" meaning context, but together they have a larger meaning context of the whole expression, which in turn has its context of assumptions linked to the linguistic tradition and the culture of the speaker and interpreter. In this case, the metaphor of man, the shadow of a dream, has a force outside its original poetic setting and thus belongs to contexts not limited to its poetic origin. But the point to be made here is that there may be a tension in the relation of a whole

[14] Black, "More about Metaphor," p. 36.

expression and the context in which it occurs, and this point must be explained briefly.

It is instructive to note Ingarden's conception of how sentences can be recognized as connected or disconnected. A consideration of his comments on the interrelation of sentences should help highlight the role of context in recognizing tension and understanding that expressions are metaphorical.

Ingarden cites examples of the importance of the presence or absence of connections between sentences.[15] The first illustrates obvious connections: "Cars make an unbearable racket" and "Freiburg is in Baden." If the latter is asserted, then one's expectations will not be undermined by the assertion of the former. Again, "My son received a good report card" followed by "He is very happy and is playing in the garden" illustrate connection. The first sentence prepares the interpreter for the second. The first makes the "he" of the second "reach out," as Ingarden puts it. By contrast, "The child is crying" and "It has two perpendicular and equal diagonals" are not connected. We are prepared for a range of sentences expected to follow, but our expectation is destroyed.

Ingarden's point that unconnected sentences establish a condition by which expectations are destroyed suggests that expectations are thwarted by the absence of connection between expressions that is not unlike the kind of tension attributed to metaphors. Certainly, Ingarden's example manifests a form of tension, although in the examples, not one of the sentences seems to be metaphorical. Sentences, presumably with literal significances, are conjoined to generate a tension like that in single metaphorical expressions. However, before pursuing this, we should notice that Ingarden does not do justice to other possible contexts in which two apparently unconnected sentences may, after all, be connected. In the example of the sentence concerning perpendiculars and diagonals, which was said to be unconnected to the sentence about the crying child, a context in which they are connected is not difficult to find. The "it" in the sentence "It has two perpendicular and equal diagonals" might refer to the child, the subject of the previous sentence, who is playing with stick toys identified as perpendiculars and diagonals and who is frustrated by the game he or she plays with them. One might even envisage a context including additional sentences that connect the two apparently more remotely related, seemingly unconnected sentences, such as "The boy is asleep" and "The angles of a triangle equal 180 degrees." These might refer to attempts to teach the child geometry. "Yesterday the boy

[15] Ingarden, *The Literary Work of Arts*, pp. 148–9.

learned a geometrical conclusion." "Today he could not remember the key to the solution, which he was supposed to have learned yesterday." "The effort tired him." In cases such as these, we make sense of the sentences by connecting them as literal statements through additional literal statements. Filling in the connections extinguishes the initial tensions.

In contrast with examples of literal sentences, the relation of sentences extracted from poems or other types of literary works to contexts outside the poems is suggestive. "The world is a stage," uttered by a friend we meet on the street, at first seems incongruous. It would require construal and, ordinarily, be interpreted as metaphorical, having an import overlapping, if not identical with, its import in Shakespeare. But suppose we found that the friend has in mind visitors who are being entertained at home and to whom he has had to strain to be polite. A hearer probably would see some such connection and understand the sentence as a metaphor founded on – but assuming that it offers a creative insight, not reducible to – some relationship between form or politeness and honest interaction between the visitors and host. The explicit function of the context, then, would influence not only the interpretation of an expression as a metaphor but also the way that an expression is construed. But the example is more complicated. The sentence is out of its original context where Shakespeare introduced it. If that context is revived in thought, the connections, and the speaker's meaning, will be different and far richer. Further, when the sentence is put into its original context, its connections are almost always with expressions that are themselves metaphorical. And the entire literary work may constitute a metaphor that serves as the sentence's immediate environment. This, like the connections it has with expressions immediately before and after its occurrence, affects the way it is understood. Let me suggest, then, that when the sentence is extracted and put into a literal context, it enriches its literal context to the extent that a sense of its original setting is carried with it. For instance, "The world is a stage," seen as having its literary origin, has a qualitatively different import, signifying that the speaker's experiences at home have a dramatic aspect and suggesting a delicate balance between visitors and the host in the speaker's attempts to adjust to these problems.

Consider another example of two lines from Steven Spender's "The Room Above the Square": "The light in the window seemed perpetual. . . . It flowered above the trees. . . ."[16] If these sentences were not recognized as components of a poem, they might be interpreted as

[16] Stephen Spender, "The Room Above the Square," *Collected Poems 1928–53* (New York: Random House, 1955).

unconnected. But the poetic context makes it clear – as clear as any such examples taken from poetry – that "It" in the second sentence refers to the lighted window or at least to the light in the window. And the idea of flowering here is seen at once as metaphorical. The context has a place for a light that flowers. What these examples show is that as already insisted, an apparent absence of connection between two sentences is itself a guarantee of neither intrinsic mutual irrelevance nor metaphorical function.

It is important to notice that the contexts under consideration have been external. They have been the settings or environments, including the circumstances and possible additional sentences within which a given expression was understood. But just as the external context may contribute to a tension between two or more expressions, another, internal tension may be encountered. The expression may be not just a literal sentence that is apparently or momentarily incongruous with its outer context. The expressions may itself exhibit incongruity among its own meaning units. This kind of situation is present in the case of the sentence "The world is a stage," uttered either when the speaker is discussing visitors at home or in most, if not all, contexts. Thus, instead of one apparent tension, there are initially two: one with the outer context and one within the sentence when it is understood literally. The outer tension may be assuaged once the sentence is understood as a metaphor. Yet what prompts an expression to generate tension in its outer context may be the inner tension rather than what otherwise would be an unproblematic sentence that happens to appear in a context in which it does not fit. This inner tension must be examined more closely, because it occurs in the most dramatic metaphors that belong to a type most readily recognized as creative.

One characteristic essential to inner tension is found in the condition that inner tensions lie between meaning units appropriate to contrasting domains, that is, to kinds or categories, in which "categories" are or are based on ranges of attributes that exclude or negate other ranges. Some of the properties of birds negate those of snakes; some properties of wood conflict with some of those of flesh.

Thus, tensions may occur between meanings belonging to a single general category, for instance, between the meanings of the terms *liquid* and *chains* in a metaphor such as "Our hopes bind us with liquid chains." The properties, fluidity and rigidity, of liquid and chains are sufficiently remote from each other to belong to different subcategories. If sentences in external tension with one another belong to incompatible categories, they might together create a metaphor and thus be constituents of an inner tension within a larger metaphor including more than one sentence. Or they might remain nonsensically associated and unproductive: for instance, on the one hand, "I am sad" and "the day is gray" and, on the other hand, "I am sad" and "water boils at 212 degrees Fahrenheit." Of course, as argued earlier, the second pair might be reconciled by a series of sentences, but unless some such context affected the sentences, we would entertain only an unintelligible relation. On the other hand, if we consider the example "The world is a stage," which exhibits inner tension, we will recognize that the world belongs (or belonged to) a kind of reality or part of experience different from the kind to which theatrical stages belong. With this rather generally acknowledged point about conflicting categories in mind, I shall concentrate on the various ways in which inner oppositions among meaning units are encountered.

One of the terms that function in the tension of the metaphor appears in a context, established by the metaphor, that includes one or more other major meaning units or key terms. As mentioned earlier, the key terms may be explicit, as is often evident in poetry ("the light in the window . . . flowered"), or a term may be implied by an outer context, such as when someone simply utters "Brilliant!" In order to describe how such terms function and how tension is exhibited, let us once again consider part of a poem, observing how the lines establish a context in which explicit terms interact:[17]

> That time of year thou mayst in me behold
> when yellow leaves, or none, or few, do hang
> Upon those boughs which shake against the cold,
> Bare ruin'd choirs, where late the sweet birds sang.

When Shakespeare says, "Bare ruin'd choirs, where late the sweet birds sang," he does so in the larger context of the verse and, in turn, the sonnet as a whole. "Bare ruin'd choirs" relates to an explicit term, "those boughs which shake against the cold," as well as other terms in the verse. The verse is a complex metaphor, containing metaphors within metaphors. The bare ruined choirs are boughs shaking in the cold; they are also places where birds sang; and they are qualifications of a time of year and of the "poetic speaker." The metaphor focused in the "ruin'd choirs" is presented within an explicit context of connected words. But there is a host of implicit meanings associated within each of the meaning units. These depend on conventionally accepted and natural or objective conditions and are the sort of conditions indicated by Black's implicative complexes and associated commonplaces and by Beardsley's marginal meanings.[18] Thus we recognize the verse as metaphorical by understanding the words and sentences

[17] Shakespeare, Sonnet 72.
[18] Ortony, ed., *Metaphor and Thought*, p. 28; Beardsley, "The Metaphorical Twist."

and whatever implied meanings they immediately have, as these are present in contrasting domains or categories.

A metaphor must bring together different kinds of meaning units, and it is because they are different kinds that the meaning units do not belong together. But it is important to notice here that the expression "do not belong together" is general and imprecise. It is chosen deliberately, however, and it reflects what earlier was called "incongruence" and "irrelevance to one another." The generality of these expressions covers utterances that may be false, that are seemingly self-inconsistent, and that are taken as neither true nor false unless reinterpreted; for instance, "Man is a wolf," "He was bound by liquid chains," and "Light travels in waves." Some may be true when understood literally, although they would then cease to be regarded as metaphors: "Cliff is an ape," when "Cliff" turns out to be the name of an ape in the zoo. To reiterate, one thing seems certain: When an expression is taken as metaphorical in a creative sense, it has terms that at least are not used together in standard linguistic expressions in the context in which they appear. There is some form of incongruity.

The presence of tension in metaphors is perhaps most clearly exemplified in oxymorons. Of course, identifying oxymorons as metaphors conflicts with views that follow a strict classification system that locates metaphor among other figures of speech, such as synecdoche, metonymy, irony, and oxymoron. But this classification presupposes that metaphors belong to one type of comparison, a presupposition that has been rejected. What is essential to my view is the point that creative metaphors at their best are figures of speech that do not depend on attaining significance by relying on antecedently fixed meanings and references. Certainly, oxymorons may be significant in the way that metaphors are when they are creative – at least through contrast of terms and generating a significance not restricted to antecedent significance. Of course, the tension or incongruity is more intense in the case of the oxymoron. "The cool heat of imagination" and "The profound shallowness of his gesture" bring together significances that seem to clash. The expressions join incompatible or, most strongly, inconsistent standard meanings. Like other metaphors that are not oxymorons, these expressions say what in literal terms cannot be. Yet the terms join and interact to say something not otherwise said under standard interpretation.

I said earlier that I do not assume that metaphors are found only in single phrases or sentences. As the illustration from Shakespeare shows, particular metaphors can interact with other metaphors to build up a quasi system that itself is a metaphor. Indeed, whole poems can function in the way a metaphor does – a view of poetry recognized by some literary critics who have made it the basis of their analyses and interpretations.

One literary critic in particular has called attention to the oppositions among meanings that contribute to the significance of poetry. In discussing poems and literary works taken as wholes, Cleanth Brooks makes a case for the tension in language that departs from its standard function. It will be helpful to discuss for a moment what he says, as it concurs so well with the claim that language used metaphorically and, more broadly, poetically exhibits oppositions among terms. Brooks states: "Yet there is a sense in which paradox is the language appropriate and inevitable to poetry."[19] Again ". . . I am interested . . . in our seeing that the paradoxes spring from the very nature of the poet's language. . . ."[20] And ". . . the poet's tendency is by contrast [to the scientist's] descriptive. The terms are continually modifying each other, and thus violating their dictionary meanings."[21] One of his illustrations is taken from a sonnet by Wordsworth:[22]

> It is a beauteous evening, calm and free,
> The holy time is quiet as a Nun
> Breathless with adoration. . . .

After pointing out that the girl who is present with the speaker in the poem paradoxically appears both less and more worshipful than the speaker, Brooks observes:[23]

The adjective "breathless" suggests tremendous excitement; and yet the evening is not only quiet but *calm*. There is no final contradiction, to be sure: it is *that* kind of calm and *that* kind of excitement, and the two states may well occur together. But the poet has no one term. Even if he had a polysyllabic technical term, the term would not provide the solution for his problem. He must work by contradiction and qualification.

Although Brooks argues that paradoxes in poetry are found in their meanings as wholes, he also suggests that the metaphors included in poems are paradoxical and may contribute to building the paradox of the poem. Indeed, he views poems as dependent on general metaphors. Speaking (metaphorically) of planes in which metaphors lie, Brooks comments, "There is a continual tilting of the planes; necessary overlappings, discrepancies, contradictions."[24] It is such overlapping that helps constitute the metaphors that Brooks says "underlie" poems.[25]

[19] Cleanth Brooks, *The Well Wrought Urn* (London: Dennis Dobson, 1949), p. 3. U.S. Copyright 1947 by Cleanth Brooks.
[20] Ibid., p. 8.
[21] Ibid.
[22] Ibid.
[23] Ibid., p. 9. Italics in the text.
[24] Ibid.
[25] Ibid., p. 10.

Subjects as Anchoring Terms

It is not unusual for writers to consider the main terms or meaning units in metaphors to be two terms (one of which may be implied). Normally, one term functions as a grammatical subject and one as a qualifying subject. Explicitly or implicitly, these are related by a copula. As we have seen, Black calls the main meaning units primary and secondary or subsidiary subjects. I shall call the primary unit the *nucleus*.

In adopting this conception of the presence and functions of subjects in metaphors, I want to comment on a point usually included by those who affirm interactionism, that is, the relationship between key terms or subjects according to which one serves as a qualifying concept or scheme for interpreting the other term. This distinction is the basis for the ideas of "tenor and vehicle" for Richards and "focus and frame" and "filter" for Black. This kind of distinction and relationship is pertinent, but I think it overlooks a point about the way in which the main terms of metaphors may be related to one another in interactionism. Either of the key subjects may, though not necessarily, function as the lens or filter, or as the vehicle of a metaphor. Some of the problems raised when one says that metaphors have one subject that is "construed" through some form of predication will be addressed later in this chapter. I shall only point out here that if, for example, the world (antecedently known) is regarded through a qualifier, a filter, "unweeded garden" in the metaphor "The world is an unweeded garden," then so an unweeded garden will be regarded through "the world." What it is to be an unweeded garden is not the same once it has interacted with what it is to be the world. Indeed, the point of interactionism, as I see it, is that it is not the antecedent world that is regarded through the screen or filter of the implicatures of unweeded garden. It is, rather, a world that is an unweeded garden and that was not antecedently there to be referred to through a filter. The world referred to is not the world of prior literal reference. This last point will be discussed at greater length in the next chapter, which concerns metaphorical reference. The main point to be emphasized at the moment is that metaphorical expressions include at least two anchoring terms or key meaning units that interact, each affecting the other.

It would be an obvious misunderstanding to conclude that all subjects or anchoring terms of metaphors must be nouns. The words that carry nonstandard and metaphorical meaning may be other parts of speech as well. A verb is a key term responsible for the metaphorical sense of "He was bathed in light" or "time flies." In "That time of year thou mayst in me behold," the preposition *in* carries a nonstandard function.[26] But again, whatever the parts of speech, it is bringing them together as meaning units with their implied meanings drawn from habitats foreign to one another that generates the inner tension. As meaning units with their implication, they thus function as focusing units or anchoring terms. Further, it is the opposition of the anchoring terms that sets the stage for a new context in which the opposing meanings function to yield a new significance. Later, this way of characterizing the emergence of new meaning and reference will be qualified and refined. For the moment, however, let us discuss the role of opposition or tension present in the functions of these units.

"He was bathed in light" joins meaning units so that their connections conflict with conceptual, literal understanding. Light is not a liquid; it does not have properties of cleansing or washing. But it and the expression as a whole invite us to expect that another significance will be present. Another significance not restricted to the given meaning units is involved. Although we cannot identify the sufficient condition for interpreting as significant what would otherwise be nonsensical or incongruous expressions, surely the resistance to our overlooking or rejecting these expressions and their fascination has something to do with a demand that these tension-ridden expressions make on thought. There is a demand for intelligent witnesses to make sense of what is encountered. What is encountered is attended to as a presentation of something to be understood. Consciousness is driven toward an order or connectedness. Thought demands advancement. What thought drives toward is a special, a unique, interrelation of meaning units. And when this end is reached, it can be seen that the influence of these terms on one another in a metaphor effects an integration that is not controlled by the meaning units viewed in their standard functions. A new meaning as a whole is generated.[27] The boughs are no longer just boughs of trees. That time of life is peculiar – as bare boughs that are ruined choirs and the like. In turn, boughs are grasped differently, and choirs and being ruined are seen in a way not specified before the metaphor: Boughs are a time of life; choirs are bare boughs that are ruined. Thus the outcome, the significance of the sonnet, is new.

---

[26] Christine Brooke-Rose, in *A Grammar of Metaphor* (London: Specker and Warburg, 1965) offers a close and extended study of the way that various parts of speech can be used metaphorically.

[27] The unique meaning is what I believe Max Black considers to be a kind of insight provided by the metaphor, which occurs because of the way that the metaphorical expression alters the association it relates to the principal subject (the thing that is viewed metaphorically). Thus, "the writer can establish a novel pattern of implications for the literal use of the key expressions, prior to using them as vehicles for his metaphor." "More about Metaphor," p. 42.

In interpreting Shakespeare's verse, I have deliberately tried to exclude terms not found in his metaphor in order to avoid as much as possible the impression that the characterization of its terms' function as a paraphrase of it. The point is that the major meaning units act on one another and that this interaction occurs against the background of the tensions among complexes of standard meanings.

Brooks's discussion, in which he considered the paradoxes found in the language appropriate to poetry, reinforces the point that metaphorical expression depends on the functions of more than one major term. There must be at least two opposing meaning units in order for the expression to establish a relation of tension. It was said earlier that one of these terms may be indefinite and depend on an implicit context. Most poems explicitly present the terms that are in tension. Yet the way that an implicit term may function as a polar meaning unit in tension with an explicit term is suggestive. Returning briefly to the example of the speaker who says "It is life" while contemplating a river, we should notice that something is ascribed to the thing that satisfies the indefinite term *it,* which functions as subject. *It* and what is ascribed to the subject do not necessitate a metaphorical expression. *It* may refer to the course of events of the speaker's personal history so that the subject is the speaker's life. The expression then could be interpreted literally. Or *it* may refer to the speaker's satisfaction with his or her situation, the initial expression thus meaning "This is the life" or "I am enjoying myself." This last interpretation, of course, formulates the significance of a frozen metaphor, as it construes the expression as a standard cliché repeated without concern for the condensation of meaning that is implied by the application of "the life" to an especially satisfactory moment of life. But of particular importance is the role that the subject term plays when its significance relates metaphorically to the ascription. Of the possibilities open to interpretation, one that is plausible and readily available is the river. If this is made explicit, a polarity will be established between the nucleus term and the ascribing term.

As already indicated one of the key metaphorical terms need not be a noun. It may be a verb or an adjective. The key term may even turn on the use of an article ("Such turning and adjustment of *the harp*").[28] The word *the* compresses the general term *harp* with one performer's harp. The metapohor may also turn, at least in part, on a preposition ("A hope *beyond* the shadow of a dream").[29] However, be-

---

[28] The line is from Browning, the first poem of *Men and Women,* quoted by Brooke-Rose, *A Grammar of Metaphor,* p. 29.

[29] The line is from Keats, *Endymion, A Poetic Romance,* Book 1, p. 857, in *The Poetical Works of John Keats,* ed. H. W. Garrod (Oxford: The Clarendon Press, 1939), cited by Brooke-Rose, *Grammar of Metaphor,* p. 257.

cause a metaphor may depend on a part of speech that is not a noun, it does not follow that an anchoring term is ruled out. At least one term or meaning unit must function as a nucleus. In every case, something is said of something else. The internal tension lies between what is spoken about, the anchoring nucleus, and the something that is said of it.

Seeing-as and the Multidirectionality of Meanings

If a metaphor is an expression in which something is ascribed to a subject, it might be claimed that a metaphor presents something *as* something else. As mentioned earlier, one term or set of terms qualifies and determines the nucleus, inviting us to see the nucleus as signified by the qualifier. Richards might be thought to suggest this by distinguishing tenor from vehicle (at least in one of his apparent interpretations of the distinction). Beardsley, as we have noted, distinguishes central and marginal meanings, marginal meanings yielding a different "sense" in which to take the primary subject.[30] Black speaks of the principal subject as viewed through a filter. One subject, it might be said, is presented *as* the second subject, or the ascribing or framing, metaphorically functioning meaning. Notice that Black uses the example "Man is a wolf," and he says that the metaphor is not a comparison of a man's face with a wolf mask (as some have proposed) but is, rather, "seeing the human face *as* vulpine."[31] However, this interpretation can be misleading. The term *as* too easily suggests either a fiction or a comparison, the very relationship that Black argues against. To see the human face as vulpine suggests seeing the human face *as if* it were vulpine, seeing it as *like* what is vulpine, or seeing it in terms of what can be readily translated as a simile. And this construal mobilizes the issues of what respects or similarities are common to compared items and of how a property can be possessed differently by the two items — "smiling" possessed by a flower, for example, if we construe the metaphor in terms of seeing the flower *as* smiling. Furthermore, the seeing-as thesis overlooks the multidirectionality of interaction in metaphors. If man is seen as vulpine, wolves may also be seen as human. Black himself suggests this. Whatever filter we start with in order to see a subject metaphorically, the filter itself changes and must screen differently; it is unlike the established lens it was at the outset.

The seeing-as view, moreover, does not adequately highlight the importance of recognizing the inner tension of metaphors. Although

---

[30] Beardsley, "The Metaphorical Twist."
[31] Black, "More about Metaphor," p. 37.

it seems correct to say that the internal relations of a metaphor's meaning units invite the interpreter to see something as something, this point does not go far enough. Every statement in which something is said of something – unless perhaps in the case of a tautology – is an instance of seeing-as. In general, an assertion says "see this as that." "The round sphere is red" says that the round sphere is to be seen as red. But more is needed in the case of seeing something in or through a metaphor. At least part of what more is needed is the tension-generating relationship in which what is seen is seen as something that is strange, remote, out of its category. Thus, the seeing-as view is not necessarily inadequate to metaphorical meaning, if we also recognize that the metaphor's impact is to present more than an *as if*, more than seeing something in terms of something else.[32]

It was noted that for Black, "Man is a wolf" succeeds as a metaphor and generates a new meaning; not only is man vulpinized, but so is wolf humanized. In the example from Shakespeare's sonnet, certainly bare ruined choirs are given the meanings of boughs, just as boughs are given the meanings of bare ruined choirs. The relationship between the terms is so interactive that it is questionable whether the subject term, which can be singled out in metaphorical expressions, is stable. Thus, if an anchoring subject is seen as another, that other will be seen as the anchoring subject. Further, in a metaphor that integrates meaning units through tension, what functions as the anchoring term may shift. The opposition between terms forces this shift. When the terms are regarded analytically, that is, by differentiating components of the whole expression, the tension forces a vacillation, or a shift back and forth, between terms and in turn among multiple meaning units. An oxymoron shows this most emphatically, at least in metaphors that are not surrounded by larger poetic contexts. "The cool heat of the imagination" forces shifting that only inadequately can be expressed as "imagination that is hot and cool," "cool imagination that is hot," "hot imagination that is cool," "coolness, which is the heat of imagination," "heat, which is the coolness of imagination," "cool heat that is the imagination."

How then does metaphor present the relation of subject term to attributing term? In grammatical form, the relationship is one of identity. "Man is a wolf" asserts an identity, even if the predicate is

---

[32] We should notice here that if I am correct, then, as argued before, similes may also function in the way that metaphors do, that is, by being more than mere comparisons or suggestions of similarities. In poetry, if nowhere else, this should be true, although the grammatical form of similes, because of the use of terms indicating likeness, makes them less immediately forceful than metaphors are. Unless the context requires otherwise, metaphors present their meanings with greater impact. And as already observed, in connection with earlier comments about Goodman, similes depend on a metaphorical function of the words compared in the simile.

construed as broader than the subject, for then the subject is identified with a part or aspect of the predicate. "He was bathed in light" presents an identity of the subject, *he,* nor with light or with being bathed, but with a subject in a certain mode, that is, with one-bathed-in-light.

What has just been said presupposes that metpahors assert identities regardless of their grammatical form. In the interaction of meaning units, which is articulated by means of an identification, there is a unification, although not a fusion of terms in tension. The tension is not extinguished. A metaphor does not say, "See this *as* that" but, rather, "See that this is what it is not." In the relationship among terms in their standard meanings, the anchor term is *not* what is said of it. Yet because the relationship does not present sheer nonsense, the relationship is *at once* nonstandard and standard. Consequently, it articulates "this is that which is not that and is this which is new."[33]

The terms that interact metaphorically succeed in establishing the metaphor's tension and newness because they are at the same time brought together and kept apart as distinct, determinate meanings. The terms interact while sustaining an independence that they have by virtue of their literal or established meanings. This resistance to losing their original identities in the metaphorical whole is important to the third key feature of metaphors.

Integration, Family Resemblance, and the Functions of Meaning Units

The kind of whole or togetherness of parts presented by a metaphor is an integration rather than a synthesis. The claim that a metaphor integrates rather than synthesizes is crucial. It is the third key feature of metaphorical structure.[34]

A synthesis submerges parts for the sake of the whole. Parts lose their independent meanings and are taken up into the whole. Their identities are lost. On the other hand, an integration orders parts so that they contribute to the whole without losing their individual integrities. They retain their significances and also participate in the significance of the whole. This kind of complex inner relationship is

---

[33] Ricoeur's discussion of the metaphorical *to be* makes a point like the one I make. What I am suggesting was initially proposed in 1975 in *A Discourse on Novelty and Creation.*

[34] Since the term *integration* first occurred to me to be appropriate for making the point at issue, I found that W. Bedell Stanford used the same term in *Greek Metaphor: Studies in Theory and Practice* (Oxford, England: Blackwell Publisher, 1936), p. 101. Stanford, however, couples his notion of integration with unity, which contrasts with my suggestion that unity, at least as closed, is not achieved. Nor does Stanford develop his notion.

what we refer to when speaking of an integrated community. In an ideally integrated society, blacks, whites, Catholics, Protestants, Jews, Muslims, Hindus, and the like all would function together for the society as a whole, without losing their own identities. The conception of metaphors as integrations suggests another characterization: The components of a metaphor are related to one another in what might be called a *family resemblance*. Both the integration and the family resemblance depend on the way that terms function internally and in terms of their contexts, past and future. In order to pursue these ideas, let us focus more closely on the elements or components within metaphors, turning again to poetry.[35]

As already mentioned, metaphors in poems may contain other metaphors and may themselves be components of larger metaphors. Because of this complexity of interacting components, a difficulty arises. When we try to extract a meaning unit by identifying it and saying something about its meaning, we inevitably distort the extracted expression.

With this caution in mind, I shall focus on two lines from a poem by Wallace Stevens, "The Man with the Blue Guitar."[36] I shall assume that the two lines form a complex metaphor, which though viewed apart from its larger poetic context, retains a certain poetic as well as metaphorical significance. The two lines on which we shall concentrate are

> Greenish quaverings of day
> Quiver upon the blue guitar.

The component expression "greenish quaverings of day" is a distinct metaphor, as is "quiver upon the blue guitar." These two component metaphors interact, and in turn, they interact together with the metaphorical sentence as a whole. Thus, meanings found in one of the components affect the meanings of the others. Meaning units in the expression "the greenish quaverings of day" may be singled out without violating the larger context, provided that we keep this context in mind as a background.

The terms in this expression, as in any creative metaphor, can be regarded in three ways with respect to the way they relate to themselves and to their contexts: as constituents, as antecedent components, and as consequent meanings. Each of the three ways of regarding terms distinguishes what may be called a *level* of meaning. And the distinctions among these levels concern three ways that these

---

[35] The next few paragraphs are based on my discussion of the components of metaphors offered in *A Discourse on Novelty and Creation*, chap. 3.
[36] Wallace Stevens, *Opus Posthumous* (New York: Knopf, 1957), p. 73. This poem was discussed for related reasons in my *A Discourse on Novelty and Creation*.

meaning units function for the purposes of analysis. The word *level* applies to stages, two of which others have recognized as conditions of metaphorical meanings: a literal but incongruous meaning (appearing as tension) and a metaphorical or "deeper" meaning appearing when the metaphor is seen to be more than nonsensical. Components regarded as terms that have antecedent meanings correspond to the first level where tension is first recognized. The function of these terms as what I have called *constituents* corresponds to the second, deeper level. *Consequent meanings* suggests an additional stage that is not deeper but, if we think of levels, is higher, higher than the first in the sense that it advances intelligibility beyond its state when associated with literal or established, linguistically accessible, intelligibility before the metaphor was created.

At the first and third levels of meaning, discrete units can be conceptualized and related to terms outside the metaphor. These meaning units abstracted from the metaphor can be used to build a paraphrase, although not one that exhausts the metaphor's significance.

Antecedent elements are the meaning units regarded as extracted from the metaphor and interpreted in accordance with antecedent meanings. The constituents are the terms regarded as components that function in internal interaction. But as constituents, they cannot be abstracted or identified as discrete units. Insofar as they are seen to function in internal relations, they cannot be identified and used in discursive speech. To do so would be to extract them and thus to return to the level of antecedent elements – or to advance to the third, consequent level. Consequent meanings are discovered when the terms are extracted again (as in an analysis of a work of art) and regarded as transformed by virtue of their interaction. Thus they are meanings made possible by the interaction of terms when they act as constituents.

The transformation of antecedents, through their functions as constituents, into consequent meanings is not simply the result of shifting attention from conventionally acknowledged meaning complexes, which are implied by the antecedents, to another set of meanings already known but not heretofore associated with the terms in the metaphor. Identifying consequent meanings is not simply shifting to marginal meanings (to use Beardsley's term) or highlighting accidental properties that may be associated with the terms of the metaphor. I am not proposing a return to the comparison view. As already admitted, comparison does take place. But it is the transformation of terms into constituents and their unprecedented functions as consequent meanings that is the metaphor's creative achievement. This achievement cannot be reduced to antecedents. It is the addition of new, consequent meaning that enables advances in the language. Without this advance toward the future, the vast body of available linguistic meanings could only have been explicitly or implicitly given, complete as a system of prior meanings that would be necessary and sufficient for our language as we now (and will) understand it.

Let me illustrate this by returning to the example "The Man with the Blue Guitar." The first line, "The greenish quaverings of day," can be analyzed as follows: *Greenish* initially can be regarded in its antecedent function. Thus it means a determinable color, whose determinates can be found on a color chart or in expanses of grass or foliage in the summer. Quaverings, interpreted as an antecedent element, means shaking, trembling, or trilling. *Day* connotes the time between sunrise and sunset, or the twenty-four hours between sunrises, or one complete rotation of the earth.

These terms can be viewed as constituents – indeed, they must be regarded in this way if the expression is to function for aesthetic and metaphorical significance. As constituents, they function internally. Consequently, as has already been emphasized, as constituents, the terms that could be translated into antecedent meanings cannot now be translated. This is especially evident in poetry, in which the meaning units most obviously interact in internal relations. Each unit is affected by, and is changed by, the others; and each unit interacting with those of its community affects the whole. Thus, each component depends on the whole complex, and the whole depends on these components. It is inappropriate at this level to single out one or the other, and to characterize the whole without identifying the components is to distort by abstraction. To characterize any one constituent completely (if this were possible) would be to say everything that is relevant to all other constituents and the whole. The issue here is not just that we have a circle – a hermeneutical circle in which the parts depend on the whole and the whole depends on the parts. We do have such a circle. But the circle is not static. Circling through the parts to the whole and back is progressive. Attempts to subject constituents and their wholes to interpretation requires attention that shifts within a spiral rather than a circle. Interpretive circling brings increasingly more meaning to the fore. Interpretation, then, must go on indefinitely and perhaps *ad infinitum.* Nevertheless, the open-endedness here is not a function of vagueness or of simple ambiguity. There are restrictions on interpretation. These restrictions are a function of the metaphor's reference, which will be the topic of the next chapter. At this point, our task is to consider how this level or stage in which the components function in internal relations – which requires regarding the terms as constituents – is related to the first and third stages.

The internal functioning of terms as constituents, seen against the background of antecedent components, is the basis for discovering and construing the components as consequent meanings. Regarded in this way, in relation to quivering, and to quavering as related to *day*, *greenish* indicates what may be unhealthy and mysterious, and immature and fragile. *Quaverings* suggests variability and uncertainty. Day means a temporally defined environment, with further suggestions of fortune and misfortune. Because of the terms' constitutive functioning, with a sense of the prior conventional meanings retained as background and with the consequent recognition of a creative interchange among terms as constituents, these consequent meanings flow from the metaphor.

It is crucial to my conception of levels of meaning, and of consequent meanings in particular, to avoid understanding consequent meanings as paraphrases that would have been possible to formulate before the metaphors occur. Nor is a description of consequent meanings equivalent to the metaphor to which they are relevant. The meaning of the metaphor itself is immanent in the constituent meanings. I think this point can be inferred from Nelson Goodman's insistence that there is metaphorical truth and falsity that are not to be confused with literal truth and falsity.[37] To use his example, the expression "This is a sad painting" is true of the painting just to the extent that the painting is metaphorically sad. I am not concerned with truth conditions. But I do think that if metaphors can reasonably be said to be true or false metaphorically, they also may be meaningful metaphorically, which is to say that they are meaningful with respect to constituent interactions, and not with respect to antecedent or consequent meanings. Metaphors enable the recognition of consequent meanings, and they do this because of the unique meaning that they introduce into language and thought.

This point should be emphasized also in regard to some of the critics of interactionism, such as Searle. The created meaning that Searle denies to metaphors is looked for at the wrong level of the meaning units' functioning. Recall that Searle failed to see that the restrictions of different subjects on the same predicate yielded anything new. But he was looking at the subjects and predicates in terms of antecedent meanings and rejecting the possibility that each expression that included a different subject but the same predicate meant just what it expressed and in no other way – which means in terms of constituents. Further, Searle did not entertain the possibility that consequent meanings were created by the metaphorical or constituent meaning. Thus, the meaning of "Kant's Transcendental Deduction," which was said to be "gravel," has ramifications for Kant's idea of dialectic, although I think here we have an instance of what, using Goodman's

---

[37] Goodman, *Languages of Art*, in particular, pp. 68–85.

terms, may be called a metaphor that is metaphorically false of "Kant's Transcendental Deduction" – if the term *false* is properly used in this way.

To appeal to another view that opposes much of the traditional literature of comparison theorists and interactionists, we should note Donald Davidson's example of the expression "He was burned up."[38] He says that when this died as a metaphor, it meant simply "He was angry." My point is that anger is not equivalent to the burning referred to in the metaphor, after it was frozen. The metaphor, whether alive or dormant, means just what it means. I think Davidson should have recognized this rather than assimilating the metaphor to a meaning antecedently understood before the metaphor occurred. Where I differ from Davidson concerns how to account for the effects of metaphors. These effects, as I have interpreted metaphor, have semantic conditions that are linked as meanings to the meaning of the metaphor. But when the tension in creative metaphors ceases to be recognized in light of an accompanying awareness of earlier literal significance, the metaphor is accepted for what it is, with whatever consequent significance it prompted and without attention to the uniqueness that the metaphor had in suggesting consequent significance.

Two features of metaphorical expressions should be recalled in relation to what has been said about the three levels of meaning. Tension is evident in the relations among the key antecedent elements, which exhibit oppositions. In their functions as antecedent elements, these terms indicate discontinuity of categories or kinds – days that quiver or trill. Days as periods of time do not themselves behave as physical objects that can engage in physical movement. Antecedent elements clash, and this yields the negative quality and tension identified earlier. There is no way effectively to consider intelligibly days as things that can quiver, unless we recognize an identity constituted by the terms' inner or internal relations. This suggests again the point that oxymorons exhibit extreme metaphorical tensions, where opposition is most extreme.[39]

I suggest that the greater the intensity of the opposition is, the richer the possible range of consequent meanings that flow initially from the metaphor will be. There are fewer restrictions on terms when they are regarded as constituents. Conceptual perspectives are the most sharply broken, and meanings are freed for different functions. The

---

[38] Donald Davidson, "What Metaphors Mean," *Critical Inquiry* 5 (Autumn 1978): 45.

[39] Albert Rothenberg holds a view similar to this. He argues on the basis of both his own experimental studies and analyses of poems, that creative acts include "Janusian thinking" or mental processes in which the opposition of images or attributes condition the key ingredients of poetic achievements. See Albert Rothenberg, "The Process of Janusian Thinking in Creativity," *Archives of General Psychiatry* 24 (1971): 195–205. More recently, Rothenberg developed this view at length in *The Emerging Goddess*.

sharper the clash is, the greater the possibilities of difference will be. If it is accepted that a contradiction in logic implies all things, then surely a metaphorical tension must suggest at least an open-ended cluster of forthcoming meanings. However, as we pointed out, the clash within a metaphor is not a condition of absolute openness. Even an oxymoron is not a logical contradiction from which, it might be said, everything follows. The interacting meanings are not wholly indeterminate, abstract concepts. They are determinate. They have definite associated meanings, and these do not express sheer nonsense.

On the other hand, the expression "Coins worm the valley" is, or at least at first seems, nonsensical. The clash here seems to lack any framework of implied meanings that are capable of interacting. The terms resist being recognized as constituents. Even so, the nonsensical aspect of this expression is not the same as the nonsensical aspect of "pleated toward if pawn," for instance. Of course, with respect to being nonsensical, they are the same. But with respect to the ways in which they are nonsensical, they are different. Each expression is recognized as nonsensical and seemingly resistant to internal interaction of meaning units – here because of violations of grammatical form. But in "the cool heat of his anger," the terms *cool* and *heat* have a framework of meanings that can interact, particularly in light of *anger*, which also has its own meaning context. And in the Wallace Stevens example, the terms *greenish* and *quavering* have contexts of meaning that interact with the meaning of *day*.

Let me point out in passing that the differentiation of the elements that comprise a metaphor offers a basis for interpreting the role of creations in the history of a tradition. Antecedent elements are drawn from the tradition and serve as the materials for forming the new meaning. The constitutive components enable the creation to become a model for the future. Because of the constituents' function, the expression yields its unique character, an identity that insists on its new presence in the tradition. Because of this new identity, the consequent elements can function as ingredients in future creations. Thus, they constitute the development of the tradition, and interpretations of works in the tradition depend on the consequent element of metaphor.

Let us return to the point that what has been said about the idea that intelligibility in created metaphors belongs to integrations and can be compared with the notion of family resemblances. By using this idea, my intention is not to adopt a faithful interpretation of Wittgenstein's notion. I want only to use certain aspects of what I think is a valuable characterization of one of the conditions of language. Thus I shall briefly suggest a way that the interrelations of meanings in metaphors function in a way something like Wittgenstein's family resemblances do.

It is obvious that in this view of metaphor, creative metaphors are not unities that take the form of general terms. They are complexes of terms, general and particular, and because they are creative, they are not instantiations or symbols of antecedent general meanings. Thus whether Wittgenstein is correct that no general terms can be defined with reference to essential characteristics or common properties is not the point here. The idea that metaphorical meanings are integrations, however, implies that even though a family does not have one or more properties or characteristics identical in all its members, it nevertheless may have a comprehensive meaning. A family is an integrated community of distinct members. However open and flexible the application of a single term – a family name – may be, and however indefinite the boundaries of the family traits may be, there is a comprehensive identity that serves as a loosely relevant criterion for the family's identification. Our inability to find a property common to all members of the family does not necessarily mean that there is no identity of coherence that enables us to recognize the family.

Complexes of the meanings of terms that constitute metaphors (what Black calls implicative complexes and implication-complexes) do not, when functioning creatively, connote meanings common to or implied by the conventional meanings of the antecedent elements. Thus, no single coherent set of meanings is common to all the antecedent elements. Similarly, no single common meaning unifies the consequent meanings that may be identified in interpretations of a metaphor. A metaphor presents familiar complexes or a network of meanings, no one of which is common to the meaning of the metaphor as a whole. Further, because the antecedent elements together appear incoherent or incongruent within the context of the metaphor, the connections among these elements exhibit contrasts as well as similarities, and these contrasts contribute to the functioning of the elements as constituents and consequently to the new import of the metaphor. The role of contrast is again a way of calling attention to the fact that the whole is an integration rather than a synthesis. A metaphor, then, is comparable to the overall character that identifies a family.

This point may be illustrated by "The world is an unweeded garden," which brings together meanings that include "the locus of our lives," "humanity," and "the whole of things," among others, with "unwanted growth," "place of beauty," "fertile ground," "uselessness," and so on. No one of the meanings or aspects of meanings is common to all the meanings. And no one is itself essential to the specific meaning of the whole. Yet each interacting with the other contributes to the whole of the metaphor. It is this mutual contribution –

including abstract concepts, particular, images, and feeling tones – that yields constituent meanings which are the originative dimension of metaphorical meaning. It is the discrimination of the outcome, together with the recognition of the differences of antecedent meanings in the background, that appears as a comprehensive character like that of a family.

Although the idea of family resemblance seems to me appropriate here, the idea must be qualified in its application to creative metaphorical expression. First, the term *family resemblance* does not sufficiently highlight the importance of the negative aspect of the relationship among antecedent elements. A metaphor does not, as a linguistic item, refer us to a class of things already recognizable as a cluster of resemblances. Rather, the meanings of a creative metaphor presents an intelligible cluster of clashing meanings. The meanings common to the terms taken as antecedent elements are in a way less important than the clash, because the common antecedent elements do not constitute the new meaning that arises from the discordant terms. The term *family resemblance* in Wittgenstein's thesis, I think, not only negates the idea of essential or universally common similarities but also stresses that families comprehend dissimilars, or differences. The term *resemblance* does not itself emphasize this point. Yet differences do contribute to the identity of families. Although the same name belongs to all members of a family, the members are different from one another, and differences as well as similarities sustain the family.

There is another way in which the idea of family resemblance is peculiar when applied to metaphors. The family character of a metaphor does not cover a set of examples to which the metaphor applies. The new significance of the metaphor is unique. Only later, if the metaphor is frozen or if it has been incorporated as literal language, can it be seen as overlapping other families and referring to more than one instance. In being new, the family constitutes a new whole. It is initially a closed family, as long as its constituents are the focus of attention. In this state, its specific members cannot be taken away, nor can more be added without changing it, although through its impact on the future and its consequent meanings, it will undergo change. If the family were not in this sense unique and initially closed, it would not be a new determination that nevertheless, as a creation and an archetype for the future, can contribute to the advancement of a tradition or to the growth of future "families" in the form of developments in language.

This account of the function of components in interaction is not, of course, offered as an explanation of the origin of a new significance. Nor has this account explained how a metaphor can create something new that at the same time seems to offer insight into something that is real. This second problem, which is an aspect of the general problem of creativity as seen in our attempts to understand metaphor, raises an ontological issue. It concerns the relation of metaphors to reality, and it will be the main topic of the next chapter.

3

Metaphorical Reference

To ask about the relevance of metaphorical insight to the world is to ask how metaphors refer to things that are in some respect independent of metaphorical expressions. An attempt to answer this question, however, calls for abandoning the commitment to metaphysical neutrality I have tried to hold until now. The idea of reference to be considered next cannot be treated apart from an acknowledgment of some form of realism. As will be increasingly obvious in this and succeeding chapters, this realism will serve as the basis for the proposal I shall make about the relevance of metaphorical insight to the world.

Paradoxes

The idea that metaphors can both create and exhibit insights concerning the world is paradoxical, that is, paradoxical insofar as they generate something that constrains them as does something already in the world. On the one hand, to create is to bring about something that was not in the world before the creation took place; on the other hand, to have an insight is apparently to discover something that was in the world, though unnoticed, before the creation occurred. As I claimed at the beginning of this book, although I do not think the paradox can be eliminated, I do think it is possible to give an account of metaphor that pushes beyond the paradox in its initial form. The first step toward providing this account was taken in the reconsideration of interactionism. The next step must include suggestions about the interactions of meaning units and also about the relation of metaphorical meanings to the world.

In its initial form, the paradox concerns understanding what is radically new. Because understanding is traditionally most often tied to tracing things to their antecedents, understanding and what is new seem incompatible. Most of the theories of metaphor considered in the first chapter slip into this way of understanding metaphors and thus minimize or negate outright the newness attributed to at least some metaphors. The various theories either explicitly or implicitly treat metaphorical meaning or sense in terms of other, antecedent meanings or senses. Accordingly, most theories center on the connotations or senses of metaphors, with minimal attention to their referents. However, in concentrating on reference, I shall try to avoid the temptation to reduce what is initially considered as new to something already familiar.

If a metaphor creates not only new meaning but also new significance or new import, then it creates its insight – its perspective on something in the world. And if significance or import includes reference, if import is more than a complex of sense or meanings taken in abstraction, apart from that to which they lead, then when interactionists affirm the creative success of some metaphors, they should affirm newness of both reference and meaning. But when interactionists offer an account of the way metaphors work, meaning rather than reference seems to be the primary condition operative in the account. Of course, one of the reasons they do this is because they assume that an account must explain how what is unfamiliar (the creation) can be traced to what is familiar (antecedent meanings). Attending to the referents of the meanings of metaphors, rather than to more meanings, may help inquiry break away from this implied reductionism.

In the following discussion, I shall suggest a way of looking more closely at the references of metaphors that are considered creative.[1] Creative metaphors will be viewed as naming or reference-fixing expressions that give birth to the referents they fix.[2] Through these referents, metaphors help constitute what may be called *the world*.

Max Black's Defense of Creative, Cognitive Insight

In Chapter 1, we considered Max Black's suggestion that the outcomes of the interaction in creative metaphors yield cognitive insights. For him, neither the insight nor the interaction can be reduced to comparisons or, more generally, to antecedently meaningful utterances. Metaphors, in a sense, help constitute aspects of reality. As we have observed, Black says that this claim "is no longer surprising if one believes that the world is necessarily a world *under a certain description* – or a world seen from a certain perspective. Some metaphors can create such a perspective."[3] The account of the sense in which metaphors can create something in the world is our primary concern. What ontological commitment is implied by Black's conception, the

---

[1] A shorter version of this chapter appeared as "Metaphor, Referents, and Individuality," *Journal of Aesthetics and Art Criterion* 42 (1983): 181–95.

[2] In formulating the point this way, I owe something to Saul A. Kripke's thesis about naming and reference, "Naming and Necessity," in Donald Davidson and Gilbert Harman, eds., *Semantics of Natural Language* (Dordrecht: D. Reidel, 1972), pp. 253–355. However, it will be abundantly evident that I do not accept or attempt to adopt his thesis as a whole.

[3] Black, "More About Metaphor," pp. 39–40.

world, which purportedly leaves room for newness? Black says that
metaphors can create, if we regard what they create as perspectives.
But what is the object of a perspective? On what is a perspective directed? On a world. But if there is only a world "under a certain description" or perspective, what metaphors create perspectives on must
be more perspectives. We seem to be insulated from anything extra-
perspectival. There is another way to put this. To say that a perspective is on something that depends on being perceived might imply
that the world is merely a system of intentional objects. The question
of existents that are independent of intentional objects – things existent, insofar as they are independent of an intending consciousness –
presumably would be bracketed. But Black does not bracket the question when he asks whether metaphors can show us "how things are."
His answer is that they can, but not in the sense that they are subject
to truth evaluations. They show us how things are with a force similar
to that of "charts, maps, graphs and pictorial diagrams, photographs
and 'realistic' paintings, and above all models."[4] Metaphors, then, can
be correct, appropriate, or faithful. And in terms of such expectations, metaphors can "convey" or "generate" insights.[5] But the question remains whether for Black charts, maps, and the like, can be
faithful only to perspectives, which themselves can be faithful only to
perspectives, and so on *ad infinitum,* or whether there is something
independent of the perspectives to which they are faithful.

In the broadest terms, Black's view seems to imply either a kind of
idealism (in the sense of equating reality with cognitively and/or linguistically determined schemata) or a form of neo-Kantianism. These
alternatives also may be seen in the question whether there is any
extralinguistic or extraconceptual condition, a condition independent
of perspectives, that functions to ground "faithfulness." If there is no
independent extralinguistic, extraconceptual condition, then the theory is idealistic. If there is, but the condition is not knowable in itself,
then the position is Kantian.

There is another question that is germane to our topic: When the
perspective is a creative metaphor, is the world (or some part of it) for
the perspective new, or is the world nothing but a system of stabilized,
antecedently unrecognized perspectives? In the latter alternative there
is something to which the metaphor can be faithful, but the world (of
perspectives) is not modified by a creation or a new constituent. The
metaphor is a discovery. Only in accordance with the former alternative can the world include something new that matches the creative
force of the metaphor. Only then can the metaphor, the new perspec-

---

[4] Ibid., pp. 39–40.
[5] Ibid., p. 41.

tive, be faithful to a new constituent or aspect of the world that itself conforms to the creative metaphor.

One of Black's defenders, Ina Loewenberg, takes up the question of how metaphors might create similarities. She advances two points that are of particular importance in her defense of Black. In "Identifying Metaphors," she suggests the introduction of a "new speech-act which we can call *proposal* for (metaphorical proposal)."[6] As proposals, metaphors are without truth-value. Although possible falsity may alert the reader or hearer to the need to interpret a sentence as metaphorical, once the sentence is interpreted as metaphorical, truth-value is irrelevant. Loewenberg does not make clear whether her view that metaphors are proposals is meant to incorporate Black's suggestion that some metaphors can be faithful or appropriate. However, presumably she intends her defense of Black to be consistent with his view, and if so, then her metaphors as proposals (metaphors) must be either faithful or unfaithful, appropriate or inapt. But again, this raises the question faced by Black's view: To what are metaphorical proposals faithful? To perspectives or something independent of perspectives?

In a later article, Loewenberg attacks this issue more directly. She prefers the originativist's rhetoric, stating "It is necessary to show that a linguistic innovation, located in a single utterance, can change or originate something in the world."[7] And she seems to affirm this stronger view just as vigorously as Black does. But what kind of object, event, relation, quality, or condition is this "something in the world" that may be originated? It turns out to be something very much like Black's perspectives. The world is a function of "observers": ". . . the 'world' is not independent of observers and language use is not a mere reporting of what there is." Things in the world are known "through some viewpoint or other, often through several, at different times, for different purposes." Such viewpoints are instruments, and metaphors are viewpoints, too, which function as instruments: to get us to view the world through what the metaphor expresses.[8] But again, what sort of thing is known or viewed through a viewpoint (metaphorical or nonmetaphorical)? Is it a cluster or system of viewpoints? Or is it something independent but viewed through these? What does the instrument accomplish? Is its function to build something new? Or is it to repair or reorganize what is already there? Loewenberg's statement that things in the world are known through (not within) some view-

---

[6] Ina Loewenberg, "Identifying Metaphors," *Foundations of Language* 12 (1975): 315–38.
[7] Ina Loewenberg, "Creativity and Correspondence in Fiction and in Metaphors," *Journal of Aesthetics and Art Criticism* 36 (Spring 1978): 345.
[8] Ibid.

point might lead us to choose the second alternative. A good metaphor, then, would be an instrument of discovery. Thus it would not be an instrument getting hearers or readers to try out a proposal that, in fact, creates its object.

This interpretation of Loewenberg's world and the things in the world viewed through viewpoints, however, might seem to be contradicted by other statements she makes. Good metaphors fit the world by making it different, and a good metaphor would "fit the world to perfection," because the world (or its part of the world) is made to fit it. Language "shapes, rather than reflects, the world." Metaphors may "change the world" by revising part of it, because the world, after all, is a system of viewpoints. The part of the world that may be changed is our cognitive framework.

Given this conception of metaphor, however, the question arises whether there is a basis for testing metaphors by any condition other than the cognitive framework itself. The standard for the fit of a good metaphor seems to be purely linguistic, lying in the metaphor's framework of viewpoints, just as the standard for deciding on the adequacy with which the world is described is the linguistic–conceptual framework to which the description refers. However, Loewenberg does suggest that there is a criterion that leads beyond language and thought, to an extralinguistic condition, although it is not clear whether she intended this. This possibility is raised when she says that the test of whether our viewpoints, which are constituents of the framework, have changed is that we have different expectations regarding them. The introduction of the idea of expectations could be understood as a pragmatist's criterion according to which expectations are anticipatory attitudes or dispositions to action — habits that have objective reference to conditions in the future.

But what could such a condition be, future or present, that brings about a change in expectations? Regarding this, Loewenberg leaves us where Black did. If expectations change because something other than a viewpoint or a cognitive framework is different, then there may be an extralinguistic and extraconceptual world or component of the world that at least contributes to bringing about the change. Yet if expectations change only because the metaphorical expression has persuasive force or only because it has some other purely linguistic and perhaps conceptual force, then it creates what it views because it is caught up in the idealism of linguistic or conceptual schemes. In the former alternative, constructing good (creative) metaphors is discovery. In the latter, it is radically creative, but at the expense of losing an independent, extralinguistic, extraconceptual reality.

The consideration of Black's originativist view and Loewenberg's defense and suggested extension of Black's account has emphasized what seems to be two irreconcilable interpretations of metaphor. If metaphors are creative, how can they provide insight into reality, unless reality is construed as excluding anything extralinguistic and extraconceptual? But then what does it mean to claim that metaphors can be "faithful" or "fitting"? Is it sufficient to see them as faithful to what they themselves constitute and, indeed, are if reality consists of just these linguistic and conceptual constructions? If linguistic–conceptual idealism is a form of nominalism, at least in comparison with realism, then it is fair to say that Ricoeur makes a similar point when he criticizes Goodman's nominalistic theory of metaphor: "The appropriateness of metaphorical as well as literal application of a predicate is not fully justified within a purely nominalistic conception of language."[9]

More fundamental than this question about that to which creative metaphors are faithful is the issue concerning whether language as a whole, as well as each instance of speaking and writing, has an extralinguistic reference. The relevance of this larger question can be seen if we notice one kind of answer open to both the nominalist and the conceptual perspectivalist in responding to the objection that faithfulness is not accounted for by perspectivalism. The answer consists of pointing out that appropriateness is justified by the acceptability of further linguistic data or further perspectives. The system of linguistic or conceptual items, regarded as a whole, has some independence of the particular expressions that are said to be apt or inapt. The larger system gives the needed objectivity. Intersubjective linguistic items connect with one another and provide all the extralinguistic ground required. However, the issue I am raising concerns whether there is no end to these linguistic or conceptual conditions.[10] The point is that some indexical or referential role needs to be played somewhere outside language as a whole if language and concepts (mind) are not wholly self-contained.

However, as suggested, the point takes a special turn when "appropriateness" is attributed to the metaphorical expression that might create new similarities. The ground of appropriateness for a new insight provided by a creative metaphor – the compelling condition of the new similarity, what suggests that it "fits" – cannot be restricted to a complex of established perspectives. For it is this complex, or some part of it, that is challenged by the new insight. Thus the world

---

[9] Ricoeur, *The Rule of Metaphor*, p. 239.
[10] Peirce faced this issue insofar as he regarded cognitive meaning as a system of symbols (generals) continuing into the future, and he also tried to make a place for a mode of reality independent of the system: individuality, found in instances of resistance to conceptual efforts (signs are indexical and iconic as well as symbolic). Peirce's view will later help in explaining my own view.

under a perspective, if it is a condition for the appropriateness of a metaphor, cannot consist exclusively in a system of known perspectives. What conditions the fittingness of a new insight needs to be something in the world that is not identical with these perspectives – unless of course, one is willing to say circularly that the object of the insight is identical with the perspective that conditions its appropriateness. The insight would then need to be self-justifying. It would be its own ground for fittingness, and in this case, we have no reason for regarding the new significance as an insight. But if a metaphor offers insight, then its appropriateness cannot be the insight itself. Its appropriateness must be conditioned by something that is in some way independent of the insight and that is, in part, independent of the perspectives.

The special turn that the appropriateness issue takes with creative metaphor suggests that when metaphorical experiences are perceived as creative, they are viewed as being at the cutting edge of language as a whole. Thus the linguistic–conceptual proposal to regard the system of linguistic conceptual data as the ground of cognitive conditions poses a special problem in the case of metaphorical expressions. Even if the perspectivalist can account for the faithfulness or appropriateness of particular literal expressions by grounding them in a larger linguistic or conceptual context, this account will reach a limit in the case of creative metaphors. Creative metaphors take a fundamental responsibility for language as a whole, making language responsible to something independent of itself, at least as it is constituted at the moment of creation. Through their creative articulations of senses or meanings, metaphors must fix references to referents that are in some way independent of metaphorical expressions. Metaphors are creative designations. To show how creative metaphors must be understood as reference fixers, it is not necessary initially to settle the ontological issue in all its ramifications. We must examine the referential, extralinguistic function performed by those linguistic expressions that are creative metaphors.

The Proposal

As I have suggested already, the problems broached in this study in part have been the result of trying to understand how metaphors function, by attending primarily to the connotations, the senses, or broadly, the intension (the concepts and properties implied by a term) and, most broadly, what I have called the major meaning units – nuclei or anchoring terms. As Black's theory proposes, "Man is a wolf" is said to offer a perspective on man through an implicative complex, a system of presupposed attributes of wolves, that acts as a filter. In

turn, attributes of humans are selected and organized as a complex
for seeing wolves differently. The referents of man and wolf are not
ignored, but it is sense or envisaged properties rather than the referents that account for a metaphorical function. This focus on the intension of terms invites the rationalist explanatory program of tracing
purportedly new connotations, intensions, or senses, to (or at least
correlating them with) relatively familiar meanings or frames of reference. This rationalist program need not be so rigorous as to demand that explanation completely subsume what is to be explained
under immutable premises. But it is a program aimed at relating explananda to concepts that refer to, or are themselves, general and
thus repeatable data that are understood because they are to some
degree more familiar than the explananda. In the case of instances of
creativity, the repeatable data may be general and fixed after they are
determined (in themselves or by cognition): they may be real *in re* and
post rem but not *ante rem;* they may be known only after they have been
"invented" by or through cognitive activity. Thus metaphors may bring
about change in the conventions of accepted language. Yet the origin
(or condition of emergence) of such generals is still at issue.

My proposal is that we should focus not only on the referents of the
component terms (words or expressions) of the metaphor but also,
and more importantly, on the referential function of metaphors taken
as wholes. This approach might appear to be a form of what has been
called *extensionalism.* In order to show why what I propose does not
fall under this label, let me briefly consider two examples of extensionalism.

There are two recent theorists who may be called "extensionalists":
Nelson Goodman and Israel Scheffler.[11] Goodman has developed an
extensionalist theory that acknowledges the creative function of metaphor. And he affirms the paradoxical character of metaphor, except
that he sees the paradox in the interrelations between language and
object rather than between a combination of formally intelligible senses or properties and a newly intelligible sense of property. His view is
based on a nominalism that replaces the role of senses and properties
that I wish to retain. Of course, my view, in contrast with nominalism,
assumes a fundamental difference in philosophical positions, which I
cannot attempt to resolve here. Suffice it to say that Goodman explicitly waives the ontological issue to the extent that he waives the question "why predicates apply as they do metaphorically," which, he says,
is "much the same as the question why they apply as they do literally.
And if we have no answer in either case, perhaps that is because there

---

[11]Goodman's extensionalism is represented in *Languages of Art,* and Scheffler's is found
in *Beyond the Letter.*

is no real question." If one considers an ontological basis for answering this question, then the problem that I want to address will be as follows: Is there a way that whatever metaphors apply to (their extralinguistic objects) can be new? Although Goodman's position avoids making clear just what metaphors apply to, he does seem to require referents that are objects and organizations of objects ("realms"). "Metaphor is most potent when the transferred schema effects a new and notable organization rather than a mere relabeling of an old one." But it is not clear what a "new realm" is apart from the schema itself.[12] Redescription is construed as relabeling. But whether one redescribes or relabels, the issue raised still concerns whether creating is only linguistic (or conceptual). In the broad sense, Goodman's view is a form of linguistic idealism as long as it is detached from the question of what is relabeled.

In *Beyond the Letter,* Israel Scheffler also offers an extensionalist thesis about metaphor. His view takes Goodman's into account, and he shows the extent to which he is influenced by and wishes to go beyond Goodman. His extension of Goodman's view depends chiefly on his own more extreme nominalism, which, early in his book, he identifies as *inscriptionalism.* Scheffler resists any acknowledgment of common features underlying either similes or metaphors.[13] Yet he acknowledges that metaphors may be creative, and he shows why they cannot be understood by any ready-made formulas. "The creative role of metaphorical utterance . . . does not simply report isomorphisms but calls them forth afresh to direct, and be tried by, further investigations. The happy outcome of such investigations is of course not assured beforehand."[14] Scheffler then observes:

It might thus perhaps be suggested that the theorist – or the producer of metaphor, more generally – does not know what he is saying ("the meaning" of what he is saying). For the metaphorical term he uses has an extension he typically cannot elucidate at the time of utterance, dependent as such elucidation may be upon contextually significant predicates determined as such only in subsequent inquiry.[15]

He adds that this predicament applies also to literal attributions that gain theoretical refinement. And finally, he assures us that this predicament seems paradoxical only if we separate meaning from fact. "The process of finding out more about one's own meaning and finding out more about the world are, however, one and the same."[16]

The proposal I wish to offer obviously does not disagree that met-

---

[12] Goodman, *Language of Art,* pp. 79–80.
[13] Scheffler, *Beyond the Letter,* p. 126.
[14] Ibid., p. 129.
[15] Ibid., pp. 129–30.
[16] Ibid., p. 130.

aphors have creative roles. Yet I do want to step beyond the linguistic confinements of Scheffler's nominalism. If finding out more about the world and finding out about one's own meanings are identical and if one consults only linguistic items, then one is surely a linguistic idealist. And this reraises the question of what, independent of language, might ground our seeing that some metaphors are more apt than others and our finding out that tests do or do not conform to our language. Furthermore, I want to consider this ontological question in conjunction with the conviction that there are occasionally novel meanings – senses as well as word tokens – that are introduced into our language as it grows in its relation to something independent of this language.

The proposal that creative metaphors are reference fixers, then, depends on the interpretation of the concept of reference. Although I shall not try to construct a general theory of reference, I do need to outline what I think are the major ways in which the notion of reference can be understood.[17]

The Concept of Reference

Reference is a relation in which there are two relata and one of them is directed from itself to the other. One relatum functions as a sign; that is, it leads to, or directs attention to, the other relatum, and the second relatum is the object to which the first relatum leads. The second does not lead to the first, at least in the same respect that the first leads to the second. For instance, the word *moon* directs attention to the moon. Because this sign is a symbol constructed within a language system, it functions as an identifying condition of cognition. The moon does not lead to the word that designates it in this respect. The moon is not a construction serving to identify the word *moon*, although seeing the moon may lead to the word *moon* with respect to reminding us of this name. Even natural signs refer in this asymmetric way. A nimbus cloud is a sign of rain. It can be said to refer or lead to rain. But rain does not refer or lead to a nimbus, although it may be a reminder that rain can come from a nimbus. The reference relation for natural signs depends on which relatum is taken to be the condition (causal, statistical, lawful) and which the result.

What is important to my proposal for metaphor is that we distinguish between reference as a relation and referent as a relatum. Failure to distinguish between referent and reference risks ambiguity in discussions of the concept. It is too easy to use the term *reference*, dis-

---

[17] A relatively lengthy discussion of the uses of *reference* is found in Mooij, *A Study of Metaphor*, chap. 4.

tinguish it from *sense,* and then forget where there is a reference there must be a referent, which is different from the relation of reference. Thus I shall consider the referent to be something other than the reference. A referent is the object (physical thing, event, conception, expression) of the referring thing – which for our purposes is a linguistic item that functions as a sign.

In the loosest, most nontechnical, and most general sense, a term refers to anything the term means. Pragmatic theories of meaning illustrate this broad sense, insofar as they (or at least some of them) understand meaning to depend on a thought leading to generalizable experiences that are consequences of concepts.[18] In turn, these consequences are meaningful with reference to further consequences. Meaning thus consists of a system of signs within which thought is referred from sign to sign. How pragmatist theories of meaning interpret reference in this way must be qualified, of course, as another, more special kind of reference may be recognized. Indeed, Peirce recognizes another kind, in the indexical function of signs, that is, the function by which a sign leads not to further general consequences but to particulars or objects that to some extent resist being general conditions or serving as symbols for further consequences. This is an important point to be discussed later.

In the most general concept of reference, every word or sentence has a reference. Fictional words such as *Hamlet* (Shakespeare's) or *unicorn* might be said to refer to null classes, because a null class can be recognized by the features not instantiated in existents. Thus, although these words do not refer to particular existing individuals, they do indicate what would be encountered if there *were* an actual person, Hamlet, designated by Shakespeare. Even connectives can be said to refer, either indirectly, as functional conditions for terms that refer directly, or indirectly, to relations. But with the exception of the indexical aspect of signs, this kind of generalized reference is so broad that it blurs the distinction between connotation and denotation, or intension and extension, or sense and reference. This distinction is essential to my proposal, and it must be developed briefly.

What I said earlier about sense and intension should have indicated how I use the term *sense.* But I should pause for a moment to comment briefly on the term. I accept in rough form the Fregian distinction between sense and reference. Note that according to Kripke, Frege uses the term sense in two ways: The sense of the meaning of a term and the sense of the way the designator's reference are fixed, which includes nonverbal conditions.[19] I use the term *sense* in the first way,

---

[18] I have specifically in mind C. S. Peirce's so-called pragmatic maxim, which James referred to as the basis for his own pragmatism.

[19] Kripke, "Naming and Necessity," p. 277.

as the meaning (connotation or intension) of a term or expression. However, what follows should make it evident that I believe that in creative metaphors how the designator's (the metaphor's) reference is fixed functions in a relation of the interdependence with the meanings that interact.

A less general way of understanding *to refer,* though not inconsistent with the first, limits the kinds of things referred to. Thus the reference of a term is its extension, or the class of objects (not senses) denoted by the referring expression. *Man* refers to all creatures denoted by the word. Here the reference is distinct from the mode of presentation, from defining or describing expression, and from properties that might be attributed to what *man* denotes. And if fictional and nonexistent objects are included as referents, they must be accounted for by special techniques.

A third way of viewing reference concerns its narrowest function. To refer is to pick out, identify, or relate an expression to a single item or single and finite set of items. It seems appropriate to call this kind of reference *designation.* In this respect, reference is, I think, what Kripke had in mind when he said he would use the term "referent of a description" "to mean the object uniquely satisfying the conditions of the definite description" and when he also proposed the term "designator" to cover both names and descriptions.[20] It is this third use of *to refer* that is of particular importance for understanding the function of creative metaphor. However, a qualification is needed. The term *object* can be used to apply to any experience toward which a name or description is directed. It may be an intentional object or a physical object thought to be independent of intentions. This interpretation seems to return us to the first or second concept of referent. And it must be admitted that what I consider to be the referent of an expression is open, as is the first concept. The referent designated need not be a physical object, or an object existing in space as well as in time. Referents may be events, moments, or what I later shall propose and explain as centers of relevance. However, I must incorporate this third use of the term *referent* because whatever else may be said about it, a referent designated or picked out must be individualized (resistant to repeatable identity). It then must be a singular, a specific locus of meaning. Thus a referent is what uniquely satisfies its referring expression. I assume that referents of this kind ordinarily belong to the reference function of names and definite descriptions. Thus the kind of reference in question designates individuals through the use of linguistic or conceptual items. In this sense they are constituents of the world to which language refers.

[20] Ibid.

It is essential, then, to insist that the kind of referent in question is both unique and extralinguistic. Being unique and extralinguistic are the conditions of individuality, whatever further ontological character a referent might have when senses are attributed to it.

Reference and Creative Metaphors

With these preliminary considerations in mind, let me turn to the proposal itself. In short, I want to apply the idea of reference to creative metaphors in the following way: A metaphorical expression functions so that it creates its significance, thus providing new insight, through designating a unique, extralinguistic and extraconceptual referent that had no place in the intelligible world before the metaphor was articulated. There are three key terms in the proposal: *creative, unique,* and *extralinguistic* or *extraconceptual* (I use the last two expressions interchangeably here). These key terms indicate that in being creative, a metaphor must meet two conditions that the adopted concept of reference makes fundamental: uniqueness and extralinguisticality. Uniqueness is necessary to the idea that the referent of a creative metaphor is new and individual. Extralinguisticality is necessary to justify saying that a creative metaphor is *appropriate* or *faithful* or *fits the world.* In this latter respect, of course, metaphors are like literal expressions when they are "true." But it is the joining of these two conditions that is special to metaphors. There is something to which the expression is appropriate, some resistant or constraining condition: yet this condition is new.

The idea of creative designation suggests also that metaphors are like naming expressions. This point does not require settling the argument over whether proper names and definite descriptions are interchangeable. What is necessary to see about creative designation is that metaphorical expressions may be construed as fixing references, which is also what names do. In this connection, it is interesting that Kripke makes room for cases in which a referent is determined by a description, "by some uniquely identifying property." It "fixes the reference by some contingent marks of the object." Later these marks may be absent; yet the reference to the object remains fixed.[21]

Names, or at least proper names, are not related to their objects by virtue of the properties of those objects, nor do they cease to apply simply because one or more of the contingent marks of their objects is (or are) lost. But in the case of metaphorical reference fixing, there is a peculiar family resemblance (see Chapter 2) applying to the metaphor and the designated referent of the metaphor as a whole, and

[21] Ibid.

the new referent appears simultaneously with the construction of the metaphor. In this respect, creative designation is different from both giving something a proper name and a literal fixing by a description.

Before attempting to expand the proposal, I shall consider briefly one of the few theories of metaphor I have encountered that proposes that metaphors may be reference fixers of something extralinguistic: Richard Boyd's "Metaphor and Theory Change: What Is 'Metaphor' a Metaphor For?"[22] It will be helpful to consider this theory as an avenue to further exposition of my own suggestion.

Richard Boyd's View

Boyd's main purpose is to indicate how metaphors may bring about changes in scientific theory. He adopts a form of realism in acknowledging "the causal structure of the world" to which language, through metaphor, may be accommodated. And he thinks that we can account epistemologically for the fruitfulness of metaphors in contributing to scientific theory-construction only if we say that metaphors refer and that they "express important truths."[23] At the same time, although he believes that Black does not give sufficient credit to the role that metaphors can play in articulated theories in "relatively mature sciences," he initiates his discussion with praise for Black's view, and he makes a point of calling attention to Black's suggestion that metaphors can create similarities.[24]

It seems clear that Boyd wants to insist that metaphors can be creative in the sense of introducing theory changes, for example, as do computer metaphors for the brain or for cognitive processes – metaphors that he thinks constitute "new" ways of theorizing in psychology. Boyd also argues that "the employment of metaphor serves as a non-definitional mode of reference fixing" that provides *"epistemic access* to a particular sort of thing or natural phenomenon."[25] More specifically, he asserts: "What I am suggesting is that – when computer metaphors in cognitive psychology are successful – the metaphorically employed computer terms come to have new referents in the context of psychological theory-construction."[26] It seems that Boyd has proposed precisely the idea just introduced that creative metaphors create new insights by designating new referents. If so, then he must recognize the two key features, uniqueness and extralinguisticality.

[22] Boyd, "Metaphor and Theory Change," pp. 356–408.
[23] Ibid., especially p. 401.
[24] Ibid., p. 357.
[25] Ibid., p. 358.
[26] Ibid., pp. 368–9.

There is no doubt, given his realism, that Boyd wants to affirm extralinguisticality. But what about uniqueness? That Boyd recognizes the uniqueness condition is suggested by his mentioning *new* referents and, earlier, by his use of the term "particular sort of thing," in the preceding quotation about "epistemic access." And his illustration of reference fixing (following Putnam), " 'Let's call "water" whatever substance is present in *this* bucket over *here*,' " seems to confirm his acknowledgment of the referent's uniqueness. However, the condition of uniqueness and thus newness soon falls out of Boyd's sights.[27] This can be seen in his interpretation of what there is about the new referents that is particular and new. His admiration for the newness of the computer metaphor is followed by a recommendation that the metaphor be understood by finding analogical relations that can "disambiguate" the referents of the terms that are given metaphorical applications. Thus, if the computer metaphor provides insight, this must be based on "features of human cognitive activity analogous in important respects to information processing, feedback, semantically addressed memory storage (etc.). . . ."[28]

New referents, then, refers to psychological states of processes *analogous* to the former (literal) referents of the metaphorically used terms. "Computer metaphors are introduced in order to make possible investigation of the similarities and analogies between human cognition and machine computation."[29] Perhaps Boyd has a special thesis concerning analogy. Perhaps he does not intend to affirm a prior structure or antecedently functioning set of common qualities connecting the terms of analogies and would instead insist that the significance of analogies is based on metaphors and that these analogies therefore generate new analogical relations that come into the world by virtue of the metaphor's power. However, he does not say that he understands analogies in this way. Consequently, his recommendation for "disambiguating" looks less like an acknowledgment of unique referents (much less of created similarities) than of a view that metaphors are instruments for discovering antecedent, common aspects of thought and machines. Boyd's understanding of metaphor seems to fit well into the mold of the Comparison Theory that Black was supposed to have rejected.

This suggestion that Boyd slips into a rejection of the uniqueness and novelty of referents not only is based on his choice of the term *disambiguate* – a term that, I think, carries with it the idea that expressions to which it is applied must be translated into liberal, previously determined, particular and precise meanings – but also is based on

---

[27] Ibid., p. 366. My italics.
[28] Ibid., p. 369.
[29] Ibid., p. 370.

what seems to me to be a lack of explanation about the relation of the analogous relation found when metaphors are disambiguated and the newness that is earlier affirmed of metaphorical referents. It is not my intention to suggest that metaphors do not create comparisons and relations – new ones – that enable theory to advance the understanding of such things as thought processes. I only want to insist that if we mean that metaphors do create new referents as they create new organizations of the senses in which things are understood, then we should be careful that we do not explain the process of interpreting the responsible metaphors by "disambiguations" that refer us back to orders of things and referents that were available before the introduction of those metaphors.

The rationalist drive is surely alive, as well it might be, for Boyd, who is concerned with retaining a realism for which there is a causal structure in the world and, as he also says, for which there are "joints" to which metaphors might be apt. But it is not clear whether what is thus in the world is antecedently there or rather, in part at least, created in some sense as metaphors contribute to the progress of theory. It seems that we are driven once more to the recurring problem of "creative" metaphor – the problem that either we must adopt a Kantian or an idealistic conceptualism, perhaps a linguistic conventionalism, in order to affirm the possibility that metaphors can create new similarities; or we must reject the view that metaphorical insight creates something new, if we wish to affirm the aptness of the insights of metaphors and the realism that this implies.

In a discussion of Boyd's paper, Thomas S. Kuhn speaks from the vantage point of the relation of language in general to the world.[30] And he hints at a possible resolution of the dilemma. He asks: Does it obviously make better sense to speak of accommodating language to the world than of accommodating the world to language? Or is the way of talking that creates that distinction itself illusory? Is what we refer to as the world perhaps a product of a mutual accommodation between experience and language?

The hint that this dilemma may be resolved lies in the question whether there may be a mutual accommodation. However, the hint shifts the issue without resolving it. Kuhn introduces a new term, "experience," and adds it to the components that want relating. But it is not clear how experience differs from the world. Experience in some respects seems to be independent of language, or the two could not interact. Such independence is what was granted to the world in the original formulation of the issue. Put another way, it may be said that

[30] Thomas S. Kuhn, "Metaphor in Science," in Ortony, ed., *Metaphor and Thought*, pp. 407–19.

whatever experience is as distinct from the world and from language, either it has constraints on and resistances to the structure that experience acquires as it is put in mutual accommodation with language, or it is some form of a system of perspectives, themselves articulated in a system of senses or symbols, without the restraints of an extraconceptual condition. Thus, we face once more either a Kantian realism or an idealist conceptualism. On the one hand, the resistance of experience to its being structured takes the place of a Kantian unknowable condition (of the world?); on the other hand, the system of perspectives is the idealistic thought-dependent world. Kuhn's suggestion that the world and language are accommodated to each other through experience, then, does not resolve the issue. Nevertheless, Kuhn's conception of an interaction between language and something extralinguistic (whether the world or experience), is the only way I can see of attacking the dilemma, even if this is not to resolve it.

Expansion of the Proposal: Uniqueness and Extralinguisticality

To expand my proposal concerning the two conditions of uniqueness and extralinguisticality, I shall comment on the realism presupposed in what has been and will be said about the conditions of metaphorical reference. Further remarks relevant to this issue will be made later in this chapter; a fuller discussion will be undertaken in the sixth chapter; and the most extensive argument showing the foundation for the realism – which, it will be seen, is the basis of an ontology – will be offered in the Appendix. However, it should help to point out here the kind of real object that I believe must be encountered as one pole in the relation between creative metaphors and the referents they are said to create. This objective term of the relation is crucial to maintaining a view that affirms that real objects, or individuals that are real, are added to the world in a way for which metaphors are in a sense responsible insofar as they are both creative and apt (or inapt).

The world of objects required consists of intentional objects and objects that are independent of the senses or meanings that comprise the objects that are intentional. The latter kinds of objects are what I call *individuals*, objects that function as the extralinguistic condition to be considered in the next section. These individuals are not determinate, characterizable objects – so called space–time objects postulated as independent of concepts or theoretical thought – but, rather, are foci of constraints, a point also to be developed in the next section. They are foci of constraints on the senses that constitute intentional objects. At the same time, however, they are not the constraints of prior theories that surely function in the context of a theory that is in development. Nor are they limited to being the constraints of social and cultural conditions, as I suppose at least some sociologies of knowledge would insist and which, I believe, strongly influence the way human intelligence works in theorizing, whether creatively or in routine ways. The constraints at issue are conditions that function independently of thought itself, as I shall explain further at later stages of the discussion. If at this stage, a reader wishes to maintain some form of the view that construes all objects of reference as centers of social–cultural constraints, or as products of common structures of the human mind, what I say can be interpreted so as to accommodate such a view. But, as already indicated, I resist accepting such forms of idealism for reasons to be sketched further later. In any case, I think that a framework within which there can be both creativity and appropriateness (or inappropriateness) must include thoughts that function at one pole of reference and intentional objects, some of which resist and constrain those thoughts as well as the thought that is enacted by whole communities of interpreters. Thus, metaphors at the same time create and discover. They create intentional objects, which are constituted of imposed meanings or intelligible senses and also under the constraints of the objects to which they are apt. As the objects of apt as well as creative metaphors, they are not wholly dependent on the creator's demands. The new meanings that are generated by metaphors and that constitute the intentional objects of theory are not arbitrarily introduced by metaphors (effective ones that turn out to be apt). The new meanings and the intentional objects they inform are under the constraints not only of the metaphor but also of the individuals, the extralinguistic, "existential" or independently functioning conditions.

Let me now return to my proposal, looking more closely at the possibility that metaphors are reference fixers that enable us to create while discovering and that do this by functioning as extralinguistic conditions that contribute to constituting the world.

I believe that the referents of creative metaphors are at once created and designated and thus must be unique and extralinguistic. In expanding this thesis, it will be necessary to address some of its consequences and the difficulties associated with affirming it.

Before proceeding, however, let me emphasize that the justification for my proposal consists chiefly in the claim that it is the key to giving an interpretive account or picture of how creative metaphors function. At the same time, there are two reasons for insisting on uniqueness and extralinguisticality. The first is that these conditions need to be presupposed to account for the created character as well as the objectivity assumed when some metaphors are said to be faithful or apt. The second reason is that there is an experiential encounter – an encounter, as was suggested, that signals more than cultural consensus – that provokes the recognition of some metaphors as faithful and others as less faithful or inappropriate. I shall return to these points later.

The Uniqueness Condition

What is it to be unique? If the referent of a creative metaphor uniquely satisfies the metaphorical expression, then no other referent will be appropriate to the reference of the expression, for no other referent could be substituted for what is designated by the referring expression, without a change in significance. A substitute would not satisfy the referring expression unless the substitute were identical with the original. In contrast, any member of a class denoted by an expression would do as well as any other with respect to belonging to the class. But such a member could not be a creation of the class regarded as a referring expression. In the case of metaphor, if another referent were appropriate, the metaphorical reference would be indifferent. But in the case of creative metaphors, what is designated is something unprecedented and thus not already designatable. Nor can we find another referring expression that can be substituted for the metaphor without overturning the unparaphrasability principle. This is not to say that the subsequent expressions are completely irrelevant to created referents. But in the first instance, the metaphor is the only designating expression, and the referent is the only designatum in one and only one interrelation. Thus, as unique, the referent is singular; it is the only instance of its type.

It is important to notice that if a unique referent is the only instance of its type, it must itself be a type. It is not an individual in the sense of a fully determinate object that somehow "possesses," or that may come to "possess," properties while retaining its independence of these properties. To refer to it as a singular is not to preclude its having the statues of a general that originates at the moment of creation – as, presumably, Niels Bohr's "atom" did at one time. If it can be the only instance of its type, it will be a singular, unique type, and it may then be a created general (some might call it a "universal"), although its inception is singular, a one of a kind for the first time. As was suggested earlier, the new instance, which introduces the new type, may be thought of as the first token that exemplifies the type. The token and type originate together. In *A Discourse on Novelty and Creation*, I discussed this relation in terms of what I called *form* and *structure*, which correspond to type and token, respectively.

The point that a unique referent may be a general needs to be developed. As something that is created, the referent is necessarily different in crucial respects from its antecedents. And to a degree it remains intelligible. Thus, insofar as it is a different, a unique, entry into the world, it is not manifestly general, nor is it manifestly some separable entity in the sense of a particular "underlying" property. Its function as a general, or as a nongeneral, particular focus for generals, depends on the participation of interpretive processes that discover while interpreting its intelligibility and on its independent tendency to invoke certain interpretations.

The point is that referents that are created are unique and thus serve as unprecedented controls on interpretation. This point is important to any view of metaphor, as this one is, that regards creative metaphors as more than ambiguous. Metaphors may be ambiguous, but they cannot, if they are creative and apt, be interpreted simply as ambiguous expressions. Their appropriateness to the world signals a control on whatever ambiguities they exhibit, so that either one of the senses becomes dominant or another sense emerges and functions as the new meaning. My contention at this stage of the discussion is that it is the created referents that perform this controlling function.

The point may also so be seen in another way. The referent of a creative metaphor may be viewed as a determination of a determinable determinateness, for the determinable is new and is determined for the first time. Red as a determinate of color can be duplicated as can color. However, "Man is the dream of a shadow" is a determinate of interlocking determinables, man, dream, and shadow, each of which relates to precedent and thus duplicable determinates, but which together do not. This suggests that the referent of a creative metaphor is an absolute determinate, the polar opposite of an absolute determinable in a hierarchy of determinables–determinates.[31] But again, if we think of such referents in this way, we should not equate them with static specifications of determinables. They are dynamic and can be specified only in the context of an evolving world.

The uniqueness condition must hold for metaphors even though their form may not make this explicit. To see the point of an expression – and one that would hardly now be received as having much if any originality – such as "Sadness spread slowly over his face" presupposes recognizing the designation of an instance of a specific mood in a unique situation and occurring for an individual. Also, the overworked "Man is a wolf" which takes the form of a generalization depends on a designating act, in this case the recognition of a singular condition (at least when the expression was fresh) and probably also of a unique situation in which a unique specification of conditions

[31] The distinction between determinables and determinates is drawn primarily from W. E. Johnson's *Logic* (Cambridge, England: Cambridge University Press, 1921), pp. 174–6. It is summarized and elaborated briefly in *Encyclopedia of Philosophy*, pp. 357–9.

functioned to provoke the metaphor. Surely this kind of initial individualizing can be attributed to "Man is a wolf," if Boyd is correct in his account of the designating function of water, or if Kripke is correct in his illustration of discovery in science: "The molecular theory has discovered, let's say, that *this* object *here* is composed of molecules."[32] In cases of this kind, the significance of each is understood in the light of a designating identification: "This substance here is 'water' "; "This object here is something composed of molecules"; and, in the case of the metaphor in question, "This instance of what it is to be human is an instance of being a wolf." The introduction of "instance of being a wolf" adds complexity; however, I want to emphasize the uniqueness of the referent within a continuum of referents. The need for this will, I trust, be made clear later.

The point about the condition of uniqueness for general as well as particular expressions can be seen from a different perspective if we turn to an important consequence of this condition.

The Uniqueness Condition and the Newness of Referents

If the referents of creative metaphors are unique, it follows that the new referent cannot be the referent of any one of the metaphor's component senses. This follows from the interaction view and the acknowledgment that the referent is created. Adopting Max Black's terminology, "primary subject" and "secondary subject," and assuming that these comprise the major components interacting metaphorically in a metaphor, we can distinguish the referent(s) of the primary subject from the referent(s) of the secondary subject, each having an antecedent place in the world. "Man" in "Man is a wolf" has a referent of the so-called literal or established sense, and this referent is understood antecedently to the metaphor. Similarly, "wolf" has its antecedent referent. But the senses of both subjects affect each other to create a new significance – a new meaning and designation. Thus, neither of these antecedent referents is the created referent. Nor can we say, with Black, that the primary subject's referent is simply understood through the filter or screen of the secondary subject's senses or "implicative complexes" or "associated commonplaces," without reverting to a perspectival view in which the object referred to by the metaphor as a whole is antecedently intelligible. Instead, the new reference must be to a third and new referent. It must be a unique, focused specification, a determination, of man, different from man formerly understood. This new referent is at the same time picked out and created,

---

[32] Boyd, "Metaphor and Theory Change," p. 366, Kripke, "Naming and Necessity," p. 321, italics added.

because the senses of *man* and *wolf* interact and call attention to it at the moment the metaphor creates it. In this connection, the view that metaphors exhibit tension is most apt. The incompatibility of the determinates – man and wolf relative to the determinable, whole metaphorical expression – jars established frameworks of determinables and dislodges preconceptions, releasing attention to a new function. The tension triggers the indexical function of the terms for transfer to another (created) locus.

Let me illustrate my point with the metaphor (already referred to) selected by Stanley Cavell (from Shakespeare's *Romeo and Juliet*), "Juliet is the sun."[33] What is the referent of this metaphor regarded as a whole? With respect to what it creates, "Juliet is the sun" does not refer to Juliet as she was known apart from the metaphor. If it did, the expression would be false, given the way proper names, human beings, and so forth were understood apart from the interaction of the metaphor's terms in its context. But if the expression in its nonliteral, metaphorical function is not false or lacking in significance and if its referent is a creation, and thus new and unique, then its referent will be something other than Juliet otherwise understood and referred to. Nor does the metaphor as creative refer to the sun, although the predicate, as it was known apart from the metaphor, does. What is the object that uniquely satisfies the sentence as it is understood in its poetic context? It should be clear that this question cannot be answered by a description of the referent, unless this description is the metaphor itself, for the referent is new. A description would have only previously established linguistic means, that is, antecedent senses, to rely on. At best, then, we might say that the new referent is Juliet-the-sun. As with metaphors that establish themselves in language or theory, if the metaphor makes a lasting impact on our understanding of human beings and nature, the names *Juliet* or *the sun* (or both) might come to be used for this new referent without recurrent recognition that it first occurred as an expression with a metaphorical function. This is less obvious for poetic metaphors, which depend so much on their poetic contexts. But as Black suggests, and Mary Hesse illustrates, such changes have occurred, as can be seen in the case of "Man is a wolf," for which "bestial" becomes more abusive for both beasts and men.[34]

An example mentioned earlier, the computer metaphor, is a relatively fresh illustration from psychology. The referent of "The mind is a computer" or "Mental activity is computer processing" is not the mind or mental activity as understood before the metaphor. Nor is it

---

[33] Cavell, "Aesthetic Problems," chap 4, pp. 74–97.
[34] Hesse, "The Cognitive Claims of Metaphor."

the referent of "The computer" computers, insofar as this expression was known before. Nor is the referent an aggregate of these two antecedent referents. The new referent is a new specification of "mind" or "mental activity," and of "a computer" or "computer processing," as these conspire to enable the creative designation to refer to a new referent.

Earlier, Davidson and Ricoeur were mentioned in support of the point that recognition and understanding of contexts are needed in order to identify expressions as metaphorical. It is important to consider this point again in connection with the argument that creative metaphors refer to referents that are new.

Ricoeur's conception of a metaphoric context leads him to give referents a locus that raises the question of how specific metaphors can be creative in themselves and how they can provide the conditions for new, individual referents and, with respect to the suggestion made earlier, how the referents in question satisfy the whole metaphor rather than any one term or subject functioning within the metaphor. Early in his book on metaphor, Ricoeur argues that reference depends on a "network of interaction" rather than on isolated metaphorical sentences.[35] Apart from a network of meanings, a metaphor would have neither the sense nor the reference it in fact does have.

Thus, to use one of our own examples, the expression "Juliet is the sun" undoubtedly is recognized as metaphorical in a context that is a network of senses. In this case, too, we know it to be from the context of the Shakespearean drama, and we understand *Juliet* to refer to someone beloved, whereas *the sun* refers literally to the center of the solar system, although it has properties such that a system of senses can interact with senses attributable to Juliet. But even if we did not know that the expression came from *Romeo and Juliet,* we would nevertheless need to have some familiarity with linguistic usage – the use of proper names that are normally applied to human beings, the reference of *the sun,* and so on. Without some context, some network that alerts us to its being metaphorical, it would not function as we now think it does. However, what must be seen, if I am correct about metaphorical reference, is that this necessity of a contextual network does not require that the referent of the metaphor itself be the same as the referent of the network. The network acts as a way to help organize the senses of the metaphor so that it refers to a new referent. But this function of the network supports the designating function of the metaphor itself. Otherwise, we would be driven from sentence to context, to broader contexts, until we could find extralinguistic reference only in language as a whole. Because the original metaphorical

[35] Ricoeur, *The Rule of Metaphor,* p. 98.

sentence is what is central, it must have a centripetal force in our understanding of the metaphor. It is the referent of this central expression that is in question.

Ricoeur's discussion includes a provocative proposal that metaphors have split references, one side referring to something not antecedently accessible to language. Because his proposal overlaps my own suggestions, I shall consider how my view of metaphorical reference differs from Ricoeur's.

Ricoeur is sensitive to the referential function of metaphor, which he thinks is shared generally with literary works. Citing Beardsley, he says that metaphors say something insofar as they are miniature poems. This, of course, challenges the view that works of literature, whose meanings are immanent, cannot refer to anything. Ricoeur insists that poems and metaphors – indeed, all instances of language – have reference. However, the reference that a metaphor has is special. Following Roman Jakobson, Ricoeur adopts the expression "split reference," which he believes characterizes the ways that metaphors refer.[36] Split reference is the basis of a tension between two functions of the copula in metaphors, a tension consisting of an interplay between identity and difference. Thus the "is" of identity in metaphors "exposes an 'is not,' itself implied in the impossibility of the literal interpretation."[37] Thus, there is tension between an "is" and an "is not." And the verb *to be* (which in metaphors is existential as well as relational between terms) has a split function. Thus reference is split, and metaphorical truth is tensional. This tension is later said to show that metaphors give us access to unarticulated fields that are referred to because of the rejections of "old" meanings that refer to established fields of reference.[38]

Ricoeur's account is fascinating and, I think, directed toward the same paradoxical suggestions I am making about metaphorical reference. However, there are two points that may mark a difference between his and my conceptions of the paradox. I say "may" because both points concern undeveloped aspects of Ricoeur's view.

The first point is that the "is not" side of the split reference of metaphor should be understood in terms of the internal tension between subject terms (Ricoeur refers to them using Richards's "tenor" and "vehicle") in the metaphor. This inner tension, I think, is the basis for the "is not" of the metaphorical copula. As Ricoeur recognizes, this "is not" is existential as well as relational. It is a referential function of the metaphor. Yet it is impossible to apply; it is "implied in the im-

---

[36] Ibid., pp. 224–225. See also his later discussion in "The Metaphorical Process as Cognition, Imagination, and Feeling," 153–59.
[37] Ricoeur, *The Rule of Metaphor*, p. 248.
[38] Ibid., p. 299.

possibility of existential interpretation." But if application is impossible, there can be no referent for the metaphorical copula in its negative ("is not") function. It is not clear whether Ricoeur sees this or whether he would agree. In his later discussion, he states, "This expression ('split reference'), as well as the wonderful 'it was and it was not,' contains *in nuce* all that can be said about metaphorical reference."[39] Presumably, the "was not" refers to the new referent that was not. But what is the referent of "the was"? It cannot be what now is, as new. Nor can it be the referent of the metaphorical copula insofar as the copula applies to a referent of the metaphor as a whole, for apparently it is this function that is impossible for existential interpretation. My suggestion is that the only way "it was" can play a role is not for the metaphorical copula as a whole but, rather, in the functions of the subject terms, each of which individually refers. In typical instances, each refers to different incompatible or incongruous domains of referents. On the basis of the tension of the relationship of the terms and the domains to which they refer, the metaphor thrusts meaning toward the new reference, supposedly to what Ricoeur views as the "is" side of the metaphorical copula.

My first point is not a criticism as much as a suggestion that the tension in question deserves more consideration and that there can be only one referent of a metaphor as a whole – that is, a referent of the terms as they are integrated in the metaphorical expression as distinct from the functions of the terms in their antecedent function. The referent of the metaphor as a whole is the unique referent that is referred to by virtue of the metaphor's creative force.

My second point follows from the first and concerns the need to examine the functions of metaphors' unique referents in relation to the thesis that some metaphors both create and exhibit insights so that they are apt or faithful. Ricoeur's discussion does explore some of the ontological dimensions of the paradox of creativity – which he too recognizes as the twofold creation and discovery that occurs where there is radical creativity. Yet my own account of the way metaphorical referents function obviously takes a different direction.

Before concluding this stage of the consideration of the uniqueness of referents, I must make a short comment about the relations among new referents and their senses. New referents are inevitably related to antecedent referents – Juliet, the sun, the mind, the computer. There is a continuity among referents through time. This relation of continuity can be intelligible only through the senses by which old and new referents are identified. Thus it might be said that in a growing language, conceptual references concern referents relevant to one an-

---

[39] Ricoeur, "The Metaphorical Process," p. 153.

other in a kind of family resemblance that controls the changing senses needed to designate the referents. New referents enter the world
of references as new children enter their families. Each takes on characters from, and contributes to, its family context. But each does so
because it has its own integrity, its own uniqueness.

The Extralinguistic Condition

The uniqueness of referents also must be understood in the light of
the second condition, extralinguisticality. The created referent of a
metaphor is both an extralinguistic and a unique object.[40] This extralinguisticality adds an ontological dimension to the uniqueness. Of
course, this insistence on extralinguisticality is likely to be challenged
from a linguistic–conceptual position. Earlier, I cited Donald Davidson's recognition of context, but without the added qualification that
the conclusion he draws conflicts with what I want to suggest. He con-
cludes that because words have no meaning function apart from how
they would play roles in sentences and, similarly, because sentences
require their contexts, we cannot directly explain reference as related
to what is nonlinguistic, for any single word's reference must be explained by its role in a sentence. I agree with this view with respect to
the need for considering context as a condition for interpreting linguistic expressions. However, I do not see why this leads to denying
an extralinguistic dimension to the required contexts. Not being able
to explain a reference without recourse to the senses (to formulate
the point in terms relevant to this discussion) does not mean restrict-
ing reference to purely linguistic considerations. However comprehensive a context must be in order to interpret an expression and
locate its referent, the significance may still be referential to something not exhausted by the context.

Further, it must be kept in mind that the kind of referent on which
I am insisting is not a condition to be understood as something existent in any ordinary sense. It has been said earlier that an object in a
reference need not exist as something physical or spatial. The term
object applies to whatever a name or description is directed. As was
suggested, it may be either an intentional object or a physical object
thought to be independent of intentions. As anything presented for
cognition, an object that is a referent can be any discrete thing whatsoever, including a sense. It may be a discrete, substantial object, a
temporal moment, a law, or whatever may be called a *center of rele-*

---

[40] This, I think, is part of the point of Ricoeur's remarks about sentence significance:
"In the phenomenon of the sentence, language passes outside itself; reference is the
mark of the self-transcendence of language." *The Rule of Metaphor*, p. 74.

vance. What the extralinguistic condition adds to uniqueness, then, is not substantiality but, rather, a controlling factor, a locus for the senses. It is a focus for influences on the range of senses relevant to it. Its function is to constrain certain senses and resist others. Some centers of relevance are more obdurate than others. They may be obdurate spatially if they are centers of relevance for the senses that make intelligible such things as physical objects. Some may be relatively unpredictable, as are many meteorological events. Some may be evanescent, as are fictions and the like. Pragmatic tests provide evidence of these differences. To describe them beyond indicating their functions in relation to senses is impossible, for there is no initial access to them except through metaphors. Nevertheless, once a metaphor is understood, further sense can be made of the referent, because other senses, senses not recognized before (consequent meanings), are relevant to the new referent. This is why the referent is called a center of relevance.

Let me emphasize that specific pragmatic tests cannot be spelled out in advance to assess the appropriateness of a new metaphorical expression as a possible insight. Rather, the determination of these tests awaits the creation of the metaphor that, as new, will require some revision of our expectations. Nevertheless, if scientific theory or hypothesis formation is at issue, there are general guidelines for the proper procedures, methodology, and requirements of some degree of coherence to the body of scientific theory, which in fact partially controls creators and those who must decide whether to support their work financially and so on. One reason this is possible is that whatever a creative metaphor may contribute to a new theory, as a hypothesis or as a component of one, it constitutes or at least prompts a larger context of theory; it may need only relate heuristically to the construction of a new theory. General guidelines can at least tentatively be applied to the larger theoretical context. Thus, although the specific application of my proposal for metaphorical reference to the arts remains to be offered, it may be said here that critics and appreciators have very general expectations when creative work in the arts is to be supported, financially or morally.

In both domains, in the sciences and the arts, these expectations will influence the sorts of tests or reasons for seeing that there is appropriateness to the referent that functions as an object into which the metaphor offers insight. Of course, the danger of imposing such expectations is that we may fail to recognize the new insight. We may be blinded to the creative advance introduced by the metaphor as it contributes to the theory. And it is for this reason that the specific expectations that guide the tests of appropriateness must await an initial appreciation of what is created. In science, I suppose, these specific tests will be part of selecting new or at least different domains of observation and devising different conceptual schemes, formulas, and the like that aid confirmation or disconfirmation. In the visual arts – with qualifications for architecture, which, I think, in many examples shares with music the kind of relation it has with its referents – I suggest that the new specific "tests" will be primarily new ways of seeing the world. These ways of seeing compel the attention of an assenting audience – in the same way that appreciators of Cézanne now see Mt. Saint Victoire in a "Cézannish" way and in light of this can "go on" seeing in a "Cézannish" way other things in the world not imaged in any known Cézanne painting. Guidelines for interpreting music will be suggested in the fifth chapter.

As pointed out, what has been said until now suggests that referents, as extralinguistic and unique, may be thought of as individuals, in a sense of individuality that I shall attempt now to explain.

Uniqueness, Extralinguisticality, and Individuals

The referent of a creative metaphor must be an individual because of the interdependence between uniqueness and extralinguisticality. Uniqueness alone does not guarantee that the unique thing is ontologically real but only that it is a unique focus of the senses or properties of the referent. However, if something has uniqueness and is extralinguistic as well, it will have a stronger (or added) function. This stronger function already has been recognized as the referent's resistance to, and constraint on, language and conceptualization. The referents of creative metaphors have roles that could not be performed if they were not independent of concepts and language. What constrains and resists the relevance of certain senses or properties is not, in instances of creativity, some sense or property already given. The constraint and resistance must transcend these, and this resistance comes from the third referent to which I have referred earlier – illustrated by the example "Juliet is the sun." It is important to recognize that this third aspect of significance is not a sense but is a second order of intelligibility. It is the referent of the metaphor that functions as an individual.

The claim made for extralinguisticality and the consequent function of the unique referent as an individual may be understood more fully in the light of the specific reasons on which the claim is based. What I have said thus far assumes that individuality is a presupposition needed to justify the attribution of fitting or faithfulness to perspectives, specifically, to some metaphors. However, as I said earlier, there is another reason for accepting the presupposition. This reason is how complexes of senses are experienced.

Extralinguisticality is encountered as a condition under which whatever can be described as "the" sense of an expression does not seem sufficient to give full intellectual satisfaction with respect to its significance. This condition is often invoked by those who deny that metaphors (and poems) can be paraphrased without loss of meaning. That there is justification for this denial is, of course, essential to my proposal: I have assumed it from the beginning. The unparaphrasability thesis and possible objections to it already have been considered.

The acknowledgment that there is "something more" is a direct experience of the extralinguistic requirement. But this condition cannot simply be a complex, a cluster, or a series of senses remaining to be identified – Cavell's way of accounting for dissatisfaction with paraphrases of metaphors.[41] I think it is correct to expect that additional senses are forthcoming. This is one of the marks of the suggestiveness or richness of good metaphors; they have an impact on future understandings of what they articulate. Nevertheless, extralinguisticality is not simply this transcendence toward future senses. As extralinguistic, the condition for the references (and for the "and so on") that is at issue must have some independence from language and thought. And its independence is illustrated, as noted, in connection with the uniqueness requirement, by an independent, extralinguistic (and unique) condition, Juliet-the-sun, that is not identical with any finite sequence of properties. Otherwise, it could not function as a condition for changes in language and thought where these changes are not more or less appropriate or faithful simply because of their consistency or inconsistency with antecedently established schemata.

This way of treating extralinguisticality and viewing it, along with uniqueness, as the function of individuality is something like C. S. Peirce's notion of resistance that marks his category, secondness, and that he sometimes associated with individuals that may be objects of signs' indexical functions.[42] It might seem unwise to use Peirce's view of individuality, which is particularly problematic with respect to whether there can be real individuals in the system that he sought. However, I think this issue need not be settled in order to capitalize on some of Peirce's suggestions. I am concerned only with proposing that individuality in some ontological sense apply to creative metaphoric reference.

Thus, following Peirce, it is clear that an individual is not a sub-

[41] Cavell, "Aesthetic Problems," pp. 79–80.
[42] Peirce's account of the category of secondness and individuality are found in a variety of papers collected in *The Collected Papers of Charles Sanders Peirce*, vols. 1–6, ed. Charles Hartshorne and Paul Weiss (Cambridge, Mass.: Harvard University Press, 1931–34, 1935), vols. 7 and 8, ed. Arthur W. Burks (Cambridge, Mass.: Harvard University Press, 1958).

stance. It is not a bare particular in which qualities may inhere. Nor is it a complex or cluster of qualities. Kripke, on whom some of this discussion hinges with respect to the idea of designation, would, I think, concur in these claims about what individuals are not. Unfortunately, he does not make clear just what he thinks they are. Nor does Peirce do more than suggest an answer. The best I can do, then, is to take seriously Peirce's suggestion that individuals are determinate without necessarily being spatial entities. An individual is a singular in experience that reacts, that acts to some extent against our will, that acts so that just any interpretation of it is not necessarily faithful or fitting. Thus, as said earlier, an individual manifests its reality as a confluence of insistent constraints, as a unique focal point of resistance in experience. And as new, referents of creative metaphors are centers or cores of possibilities. They are focal points of relevance for qualities and, in turn, senses that *would* give absolute determinateness to the focal center *if* they *were* fully actualized.

It should be clear that the idea of relevance to extralinguistic conditions does not necessarily construe metaphors as having truth-value. I shall digress briefly to suggest a way in which the question of truth-value may take the study of metaphor in another direction. Although I shall not follow this direction far, I do want to indicate a way of enriching metaphor studies without, it seems to me, conflicting with the main theme of this study.

Truth-value and Metaphor as Illocutionary

The paradox of metaphorical designation may be looked at from the perspective of the way that metaphors are truth-value free. That they are thus free, in the sense of truth as a correspondence to fact or as coherence to established theory, follows from claiming that they fix new referents and from accepting faithfulness or appropriateness (which in Black's view is set off from truth in any strict sense). The idea that metaphors in their initially metaphorical function are free of truth-value is one reason that some writers have maintained that metaphors have performative illocutionary functions. My proposal implies that creative metaphors are performative in several interrelated ways. They are performative as instances of naming. Thus, they have the force of acts of generating or bringing something into being. And they have the force of instructions to recognize what they create and pick out.

The idea of creating – under conditions of the illocution of naming – may be seen in the light of John Searle's (and Austin's) "direction of fit" criterion for classifying illocutionary acts.[43] Thus it can be said that creative designation has two directions of fit, getting the world to match the words while getting the words to match the world. Creative metaphors are thus bidirectional. If they have the force of naming and instructing an audience to witness the naming act and what it creates, then they will demand that the world match the words. They also have the form and force of assertions, which match words with *this* or *that* individual in the world that has and will have an intelligible impact in the world. The first match is required by the creative point (or purpose) of the metaphorical activity. The second is required by the realistic purpose.

The closest of Searle's classified types of illocutionary acts to the construction of metaphors seems to be a species of what he calls "declarations," which are bidirectional in matching words and world. Searle observes, "It is the defining characteristic of this class that the successful performance of one of its members brings about the correspondence between the propositional content and reality, successful performance guarantees that the propositional content corresponds to the world. . . ."[44] Declarations are peculiar because "the performance of a declaration brings about a fit by the very fact of its successful performance."[45]

Searle asks, "How is this (peculiar bringing about a fit with the world) possible?" His answer is that most declarations involve "extralinguistic institutions," that is, systems of rules – the church, the law, the state – and a speaker who has a special place in the institution – a priest, a lawyer, a member of the administration. Presumably the institution is by convention believed to make or guarantee the fit. However, Searle sees exceptions to this, one of which is a declaration that concerns language itself, naming or dubbing.[46] Declarations of dubbing have the bidirectional fit, but not through an extralinguistic institution, or by describing an existing state of affairs, or by trying to get someone to bring about a future state of affairs.[47]

With respect to naming, although Searle's comments suggest otherwise, it seems more plausible – to rely on a standard that Searle himself uses in other contexts – that the declarer who names or dubs

---

[43] John Searle uses this expression in "A Taxonomy of Illocutionary Acts," ed. Keith Gunderson, *Language, Mind, and Knowledge, Minnesota Studies in the Philosophy of Science*, Vol 7 (University of Minnesota Press, 1975), pp. 344–69. J. L. Austin uses the term in "How to Talk," *Proceedings of the Aristotelian Society*, 1952–3. Reprinted in J. L. Austin, *Philosophical Papers*, ed. J. O. Urunson and G. J. Warnock (Oxford, England: Oxford University Press, 1979).

[44] Austin, *Philosophical Papers*, p. 13.

[45] Ibid.

[46] Ibid., pp. 14–15.

[47] Ibid., p. 15.

indeed is established as an extralinguistic agent in treating language as an object. It seems to me that there is reason to regard uttering metaphors as like dubbing when they are understood as illocutionary in this way.

It is interesting that Searle's own comments about those declarations that overlap what he calls "representatives" – acts in which the speaker is committed to something's being the case – are suggestive with respect to a way of looking at declarations, if not at naming, then as creative. Representatives are illustrated by umpires who proclaim, "You're out," and by judges who judge, "You're guilty."[48] In these cases, the declaration constitutes the situation or referent toward which the declaration is directed. What is constituted is not new except as a particular instance of a general declaration, because the speaker represents an institution, and what the speaker says is supposed to express the general authority of the institution.

A metaphor creator would also speak from a linguistic institution that overlaps those of umpires and judges, what may be called the institution of "poetic license." Some (and perhaps all) cases of naming (christening) are like declarations based on some such kind of extralinguistic, institutional requirements. Some naming, at least, presupposes authorization. One who names the ship *Queen Elizabeth* does so institutionally and would not belong to the exceptions included in the naming or dubbing that Searle mentions. So the metaphor speaker names (reidentifies) on the basis of the institution of using figurative language. There is a difference, however, for metaphorical naming does more than express the institution of figurative speech; it creates something that contributes to changing the institution. Of course, my suggestion does not answer the question raised earlier about whether the world may change apart from human imposition, but it does suggest that something occurs on the human side of creative designation that is faithful to the world.

Others who have tried to classify metaphors as illocutionary rely on the general category of invitation or recommendation. Metaphors invite or recommend to us to view the primary subject in a metaphorical way. Such attempts to use the latest fashion in philosophy seem to me to be a bit too facile. They bypass the central issues of appropriateness to the world. In a sense, I am guilty of this, too, because I do not take space here to examine the idea that metaphorical expressions may have bidirectional, performative force. I hope only to have offered a suggestion. However, the question of metaphors' constantive element, or the faithfulness of their cognitive insight, which is the main issue in this chapter, still needs to be explored.

[48] Ibid., pp. 10, 15.

According to the view proposed in this book, creative metaphors are appropriate for objective reasons that contribute to the force of performative, institutionalized acts. Thus, even though the reference fixing of creative metaphors is not itself true or false, it is relevant to truth or falsity. What it designates, as a center of relevance, constrains the inclusion and exclusion of senses, present and future, attributable to it. With respect to the Newtonian concept of gravitational forces, for instance, "The earth and sun are mutually attracted through gravitational forces" is faithful to a network of relevant senses. These are discovered as the concept itself, in its original metaphorical form, is examined for its implications and developed into a theory. If its consequent meanings are tested so that predictions concerning observations are confirmed and if the theory can be made coherent with its addition, the theory will be called "true" or at least acceptable as an indication of "the way things are." Truth assessment, then, is indirectly relevant to the truth-value–neutral creative designation, at least in theoretical inquiry. One of the implications of this point concerns the ontology that underlies the view of metaphorical reference being advanced here.

The Role of Metaphor in the Implied Ontology

The view of individuals proposed in order to accommodate the conditions of created referents depends on an ontology. I shall not attempt to develop the ontology here. I shall only anticipate such an attempt, leaving a short sketch for the last chapter. My purpose in this section is to indicate the interdependence of the ontology and the creation and interpretation of metaphor. With respect to the proposal about how creative metaphors function, the kind of ontology to which the proposal commits us should be admitted.

Thus, the view that created referents function as individuals in the sense of constraining centers of relevance leads to an ontology for which the world must be understood as an evolving system of dynamic individuals. These are "known" or experienced directly or immediately as reaction, resistance, and constraint encountered when the meanings are differentiated and interpreted. When interpreted, they are also known discursively, through the mediation of fixed concepts and relations. Known in the latter way, they are inferred in the sense that they are postulated as the particular nodes in a network of qualities that are intelligible as systems of interrelated senses. These qualities and senses form an evolving network or loose system because they relate to one another not only by virtue of purely logical or formal requirements but also in terms of the restraints or resistances of the individuals that function as their referents. It is these restraints that impress us when we acknowledge the point of asking whether our perspectives, or our networks of senses, are apt or faithful.

This picture of the world and its intelligibility obviously depend on regarding at least some instances of creative cognition as objectively grounded. The way in which created referents constrain interpretations and present themselves as discoveries for audiences – audiences including experts in the field in which their metaphors function, as well as for the creators of metaphor – indicates that the created individuals are not invariably the result of arbitrary human acts. Indeed, they are conditions of intelligibility. For they are conditions for future systematic growth and for the necessities of theories. They are conditions for future cognitive and linguistic habits on the part of a general public – and in the domain of art, of the basis for the accumulation over time of what are accepted as masterpieces. Though individuals are "born" as outcomes of creative expressions (metaphors themselves), they also may be objective conditions that "emerge" in the world. This must be so if the metaphor functions in scientific theory and if theory concerns "what there is." Such metaphors play a role in their relations to other constraining conditions, that is, other individuals and the intelligibility requirements of cluster of senses.

A creative metaphor that is integral to a developed and established scientific theory will have been tested indirectly by the tests that established the theory to which it contributed, although at one time it intruded into the theory that was accepted until its inception. The computer–mind metaphor remains to be tested, insofar as the psychological theory to which it contributes has not yet developed sufficiently to be established.

The role of metaphor in science was also confirmed by Owen Barfield and C. S. Lewis, who have written fairly extensively about the growth of language and cite many examples of the changes that words have undergone.[49] One such example is *gravitation*. Barfield discusses the word in connection with *attraction*, surmising that until the discovery of gravitation, the concept connected with *attraction* (from the Latin *ad-trahers* "to draw" or "drag toward") must have been practically beyond the range of human intellect. There was formerly "no half-way house in imagination between actual dragging or pushing and forces emanating from a living being, such as love or hate, of those 'influences' of the stars which have already been mentioned."[50]

The metaphors of gravitation introduced into the field of physics have been tested. Their referents play the role of being constituents

---

[49]Barfield's discussion appears in various places. Those of use here are in *History of English Words* (London: Faber & Faber, 1954). See also C. S. Lewis, *Studies in Words* (Cambridge, England: Cambridge University Press, 1960).
[50]Barfield, *History of English Words*, p. 143.

of the world. Still other metaphors, such as that designated by "electricity is a fluid," were relatively weak in their interactions with the other referents of developing theories of electricity. Eventually the fluid—electricity metaphor became dormant or perhaps dead with respect to its role in the world to which the theory applies. The referent or constraints that seemed to be a basis for the theory were inadequately interpreted. And the referent no longer plays a role in the world as the world is now understood.

The use of the terms *centers* or *focal points of relevance,* mentioned earlier, bears on what has been said about the roles of individuals that are objects of theory. Focal points of relevance function so as to require the relevance of certain senses or properties of the referent and the irrelevance of others. Thus theories, which are systems of senses, are aimed at matchups with individuals. Also, works of art, with their own senses proper to the media in which they are formed, are aimed at matchups with the individuals they create, a topic to be discussed later and which was mentioned earlier in this chapter.

In the case of creative metaphors, what is relevant marks change and the possibility of new relevance in the future. Like growing infants, metaphors create referents that generate forthcoming senses, meanings that would not have been recognized without the metaphor. The Appendix at the end of this book extends this discussion of reference specifically in light of some of Peirce's ideas about indexicality and metaphor. Also, the sixth chapter and the fifth chapter, indirectly, will examine the problems of securing the realism of the implied ontology and, in that connection, will look at the difficult issue of how normative considerations affect the way the constraints of referents function for interpretation.

Recapitulation

This discussion has proposed a view of metaphorical reference that is intended more to be suggestive than complete. My purpose is to lay a basis for developing the interaction theory beyond its outlines in the second chapter and to apply this expanded interactionism to some of the nonverbal arts. Before proceeding, however, I shall summarize the discussion in this chapter, reviewing my main suggestions.

I considered again Max Black's interaction theory of metaphor, with respect not only to its concession that some metaphors create and do not simply reveal antecedent similarities, but also that some metaphors offer cognitive insights that are unique in relation to established knowledge. Black's form of interactionism, however, emphasizes the function of senses and thus reaches a limit in giving an account of what is that is created. This limit can be seen as the result of minimizing the referential function of metaphors. Consequently, Black does not make clear whether the intelligible world to which meta-phorical insights are directed and to which they are faithful is nothing but perspectives. To respond to this point, I proposed that a theory of metaphor move a stage further and treat metaphors as creative designations of extralinguistic conditions. These extralinguistic con-ditions are individuals that provide independent constraints on our system. At the same time, the individuals that are creatively desig-nated are unique.

The implied ontology is a realism – patterned in part on sugges-tions by C. S. Peirce – that leaves room for unique individuals that are centers or foci of relevance. These resist and constrain the appro-priateness of qualities and properties to one another as these are ap-prehended in terms of senses. Individuals sustain clusters of proper-ties and, in turn, of senses. Thus, the significance of creative metaphors cannot be reduced to one or more systems of senses. And their signif-icance is not limited to linguistic or conceptual conventions. They can be creative in interacting with an independent reality that they help create – with individuals that constitute a dynamic, evolving world. An approach based on the treatment of metaphors as illocutionary naming acts is consistent with the conception of an interdependence of linguistic acts and the object of those acts. But consideration of the role of extralinguistic conditions moves beyond the illocutionary function of language.

This proposal, of course, passes over questions about differences between creative designation in poetry or the literary arts and the sciences. I have been concerned primarily with making the suggestion in connection with Black's much-cited view, which assumes that cre-ative metaphors operate in both the sciences and the arts. There are, of course, those who see significance in the arts as immanent in each work, and I am sympathetic to this view. Yet I also think that art works do have relevance to something extra-aesthetic.[51] Their faith-fulness may be assessed in ways other than in science, but they do bear on reality in some respects. Whatever may be the most adequate ac-count of this issue, I think the proposal concerning creative designa-tion is applicable to the arts. Indeed, it may be easier to conceive of the referent of a work of art as an individual, that is, as a focus and center of relevant senses, than it is to conceive this for a scientific theory. In any case, the application to the arts needs further study, which is the subject of the next two chapters.

[51] I have suggested this view in "Art and Symbol," *The Review of Metaphysics* 15 (Decem-ber 1961): 256–70, in *A Discourse on Novelty and Creation*, and, most recently, in "Philo-sophical Creativity and Metaphorical Philosophy," *Philosophical Topics* 12 (n.d.): 193–211.

4

Metaphorical Interaction and the Arts

Difficulties in Applying Verbal Metaphor to
Nonverbal Contexts

The application of the preceding analysis of metaphor faces two related difficulties that should be mentioned at the outset. First, the characterization of metaphor needs to be modified when transferred from verbal examples, and the extent of modification required may prompt the criticism that using a theory of metaphorical expression as a way of understanding art in general lacks any special conceptual utility. A theory of metaphor, then, would seem more properly a species of, rather than a foundation for, a theory of art. The components of verbal metaphors are words, phrases, and sentences with grammatical rules that are peculiar to verbal language. Because nonverbal components are not words, they are not included in larger units that use verbal, linguistic, grammatical rules. Thus a common ground between verbal and nonverbal meaning reference might be denied. In short, it might be said verbal and nonverbal meanings are intrinsically different.

The first difficulty raises a question that can be answered best after the application to the nonverbal arts has been made. The reader can then decide whether the approach to these arts through metaphor sheds light that otherwise would be missing. In anticipation, however, let me point out that if metaphors are aesthetic wholes, and thus works of art, then they represent condensed and relatively obvious delineations of the structures of art works. Thus they should serve as models of works of art in all media. And even if the differences between verbal and nonverbal constituents is essential to this structure, we may nevertheless be able to see something common to the model and what is modeled that might be overlooked if it were not regarded in terms of that model. In any case, I hope that this proposal will at least suggest a point of departure, providing one fruitful basis for an aesthetic of the nonverbal arts.

The second difficulty is that applying what has been said about verbal metaphor to nonverbal contexts may seem strained, particularly because the application is made through a discursive account, which may be thought inappropriate to the examples from various art forms. With respect to the second difficulty, which shares the suspicion of treating alike what is verbal and nonverbal, I again proceed on a hope, a hope that the discussions of nonverbal works of art will be sufficiently faithful to them to overcome the discursive manner in which the application of metaphor is to be made. In general, a response to the point that the application may confuse two linguistic domains – verbal and nonverbal – depends in large part on my attempt to show that verbal and nonverbal elements may be alike in that they both function to articulate significance. I acknowledge, then, that my discussion rests on the assumption that verbal and nonverbal significances are at least relevant to each other. This assumption should be considered. But in order to do so, it is necessary to anticipate some of the discussion to follow.

The application of verbal metaphor to nonverbal expressions will center on the relationship between what I have called *antecedent elements* and *constituents*. As indicated, in the case of nonverbal meanings, the transformations that must be undergone by elements that enter into contexts where they function as constituents pose special descriptive tasks. We cannot say what the particular constituents in a nonverbal context are because we have no ready-made language for this purpose. Although in verbal examples, constituents cannot be described with respect to their distinctive functions as constituents, verbal language is at least appropriate to their verbal meanings as extracted from their interacting contexts. In nonverbal instances, attempts to say anything about their components require that we rely on a medium to which they do not belong. Yet critics do discuss, interpret, and "explain" works of art. What makes their commentary applicable to a specific work is the special way in which they use words. In order to succeed in this, they sometimes find expressions that were new when the authors introduced them. Critics in Cézanne's own time did not have available the words to write about his style that we now have; but later critics originated certain uses of terms that stretched the critic's language and helped us gain insight into Cézanne's style – *plasticity* and *architectural,* for instance. A good critic at some point must be creative when the work to be criticized is itself a creation. This, of course, reiterates the point made earlier that metaphors can be used to enable the appreciation of other metaphors.

Identification and description, then, must employ senses and references already known, or one must invent or discover new senses and new referents. If this can be done, it must be done through an attentive response to the impact of the aesthetic object. And if this response can be expressed intelligibly by means of new articulations, these are at least candidates for being metaphors, because metaphors are kinds of expressions that contribute to the growth of language through the origin of new significance. Metaphorical description is the proper language of criticism, that is, if criticism is to approximate the new intelligibility originated in the internal relations of the aesthetic object. We thus must resort to verbal metaphor. We must do so because of metaphors' help to those who wish to approach and understand aesthetic objects, nonverbal and verbal, through a verbal approach.

In considering this issue, we should remember that the terms *meaning* and *significance* or *import* – which I use to include meaning as well as reference – have a use so fundamental to our attempts to find intelligibility in experience that the question of common verbal and nonverbal significance itself may be improperly formulated. Theories of meaning (and significance) are generally attempts to understand the conditions of belief, of true and false propositions, or of what is verbally expressed. But significance may be more fundamental than whatever can be found appropriate to verbal expression alone. This suggests why the terms *meaning* and *significance* may be attributed to nonverbal and verbal determinations of experience. And it should also suggest that with respect to meanings and significance, nonverbal components of articulated experiences may share a way of being significant. Meaning and significance thus must be understood in the same way that intelligibility is understood. Meaning and significance are more general than are verbal meaning and significance. Indeed, nonverbal significance is taken to be one of the necessary conditions of verbal significance.

This way of understanding significance, it may be noted, is not unlike Benedetto Croce's and R. G. Collingwood's account of how experience must first be aesthetic if it is to be conceptual. And it is not unlike most contemporary writers who insist on preconceptual or precategorical intelligibility. It is assumed that meaning and significance provide the ground for meeting the demands of thought. Like the condition of intelligibility, they are a foundation for intellectual satisfaction. This assumption is shared, although it is not acknowledged in this form, by theories that distinguish kinds of meaning but that base all meanings and, in turn, intelligibility, on truth conditions, on consequences in sense-experience or in broader experience in general, or on psychological conditions and symptoms. This assumption is also implicit in use-theories of meaning, because sorting out uses of the term *meaning,* or *significance,* must depend on the condition that these uses are identifiable and intellectually satisfying (or useful) for those sorting purposes. The uses of the term *meaning* itself must be meaningful, and the words employed in writing or talking about these uses must refer to something (identities that are repeatable).

The upshot of this way of construing meaning and significance is that the assumption on which my account of metaphor and art is based is that nonverbal experience can be significant; it can be meaningful and referential insofar as it approaches being determinate and thereby identifiable. It is thus intelligible. Such identities are the resources of verbal articulations that develop these identities and that may bring them into relations with other identities for conceptual communication. However, I suggest that the preconceptual meaning that may be taken up by verbal languages is also significant. That is, it has a kind of referential function that makes it preconceptually, and often subsequently, relevant to the world. This suggestion will be the main topic of the fifth chapter.

In this chapter, I shall proceed on the assumption that even though nonverbal arts may have meaning functions that are (by definition) nonverbal, nevertheless, the significances that these functions achieve may be compared with the functions of verbal metaphors, for they function to provide intelligibility to that on which attention focuses. Thus the proposal that there is an isomorphism need not violate either form of expression.

The interpretation of metaphor outlined in the previous chapters will be extended in two phases corresponding to the two dimensions of significance: sense and reference. The first phase, which is the subject of this chapter, will discuss how the function of the components of nonverbal artworks is isomorphic with the interaction found in verbal metaphors. The second phase, to be treated in the next chapter, will focus on the way the relationships between nonverbal artworks and the world share a structure with the relationships between a verbal metaphor and its designation.

From the side of the nonverbal arts, there are distinctive, nonverbal characteristics that must be considered before what is isomorphic with verbal metaphor can be discussed. But consideration of these requires an adumbration of a theory of art, which, introduced at the outset, will help the discussion converge on the isomorphic relation of verbal metaphors to metaphorical functions in the arts. For the sake of convenience, the nonverbal arts hereafter usually will be called simply "the arts," "works of art," or variations thereof.

A General Theory of Art

The conception of art to be outlined assumes a quasi-ontological commitment in the sense that it is based first on the functional approach already adopted for verbal metaphors and second on an assumption about the ontological status that may be assigned to works of art on the basis of function for those who experience them. Thus, in accord with the functional approach that I have assumed from the beginning, my conception of works of art is based on how these function for those who direct attention to them. Just as an object's reality is a condition of how it functions, so what appropriately indicates the ontological status of an object is its mode of functioning. Moreover, there is a relationship of reciprocity between an object and the way it functions as an object of attention for a conscious agent. This relation determines what can be said to be real, unreal, or ontologically neutral. The claim that there is reciprocity should be sufficient to show that the conception of art here is intended to avoid both subjectivism and relativism. The view that the ontological status of a work of art is correlated with modes of attention to objects is not a subjectivism; nor need it be wholly relativistic in the sense that it can be said that either pole in the relation of reciprocity is arbitrary. To be sure, there are instances when factors affecting the agent attending to an object are conditions for the way the object is apprehended. Fatigue, for example, may cause blurred vision. And every moment of conscious attention to an object includes an increment of interpretation. Nevertheless, there are resistances and constraints on the object side of experience when attention is directed toward an object that functions as in some sense "real." For instance, physical objects persist throughout instances of opening and shutting one's eyes. Even fantasies resist to some extent the configurations of images that the conscious agent can entertain. This point is a reminder of the resistance that was said to be encountered in the extralinguistic and extraconceptual aspect of referents, referents functioning as individuals.

The connection between the constrained function of individuals and the constraining function of objects regarded as real is, of course, an ontological issue in its own right. The degrees of resistance and the respect in which they function characterize the kind of reality an object appears to have. Additional consideration relevant to adopting an antisubjectivist view will be offered later. But what is important to art in the implied ontology will be discussed later only as it bears on creative reference fixing. At this juncture, I wish only to emphasize that an object regarded as real functions so that the object has conditions that are in part independent of the determining condition of attention.

In adopting an ontological framework, it also is taken for granted that the kind of art in question is creative or created, just as it has been taken for granted that the verbal metaphors being considered are creations.

As a first step in outlining the conception of art that hinges on these assumptions, it will be helpful to consider what may be identified as the "major conditions" or "factors" in an "art situation." An art situation occurs when things called works of art, or things that function as art, are present in some context. Such things are capable of evoking aesthetic experiences on the part of observers who are not, at least in every respect, creators of, or responsible for, the origin of the objects to which they attend. There are three primary factors that serve as conditions for an art situation: the work of art, the creator, and the aesthetic observer. In turn, these three factors function in a context that affects them and is affected by them. Society in general, including family units, religious and civic organizations, the state, and civilization with its inherited values all are present as a surrounding milieu fading off into a horizon of peripheral conditions. Yet each factor of the art situation has its own integrity and makes its own contribution to the constitution of what seems important to social, religious, and political life, and to experience in general.

The first part of this book concentrated on one of the major terms in the art situation, the work of art, in the sense that metaphor serves in this capacity. The other factors or conditions will be taken into account as the view of metaphor is broadened in terms of nonverbal art. The role of the other factors can be seen when we observe a distinction that has been implied as well as made explicit in various aesthetic theories: a distinction between the work of art and the aesthetic object. In the context of the art domain, the aesthetic object is the work of art insofar as it is regarded in aesthetic experience.[1] In turn, the way of regarding the work of art is a function of the observer's attention, what the creator does in producing the work, and the cultural context in which both the observer and the creator live. Aesthetic objects are apprehended in other contexts – in nature, sometimes in human actions and characters, and in manufactured objects that are not made with aesthetic values as their goals. This function of aesthetic objects "outside" art will not be of concern here. On the other hand, the possibility that things called *works of art* may function nonaesthetically needs to be emphasized. My main task at the moment is to identify the differences between objects that function independently of art situations and these same objects functioning within art situations.

Earlier, the point was made that there is a reciprocity in aesthetic experience. If the way the work functions is relative to the purposes of those who see it and use it, there is an interdependence between work of art and observer. The work then is a condition or set of conditions that cannot be effective without the presence of an observer. A work would not attain economic value unless observers regarded the work from the perspective of consumers or potential purchasers. A work would not have a function for chemists unless they ap-

---

[1] One of the most thoughtful and extensive defenses of this distinction is found in Dufrenne's *Phenomenology of Aesthetic Experience*.

proached it with the purpose of using their own methods of analysis. The work could not be aesthetic unless someone took an aesthetic attitude toward it.

It might also be claimed that the aesthetic object is a projection of the observer's consciousness. Consequently, it might be construed as identical with an image or only the intentional object, or as the contents of perceptual and perhaps intellectually functioning imagination. This way of construing the aesthetic object as exclusively internal to consciousness, however, is an interpretation of, or a hypothesis about, what is observed when the work of art is regarded from different perspectives. The description of the work of art and aesthetic object offered here takes the form of describing these in their own terms, in a way that prescinds them from the observer's direct action, and this form of description is continuous with the phenomenological, or metaphysically neutral, approach adopted earlier.

Whether the object of attention exists independently of attention is not the point at this stage. What is important is that the description in terms of the object reflects how works of art impose themselves on us. This is to say that as far as what occurs in experience is concerned, as far as there is immediate evidence, works of art and aesthetic objects are *there*. They are not, as given, projections of consciousness. To reiterate, the claim that works of art and aesthetic objects are wholly subjective is a hypothesis introduced to explain the way they appear and function for us. But before such an interpretation, what we encounter is something that appears to be objective. Works of art and aesthetic objects, for aesthetic appreciation, are initially confronted rather than invented. The way they are experienced, as particular experiences that are given or that appear before us as things demanding attention, is one reason that some theorists interpret them as objective or as having some kind of independence relative to the observer's consciousness. Those who would subjectivize them have other reasons for their approach, such as variations in taste and difficulties in specifying definitive tests of imputed traits. But before either objectivism or subjectivism is proposed, works of art occur in experience as having their own autonomy in relation to the observer. They do so independently of any philosophical ontological theses or methodological attitudes. The work sets itself off. It frames itself for us. As Dufrenne explains, it creates its public.[2] It "enlists" the aesthetic life of both the observer and the creator.[3] "[T]he aesthetic object is within consciousness without being of it; and, conversely, the work of art is outside consciousness, a thing among things, yet it exists only as re-

---

[2] Dufrenne, *Phenomenology of Aesthetic Experience*, in particular, pp. 63–71.
[3] Ibid., p. xlvii.

ferred to a consciousness."[4] "Aesthetic perception completes but does not create the aesthetic object."[5]

The work of art – its appearance as a thing with aesthetic character – thus is phenomenally objective. It attracts attention just as other perceived objects abstract attention. It can surprise us, for instance, if we unexpectedly hear the sounds of a piece of music being performed in the distance. It can serve as background for other activities – which is unfortunate if we respect these works' specific structures. It can dominate our awareness, as sometimes happens when we enter an imposing architectural structure or when a mural persists in drawing our eyes from one part of it to another.

Works of art and aesthetic objects have phenomenal objectivity. But the distinction between works of art and aesthetic object needs to be examined more closely. The distinction is the outcome of other, finer distinctions that can be seen in the way that works of art function.

The following account of the way a work of art functions aesthetically and nonaesthetically will depend on its relation to the other factors of the art situation. The central point to be made is that a thing becomes aesthetic when its features are regarded for their own sakes, that is, without concern for their relations to things and qualities that are independent of the object of attention. A vase, for instance, may be considered for its qualities such as line, overall shape, color, texture, and sense of mass. An appreciation of features such as these, regarded independently of putting the vase to a specific use, is necessary for it to be an aesthetic object. This is not to say that the general idea of the function of vases has nothing to do with these other features. Indeed, the general function of being a vase may be admired for its own sake. Further, there are additional conditions to be met before an object can be regarded aesthetically, conditions having to do with the inner relations of the features that are the objects of attention. These conditions will be considered later. What is important at the moment is simply to observe that things called works of art may or may not be aesthetic objects and that they become aesthetic objects when a certain attitude is taken toward them.

A thing called the work of art can be other than aesthetic. It can function for other ends; for instance, it may be an economic object if it is marketable. Of course, if it is also aesthetic, its value on the market ideally will be determined by its aesthetic function or its aesthetic value, although I suspect that most works of art are valued economically (as investments) only indirectly and remotely on the basis of aesthetic considerations. If they were aesthetically valued initially, they

[4] Ibid., p. lii.
[5] Ibid.

would soon lose this value, which would be replaced by considerations of rarity, demand, and psychological motives such as competitiveness and pride.

A work of art may also function extra-aesthetically for the chemist who, in the case of paintings, analyzes pigments and physical properties as a way of dating or gathering information about the materials available to artists in a certain historical period. A building functions extra-aesthetically when it serves solely as a shelter or as material to be taken from the building after its destruction. This happened in the past when, for instance, monarchs or popes wanted the marble in Roman monuments. When a work of art functions aesthetically, however, its features appear for contemplation and as a condition of aesthetic experiences. It is in this function that the work becomes an aesthetic object. This idea is hardly original. Mikel Dufrenne emphasized it, and up to a point, what I shall say agrees with his account.[6]

The Hierarchy of Attention and Its Objects

The ways of regarding objects called works of art and those called aesthetic objects can be ordered hierarchically. Thus, each way or mode of attending to an object can be understood as a level at which attention functions. As will be seen, the importance of distinguishing levels in a hierarchy lies in proposing an isomorphism between the distinctions between verbal and nonverbal metaphors. Approaching the work of art or aesthetic object in this way will outline the theory of art to be united with the picture of metaphor offered earlier.

Correlative to the hierarchical modes of attention, those things that are regarded as works of art and aesthetic objects also can be identified at distinct levels. The number of levels depends on how finely the distinctions are to be drawn. But whatever the number, the levels inevitably overlap. One level of attention is related to another in an order of dependency. The lowest level is a necessary condition for each higher level, although with a qualification to be made concerning the first and second levels. Each higher level depends on the lower and is a necessary condition of the higher.[7] Thus they need not be temporally distinguished, for the point is that they are logically distin-

---

[6] Ibid.

[7] The relations among levels reflect the kind of relations that C. S. Peirce describes for his three categories by a process of prescision. Although the term "prescision" undergoes subtle changes in Peirce's thought, here it is used to indicate that we cannot abstract the richest from the most abstract, although we can do the reverse. The hierarchical order is also like that of Nicolai Hartmann's ontological and axiological strata. See his *Ethics,* trans. Stanton Coit (New York: Macmillan, 1932), especially vol. 1; and his *New Ways of Ontology,* trans. Reinhard C. Kuhn (Chicago: Henry Regnery, 1952).

guished in that one can be thought of on condition that another is thought of.

There are five overlapping levels of apprehending (and correlatively five aspects of objects of attention or intentional objects) that can be distinguished for objects called works of art: the work of art is (1) a physical object or presence, (2) a perceptual thing, (3) a representation or symbol, (4) a formal-expressive thing, and (5) an aesthetic object. These levels are most easily distinguished in the visual arts. The visual arts serve as the primary model for my account, because they show all the aspect of works of art that can be found in any art form. If one claims that music has no physical dimension, it should be noted that the need for distinguishing levels is still necessary for music because it is at least perceptual and formally expressive.

If it is said that by using the visual arts as the model, the dimension of time is neglected, I must point out that temporality is a condition according to which works are related in terms of the five levels. Paintings, for instance, have temporal relations to their history; they often have referential elements that suggest time in represented movement; and their components cannot be differentiated all at once. Time is obviously intrinsic to an art form such as music. The main point in this connection, however, is that temporality is a perceptual factor in the things regarded as works of art. Further, the first, physical level, which might be denied in regard to art forms such as music, is present in these other forms to the extent that physical properties such as measurements of volume and pitch are understood to be correlated with perceptual qualities.

The distinctions at work here owe much to Mikel Dufrenne's and Jean-Paul Sartre's discussion of art.[8] The distinctions also reflect many of the ideas of Benedetto Croce and R. G. Collingwood.[9] But there is, I think, a more basic conception underlying the distinctions. This underlying conception is common to philosophers who hold opposing fundamental philosophical outlooks but who have recognized parallel ways of attending to the things called works of art. Let me pause here to observe how a writer from a different philosophical position acknowledges distinctions of the kind that I assume in marking off the levels of works of art. Paul Ziff – in opposing the view that there is a class of things existing as special objects of art – outlines distinct "families" of descriptions that use the same terms and sometimes the same sentences in different ways to apply to the same painting: for ex-

[8] In particular, Dufrenne, *Phenomenology of Aesthetic Experience;* and Jean-Paul Sartre, *Psychology of the Imagination* (New York: Citadel, 1961, originally, New York: Philosophical Library, 1948).

[9] Benedetto Croce, *Aesthetic,* trans. Douglas Ainslie (New York: Macmillan, 1922). R. G. Collingwood, *The Principles of Art* (Oxford, England: Clarendon Press, 1938).

ample, "The painting is flat" uttered by a carpenter who is building a crate for the painting and "the painting is flat" uttered by a critic describing the painting stylistically. Ziff's account of the different uses for the same descriptive sentence brings out with admirable precision the kind of point I am making about levels of apprehension.[10]

Ziff builds his case on the idea that there are distinct uses of language, which account for the way that we view works of art. Of course, his analysis concerns primarily the uses of language. The exclusion from consideration of objects correlative to the language in its different uses is simply an avoidance of the ontological issues. In contrast, I think it is meaningful to ask: What kind of thing is the object or thing that can be described for different purposes? Is it a substance or singular substratum? Is it a bare particular? Is it an unknown thing-in-itself? Is it nothing but a cluster of properties? For any of these options, the painting must be understood – described, interpreted, and given determination in relation to other things we understand – by clusters of attributes of the kind referred to by carpenters, critics, art historians, auctioneers, and so forth. As will be seen, it is in terms of the types of clusters of attributes that the following remarks about levels of art works will be offered.

The objects at each level of attention function at least as intentional objects, although to reiterate, in view of the limits and constraints on attempts to interpret what appears as an object of attention, to be an intentional object is not to be a mental counterpart of a mental activity. As Harold Osborne commented,

Whatever your philosophical position about the nature of material things and their qualities, you must recognize that there are groups of sense impressions having qualities analogous to those which we ordinarily attribute to material things, that some of these groups are comparatively abiding, and that they occur in connection with those regions of space which in ordinary language the material thing would be said to occupy.[11]

Let us return, then, to an explanation of the levels I have mentioned.

The first level of the work of art is its function as a physical thing. This is a level at which the object is not regarded as an instance of art. The point about this kind of object is that by appearing as a physical thing it does not prompt an interpretation of it as art. What does prompt such an interpretation is found at a higher level or mode of attention. The work of art as a physical thing is simply a spatial—

[10] Paul Ziff, "Art and the 'Object of Art'," in William Elton, ed., *Aesthetics and Language* (Oxford, England: Blackwell Publisher, 1970), pp. 170–86.
[11] Harold Osborne, *Theory of Beauty: An Introduction to Aesthetics* (London: Routledge & Kegan Paul, 1952), p. 93.

temporal object. In this respect, it has what Dufrenne regarded as the status of a "thing."[12] Of course, as a spatial and/or temporal object, it is more than something that can be located by spatial coordinates on a grid. It has properties that include some or all of the following: weight, size, shape, identifiable matter, and duration over measurable intervals. However, such properties are identifiable through publicly accessible observations. Thus the physical object is also a perceptual object, so that the second and first levels are linked in a special interdependence with respect to the order in which they are distinguished for cognition. Yet physical objects are given as phenomenally prior to perceptual qualities when these are abstracted from the object. Physical—perceptual properties, of course, can also be attributed to non—art objects.

This physical and perceptual aspect of a work of art is important to objects that are attended to as art, because works of art can be and are, for certain purposes, treated as things in this sense. We have already noted Ziff's account that refers to the way carpenters use language regarding paintings. Shippers who wish to crate a painting must see it as a physical object with perceptual properties. Printers preparing type for a set of inscriptions called a poem must see one of the conditions of the poem as a cluster of physical properties. Acoustical engineers and many hi-fi enthusiasts regard music in terms of sound properties — wave frequencies, loudness, response to transients, measurable distortion of pitch, and the like.

The respect in which a thing is a perceptual object should be distinguished from the physical dimension so as to call attention to instances in which interpretation is not so closely connected with quantifiable properties but is tied to qualitative characteristics, characteristics thought of as partly dependent on an observer's sensitivity. An obvious characteristic of this sort is color: Some observers are more sensitive than others are to differences in hue, value, and saturation. Some observers are color-blind. Similarly, heard sounds obviously are qualities that function differently for different perceivers. If the object is perceptually apprehended, it is less stable than is the object regarded in its function as a physical object. The object as physical endures in more predictable ways than does the object as perceptual. Furthermore, attention to the quantifiable properties at the first level can frequently exclude qualitative aspects: The shippers need not consider the color of the painting they are to crate; the printer of a score need not consider what the music that is to be performed sounds like. Yet on occasion, quantitative and qualitative properties overlap, and as I

---

[12] Dufrenne, *Phenomenology of Aesthetic Experience*. The distinction between thing and aesthetic object, and works of art is first introduced on lxv.

shall try to show later with respect to works of art, this second, perceptual level helps bridge the first level and the level at which features explicitly prompt seeing an object as aesthetic. An archeologist analyzing an artifact in terms of its physical properties may well be concerned with physical correlates of color found on the artifact, for instance, they may provide evidence for the data on the social use of the object. Further, qualitative characteristics may correlate with quantitative properties, for instance, the measurable height and dimensions of a Gothic cathedral as distinct from but correlated with the perceived rising height and verticality that gives expressive power to the structure.

The last example points to a way of regarding the object as it incorporates the third level, the work as representational or as a symbolic object, which is presupposed when the object is viewed as having cultural significance. Seeing the object as representational reveals senses or meanings and references it has in terms of its context, the object may represent something in the sense of indicating certain domestic or social purposes. It would then be regarded as an artifact or as an example of the functional arts. In this sense, a cathedral may represent a religious commitment in a society. It expresses this by being interpreted as a symbol of human aspiration for the divine.

It should be reiterated here that these levels are distinguished without regard to the temporal order in which things are noticed. Thus the representational level may be attended to before (temporally) the other two levels. In most cases, I suspect, such objects when initially attended to have been interpreted as representational artifacts by the archeologist or perhaps the art historian. They were thus classified according to representational functions before they were viewed analytically, in physical–perceptual terms.

Occasionally objects may be found accidentally and may appear to be unclassifiable, for example, unworked stones. These would be preanalytically regarded as physical–perceptual things. Only later would someone recognize that some of the perceptual qualities suggested representational significance or purposeful design, in which case they would begin to function for attention as objects that are artifacts. Further, this third, cultural level may be recognized temporally only after an object has been regarded in terms of the fourth level. The point I am making is that temporal considerations are not essential to the distinctions.

The fourth level is the one at which attention is focused on formal-expressive aspects of an object. Because this level is constituted by a special relation between form and expressiveness, a relation that is easily misunderstood, it will be helpful to refer to several fairly well known aestheticians: R. G. Collingwood, John Dewey, and Susanne

Langer. The basis of my proposal for interpreting the concept of the formal-expressive can be seen in both Collingwood's and Dewey's insistence that artistic expression is not an uncontrolled disclosure or ejaculation of feelings. It is not a revelation of symptoms. It is an activity of controlled attention without the intervention of preconceived or preimagined experience. Expression in a work of art is both a discovery and a creation or generation of what is expressed. To express is to experience and act in a unique way. What is expressed is unprecedented. It is an articulation of what may be identified and experienced for its own sake. According to Susanne Langer, expressiveness has its import in what she calls "presentational symbols." Based on this conception of expression as exhibiting rather than representing, what is expressed must be understood as inseparable from the object's perceptual properties.

The importance of the formal-expressive function of elements that may be symbolic should be clearly evident in music. Simple rises in pitch in a series of tones tends more toward an uplifting expressiveness, toward growth or heightened intensity, than toward relaxation or diminishment of intensity and growth. Ending a composition on a chord that is not the tonic leaves the end less settling than it would be if the conclusion were to culminate with the tonic chord. I do not mean to ignore changes and variations in human responsiveness to sound relationships, but I do assume that even in a time when atonal music and other musical sound patterns have broken with the nineteenth-century traditions of harmony, there are some fundamental psychophysical dispositions to respond to sound patterns that are common to all humans. What we like may vary – for instance, whether we prefer to hear compositions end in a query rather than a resolution – but our response is basically the same.

If formal-expressive qualities are exhibited in a musical composition that is interpreted as having a kind of representational function, in the way, for instance, that Beethoven's Third Symphony is construed as at least relevant to heroism, then it is the formal-expressive properties that are crucial to prompting such interpretations. Attention to the integrative contributions of the formal-expressive functions of sound patterns to their representational functions is essential to appreciating so-called content. The interanimation of functions is what delivers a significance that is, through internal interaction, exhibited rather than represented. Thus a work of art presents something formally expressive that can be discovered only within its own boundaries, something not available elsewhere before the advent of the work.

The fourth, formal-expressive level depends directly on the second, perceptual level as its necessary condition. There must be something physically present, or at least with a minimal perceptual or virtual physical presence ordinarily associated with images (even fictional) that can be identified temporally and virtually spatially. The patterns or relationships signified by musical scores are patterns of virtual sounds – patterns that would attain actual physical presence if performed by instruments or voices and that for many who can read scores would attain actual imaginary sonorous presence. What is thus virtually and imaginatively present is in part virtually quantifiable, although, of course, not exhaustively, as an actual perceptual–physical artifact.

Although the fourth level depends on the first and second, it should be noted that properties regarded in physical–perceptual senses are in themselves not formally expressive. Insofar as properties are purely physical and perceptual, as they are at the first and second level, they can be quantified or correlated with quantified measurements. For example, when a color is seen according to perceptual considerations, it can be correlated with wavelengths or a color chart. Thus some additional aspects of the object must be present when it functions at the fourth, formal-expressive level. Some formal, ordered character must be present with the expressive aspects.

The fourth level was illustrated in the example cited earlier of the description "the painting is flat." This has one meaning at the second level, say for a furniture packer. It has other meanings for the purposes of art criticism. For instance, *flat* may suggest the absence or minimizing of three-dimensional representation. Or it may suggest the absence of exciting colors and shapes or a general lack of effectiveness. Other expressions appropriate to the formal-expressive mode of attending are "The painting is powerful in its dynamic balance," "In the trio section, the music moves into lyrical gaiety," and "The poem's use of consonants in this line intensifies the developing tension."

These examples suggest that what is formal-expressive manifests characteristics that are most readily articulated in words used to apply to feelings or emotions. However, the term *formal,* which is linked to *expressive,* should indicate that *expressive* is not simply a communication or outflow of feeling. Certainly, what is formally expressive exhibits something comparable to what emotional expression may also exhibit and communicate. Whatever is formally expressive is effective in a way not limited to purely abstract articulations – if there are any such articulations that are pure. At the same time, what is formally expressive, as formal, exhibits a controlling order, a formal dimension that requires that the expressive aspect be dependent on the formal, and vice-versa. The expressive and the formal are interdependent. *Expression,* of course, can be used broadly enough to apply to anything that is uttered or provokes some emotional or cognitive content. My purposes require only that the term be understood as covering both cognitive and emotional conditions and that the thing said to be expressive exhibit (as distinct from represent) its expressiveness – whether or not it also communicates or whether it is responsible for provoking actual ideas, images, or emotions in those who find the thing expressive.

My view implies that the fourth level of the relation between attention and its object is a necessary condition of both abstract and representational art. This relationship was implicit in what was said about absolute music. Even computer-generated musical compositions exhibit some expressive qualities as the appreciator interacts with them. And a Mondrian composition, as well as more recent examples of paintings dependent on subtle color and textual contrasts, manifests some degree of expressiveness of the sort just described. We shall consider later the way the formal-expressive level functions in art objects that are aesthetic.

The point made earlier about the inseparability of formal-expressive and perceptual properties anticipates the way that an object's features function at the aesthetic level. As I shall indicate, the main character of aesthetic attention is found in the way it regards the qualities of an object both for their own sakes and as interdependent. Furthermore, it will be important to see that to attend to objects in terms of the formal-expressive level is integral to aesthetic attention. Nevertheless, formal-expressive qualities may be apprehended independently of aesthetic concerns, for instance, if formal-expressive characteristics function only as cues to reverie or to stimulate courage, as in the case of a military march. Moreover, attention to an object's formal-expressive qualities may be, and most often is, prior to the other, analytic and symbolic interpretations of the same object. This point is nicely suggested by Rudolph Arnheim: "But if I sit in front of a fireplace and watch the flames, I do not normally register certain shades of red, various degrees of brightness, geometrically defined shapes moving at such and such speed. I see the graceful play of aggressive tongues, flexible, striving, lively in color."[13] Formal-expressive characteristics may also be the basis for an art historian's classification of art by period or style and the interpreter's descriptions of the symbolic significance of artifacts.

This point is a reiteration of what was said earlier about the independence of the levels from temporal occurrence. However, the point about the irrelevance of occurrences in time as applied to the relation between the fourth and fifth levels might be questioned. Thus, on the

[13] Rudolph Arnheim, *Art and Visual Perception: A Psychology of the Creative Eye* (Berkeley and Los Angeles: University of California Press, 1954), pp. 454–5.

one hand, the possibility that formal-expressive attention may follow as well as precede the fifth level of aesthetic attention may be challenged, for one might think that we cannot appreciate something aesthetically without first recognizing its formal-expressive qualities. Thus we may think that the expressive qualities of Cézanne's *Mt. St. Victoire,* such as monumentality, strength of spatial structure, and the solidity of color patches, are what provokes or at least prepares us for appreciation. The important role of the formal-expressive in such instances of aesthetic appreciation should be acknowledged.

The recognition of formal-expressive qualities, however, may just as well depend on an initial act of aesthetic attention that prepared the way for noticing the formal-expressive aspects of the aesthetic object. For example, it seems possible, perhaps likely, that the Altamira Cave paintings may well have had an aesthetic appeal before they were subjected to historical, chemical, and sociological analysis and before particular formal-expressive characteristics were selected for attention. Attending to formal-expressive qualities so that they are explicitly discriminated within their settings in works of art may thus be either subsequent to or prior to the aesthetic activity of appreciating the work as a whole. But what is this fifth level of aesthetic activity?

The Conditions of Aesthetic Attention

The basis for distinguishing the aesthetic level lies in two interdependent conditions: The first is what some theorists have called *distance,* and the second is the functioning of elements in internal relations. Because of the interdependence of these two conditions, the idea of distance must be understood in a way that to some extent qualifies its more commonly accepted significance. This qualification is best seen in the light of the classic interpretation of distance and a recent criticism of its application to what is called the "aesthetic attitude."

The classic statement was made by Eduard Bullough.[14] What Bullough calls "phsychical distance" refers to the condition under which an attitude constitutes aesthetic experience so that all considerations of practical concerns, moral interest, desire for pleasure, and, generally, all considerations of means and ends are made irrelevant to attention and its object. However, the basic idea of disengaging one's interests and attention from practical purposes and knowledge is found in a long tradition traceable at least as far back as Kant.[15] Essential to this idea is the conviction that there is an aesthetic attitude, a way of looking, listening, imagining, or thinking that is distinctively appro-

---

[14] Edward Bullough, "Distance as a Factor in Art and in Aesthetic Principle," *British Journal of Psychology* 5 (1912): 87–8.
[15] Immanuel Kant, *Critique of Judgment.*

priate to apprehending aesthetic objects, especially works of art. The mark of this attitude is its disengagement from purposive responses and intentions that guide attention in nonaesthetic – ordinary, as well as refined, reflective theoretical – experience. In disengaged attention, qualities and their organization within the object of attention can be noticed without the interference of related consequences and antecedent conditions. Attention to its object becomes intransitive rather than transitive.[16] What is there, in the object, can be recognized for its own sake. Without distance, what is there would be noticed only as it led to other qualities and relations in other objects. Attention thereby would be drawn away from the given object for the sake of that to which its recognition is instrumental.

One recent critic of the view that there is such a thing as a distinctive aesthetic attitude has argued that there is nothing aesthetically distinctive about giving undivided attention to something. Thus, he says, there is no reason to call this attention "aesthetic." This criticism, offered by George Dickie, is directed particularly toward Jerome Stolnitz's version of the aesthetic distance theses, although Dickie mentions others besides Stolnitz, including Bullough.[17] We need not discuss the variations among the theorists who believe that aesthetic attitudes depend on a form of distancing. But we should consider an aspect of the view that apparently neither the critics nor perhaps the more recent defenders of the idea of aesthetic distance have sufficiently emphasized.

Attending to an object with undivided intransitive attention or distance, disengaging attention from purposive reaction, is not alone what guarantees an aesthetic attitude. For instance, Kant's way of distinguishing judgments of beauty from other responses and judgments requires more for aesthetic disengagement than simply the assumption of an attitude of undivided attention. Aesthetic experience is positive and pregnant with possibilities not necessarily given for pure attention. Aesthetic judgment acknowledges *purposiveness* without concern with some determinate purpose. It depends on a kind of *interest* that is not directed toward an end independent of the object of attention. And most important, aesthetic attention is responsive to what Kant calls "aesthetical ideas," which are the products of genius and which are expansive beyond the limits of any conceptual understanding.[18]

---

[16] See Eliseo Vivas, *The Artistic Transaction: Essays on Theory of Literature* (Columbus: Ohio State University Press, 1963).

[17] George Dickie, "All Aesthetic Attitude Theories Fail: The Myth of the Aesthetic Attitude," *American Philosophical Quarterly* 1 (1964); 56–66. Jerome Stolnitz, "Some Questions Concerning Aesthetic Perception," *Philosophy and Phenomenological Research* 22 (1961): 69–87. See also Stolnitz's *Aesthetics and Philosophy of Art Criticism, a Critical Introduction* (Boston: Houghton Mifflin, 1960), especially chap. 2.

[18] See Kant's *Critique of Judgment*, trans. J. H. Bernard (New York: Hafner Press, 1972), sec. 49.

Distancing simply provides a frame for attention, marking off extrinsic from intrinsic concerns. Thus an aesthetic attitude includes more than just being alert to qualities for their own sake, in their own terms. An aesthetic attitude is not just seeing (or listening to or imagining) what is there to be noticed apart from conditions and consequences or from practical needs and purposes. It is noting what is there having an intrinsic order, which is precisely what distinguishes the fifth from the other levels of attention.

This positive aspect of the object of aesthetic attention is to be found in the internal relations of the object's components. And what marks an instance of disengaged attention as aesthetic is that attention dwells on the ordering of the components of what is discerned. This Dickie overlooks.

An object's internal order, as was pointed out, is the internal relatedness which is the second condition of the fifth, aesthetic level. The aesthetic level will be discussed in connection with the application of the general theory of art to the proposal that there is an isomorphism between verbal and nonverbal metaphor.

The Application to the Arts

In order to explore the application of the view of metaphor proposed in the previous chapters, it is necessary to reflect on an aspect of verbal metaphors that was not mentioned before, although it was implied in the discussion of interactionism. This aspect of metaphorical expression can be seen when we observe that the verbal meaning units comprising metaphors belong to a medium – verbal, as distinct from pigment, stone, musical tones, and the like. In bringing together the elements of its medium in a relation of interaction, a metaphor modifies its medium, or more accurately, it modifies the usual function of its medium. A medium is not simply matter or a collection of materials or elements. A medium consists of materials having a certain function, a function that will contribute to and be changed by the particular use to which the materials are put. Thus, a metaphor modifies a medium in that it gives another use to a medium, whose usual function in everyday experience is practical. The medium of verbal language is ordinarily thought of as functioning to impart information or to communicate in some way, even if what is communicated is not conceptual. But when words are brought together in a context so that they yield metaphorical expression, the words become prominent for their own sakes to the extent that their significances are played with. Such play is not trivial, because it loosens the usual semantic rules for joining words and because the outcome is a new significance.

This outcome is initially a semantic immanence that exhibits a transformed medium. At the same time, there is a transcendence of what was significant. Thus, the semantic immanence is the bridge by which the new significance can be reached. The reason for considering metaphors in these terms is to indicate that there is a basic ground shared by verbal metaphors and art: the manipulation of the medium so that there is a stage in which significance is made immanent or internal to the expression that functions metaphorically and aesthetically. In the arts, this way of gaining significance is the outcome of the interplay of the levels of attention.

The contrasts between the levels of attention and their correlated objects show the patterns common to verbal metaphor and nonverbal expression. These contrasts depend on the difference between how components of both verbal metaphors and aesthetic objects function internally in relation to one another and how those same components function independently of the aesthetic object. Functioning internally, it may be recalled, is essential to the interacting terms of verbal metaphors when the terms are understood as constituents rather than as antecedent meanings. In order to develop this account of the common ground between verbal metaphors and aesthetic works of art, let us examine further the aesthetic functions of components at the fifth level of attention.

The aesthetic function of components at the fifth level will be viewed in light of the three key features of verbal metaphor: (1) the presence of at least two major terms or subjects, (2) tension, and (3) integration. Although most of the remainder of this chapter will be devoted to exploring the role of tension and integration in the arts, it is necessary to describe the first feature briefly. The possession of two subjects can be dealt with quickly, for in the aesthetic arts, the presence of the two anchoring terms is intimately bound up with the other key features of the aesthetic level, which will be discussed more extensively.

The Presence of Two Subjects

In most if not all the arts, one can distinguish multiple subjects. Each representational component can be regarded as a subject or term interactng with others, as "world" and "unweeded garden" interact in "The world is an unweeded garden." Art historians often analyze works of art in terms of various symbols that can be identified within the works. And components such as these may be regarded as subjects. However, in nonverbal expressions, as in verbal metaphors, there are certain meaning units that have prominence. There are two ways in which prominent meaning units function as two subjects. The first way is obvious. One unit helps control the way the other is seen or heard. In Cézanne's *Mt. St. Victoire,* a mountain image is seen architecturally in part because of the solidlike carved space of a sky as well as the buildup of overlapping color patches. In a sonata-allegro form, a second musical theme affects the first, as may be emphasized in the development section. But there is a second way that two subjects function in the arts, and this is not as obvious as the first.

In the second way that subjects occur, the prominent terms may require constructing a context in order to be recognized as functioning like subjects. Thus, nonverbal expressions parallel verbal expressions such as "Brilliant," which is understood metaphorically in that it has a context that invites nonliteral interpretation. As was pointed out earlier, the expression "Brilliant" is not, in isolation, an assertion, although it is construed as an affirmation in relation to an implicit context. Similarly, paintings, musical compositions, and even poems regarded aesthetically do not assert anything. They are not arguments or conclusions of arguments. Nevertheless, if we consider a painting such as Cézanne's *Mt. St. Victoire,* I think it is obvious that the painting's subject, the painted Mt. St. Victoire, is at least relevant to the extra-aesthetic part of the landscape, Mt. St. Victoire in southern France, which can be seen apart from the painting. The actual mountain obviously does not enter the painting as a subject. Nor is the painted mountain to be construed as a representation (as a photograph would be) of the actual mountain. Yet the significance of the extra-aesthetic mountain is relevant to one distinct component of the painting, the painted mountain. Otherwise, Cézanne's transformation of its form could not be recognized. Even if one has never seen the actual mountain, the apprehension of the representational form of the mountain in the painting signals the possibility of a model, a landscape in space and time that is independent of the painting.

An external object that has such a role often is something envisaged rather than perceived. And because it may be envisaged as independent of the painting, it is not inappropriate to use the term *extra-aesthetic image* to refer to it. Thus, it can be said that corresponding to the implicit subject in the expression "Brilliant," there is a second subject or key term for Cézanne's painting – in this case, the extra-aesthetic image of the actual mountain, an image that is assumed to be available to normal vision and that is subject to pragmatic tests of confirmation in case we want to test our attempts to communicate information about it. Once the painting is regarded as a presentation of a prominent image (among others) that functions aesthetically and as a transformation, for aesthetic purposes, of a counterpart preaesthetic image, then we have an interaction parallel to a verbal metaphor.

Considering once more "Man is a wolf," it can be said that man functions initially in the same way that a preaesthetic image of a nonverbal metaphorical expression does. In the case of this verbal metaphor, the metaphorical image, man, is a conceptualizable image referring to man but, at the same time, having this reference changed as it interacts with wolf.

It might be asked whether the proposal regarding subjects can be applied to nonrepresentational painting. The answer, I think, depends on our willingness to grant that even aesthetic works such as these have relevance to the world. If they do, as will be pursued when the question of metaphorical reference is raised for nonverbal expressions, then they can be understood as relating to some extra-aesthetic subject comparable to the actual Mt. St. Victoire. For instance, Mondrian thought of himself as distilling and abstracting from objects in nature when he painted his purely abstract compositions. And as I shall propose later, composers of music have in mind human conditions and sometimes events in nature even in nonprogrammatic music.

In cases of abstract art, I think that structures of human actions, cognitive and emotional, are necessary but not sufficient conditions of the significance of aesthetic works, although such works help constitute those same conditions through the interaction of components that are subjects relevant to the various visual and/or dynamic rhythms and psychophysical processes that we experience. Structures of human life are preaesthetic subjects like the literally understood things in the world that function for verbal metaphors. The role of extra-aesthetic images for abstract art will be illustrated in the discussion of the relevance of the arts to the world. At the moment, the point is that subjects recognized as internal to aesthetic art works must be considered with respect to how components function in internal tension at the aesthetic level of attention.

Tension and Internal Relatedness

It should be clear that what I mean by "functioning internally" is a kind of interaction in which parts and whole are dependent on one another. But within the whole, the dominant components, the key terms, play the most important roles in interaction. And it is their interaction that sets up the second main feature of verbal and nonverbal metaphors: tension. This section will deal with the inner relatedness that establishes tension. Special attention will be given to the way the elements that can be differentiated and identified in terms of their antecedent meanings function in relation to one another as interdependent components or constituents. Let me emphasize again that such constituents interact in a special way, a way that cannot be understood insofar as the elements are construed as if they were independent and as functioning in external relations. Thus, when an element is drawn into an internal relation with another element, both are dependent on each other, and all elements within the whole cooperate together. In this interdependence, interaction occurs.

Internal relatedness can be illustrated by absolute music. Normally, it is neither each tone nor the summation of tones that attracts attention so that the aesthetic attitude is established. Texture, melody, rhythm, and the like all are part of the ordering that is confronted by aesthetic attention. To be sure, there are instances when what seems to be a pure tone in a single pitch, sounded continuously, calls attention to itself and may even provoke the expression "It is beautiful." This kind of reaction may occur, too, when someone admires a certain hue without considering its setting. But if such responses are aesthetic, they are at one pole of a scale that covers the simplest to the most complex aesthetic objects. The ordering internal to a single tone or a single color approaches unity. And the gestalt, which for tones and colors necessarily emerges from a relatively simple order, does not have as much power in provoking admiration as a complex order does.

It should be emphasized that shapes, lines, and colors, when outside objects of art, may appear not merely as pragmatic, conceptual items of experience but also as interesting patterns or attractive shapes. When this is true, however, these visual, graphic things function aesthetically, as they must for an artist who uses them as material for an aesthetic work of art. They are ready for incorporation in a work. The one who can translate this through the hand and integrate such qualities in a larger meaning unit that exhibits an expressive order is one who is an artist. Qualities that are present outside art may be expressive. Red may be harsh or vigorous both inside and outside a painting. Formal-expressive elements such as gracefulness of line and harmonious relationships may have a place both outside and inside aesthetic objects. These become aesthetic when "framed" by larger contexts of formal-expressive qualities interacting with them.

Every component of an object that appears for aesthetic attention is an element that functions in ways proper not only to the aesthetic but also to one or more of the other modes of attending. Thus, not only the entire object but an element as well may function at different levels. The "same" element may, for example, appear as an area on a painting, and this area may be identified by color theory as a specific hue, with a specific saturation and specific value of lightness or darkness, correlated with light rays of a specific frequency of vibration. In turn, this area of the painting is a visual quality to which we can point.

But at the same time, it may appear against a background that is a shape or visual form that represents something. In turn, the area not only may contribute to representational elements, but it also may be formally expressive. And most important, the element may interact with others, all affecting one another according to their various functions, to yield the aesthetic level. It is when an element functioning at the formal-expressive level, as well as at other levels, interacts and relates internally with the other elements that it becomes an aesthetic component.

Elements that can be distinguished at more than one level will have distinct functions appropriate to those levels that, in turn, are themselves interacting with one another. For instance, the properties of a physical–perceptual element, or the properties of an element in its physical–perceptual function – say, colors or shapes – make differences to the properties of representational components, or the properties of this and other components in their representational functions. The gilt color of the sky in a Byzantine painting carries a perceptual strength in its composition, but it also is a symbol of heavenly presence, and both functions mutually support each other. Or to consider a function itself, instead of an element with several functions, the iconicity of the golden glow in the Byzantine painting is an obvious general property attributable to the same element in more than one function: The gold resembles golden color outside the painting, wherever it appears, and it resembles something precious. Flatness may be a property of a two-dimensional, rectangular shape of a tabletop surface, and it may be shared with flatness of a portrayed surface of a tabletop in a Matisse painting, whose formal-expressive flatness is enhanced by the represented tilting of the surface and by other broad color surfaces. More obviously, flesh colors on a human figure in a painting are iconic, perceptual, and representational (of color on an actual or possible model), and if the painting is more than a simple imitative photographic piece, the colors will assume a unique formal-expressive function, perhaps exhibiting rugged courage or a delicate warmth of personality.

In their aesthetic capacities, components work together so that aesthetic works of art exhibit significances that "emerge" from, or are transformations of, the meanings and references that have antecedent independence of the aesthetic object. The arches extending backward from Plato and Aristotle in Raphael's *The School of Athens,* for instance, simultaneously exhibit a pictorial framing while representing an ancient architectural structure that contributes to a suggested historical setting for the scene. But this setting is affected by other indications of time that do not fit the architectural style: the time of Plato and Aristotle themselves, as well as that of other representational figures. Such historical discrepancies are subordinated by formal properties seen in the grouping of figures and the unifying features of the composition.

Another illustration is found in the writing of the art historians David Robb and J. J. Garrison, who interpret Rembrandt: "More and more he grew to look upon objective reality as something to be translated into intrinsically expressive rhythms."[19] They assume that the function of components affects and transforms the representational basis external to Rembrandt's paintings. One might quarrel over the exact terms of the appraisal, questioning, for instance, what "objective reality" and "intrinsically expressive" mean. But surely we can recognize some distinction between something that satisfies "objective reality" and something that is "nonobjective" by being a characteristic intrinsic to painting. Objective reality presumably is what the authors take to be independent, in part, of human interpretation and what is public or common to all who can see with normal vision. More important here is the main point of their appraisal of Rembrandt. The artist is said to transform what is independent of the painting and is common to normal vision. The artist transforms the perceptual qualities that delineate faces and torsos into images that are not found in the world but that function in a different way so that the qualities constitute a different kind of object of attention. Similarly, in music, the composer transmutes perceptual qualities (sounds) of the world from the second level to the fourth, formal-expressive level and, in turn, to the fifth, aesthetic level.

Art shares with verbal metaphors the incorporation of meaning units from the world as it is apprehended literally, that is, in terms of standard, conventional contexts. Meanings are brought together in contexts that are strange in relation to the literally understood world. And they are transformed through a kind of interaction that is constituted by internal relations, just as the elements or terms of a verbal metaphor understood as antecedently significant have their significance changed when they interact internally with the other terms in their constitutive functions.

It should be emphasized that although each level is distinct and consequently can be contrasted with each and all of the others, the contrast between the fifth and the lower levels is different in kind, because it is based not simply on a function correlated with a mode of attention but also on the special interaction that marks the aesthetic level. The contrast that is effected is essential to the tension present in nonverbal metaphor.

[19] David M. Robb and J. J. Garrison, *Art in the Western World* (New York: Harper Bros., 1942), p. 729.

Before concentrating specifically on the tension generated by the interacting levels of aesthetic objects, several points related to what has been said about aesthetic objects should be considered. These points have to do with a possible objection and certain conditions associated with internal relatedness that have possible consequences for criticism. The latter also pertain to the referential function of nonverbal metaphors, to be discussed later.

It might be objected that nonaesthetic objects can also be thought to have internally related parts, say, in a living organism or perhaps in some deductive arguments formulated in a logic of relations or in an objective idealist's Absolute. It is tempting to say with the objector that whatever is regarded as in internally organized object – every organically related object – is, in respect to its organicism, aesthetic.

We should be cautious, however, about spreading and thinning the notion of what is aesthetic. I think this difficulty is avoided, because in an aesthetic whole the internal organization must include components that have formal-expressive functions. Understood in terms of biology, a living organism may have internal relations that, it may be said, are a condition of life. Unless the functions of the vital organs were mutually supportive, life would cease, and each organ would be different with respect to function. Even nonvital organs will affect one another and change if they lose their normally functioning context. Yet these components are not, for biology, formally expressive. If a sculptor created a statue of a living organism, and if it were responded to by an aesthetic attitude, then its components would have formal-expressive significances. And so would a living creature viewed in this way by the sculptor. We can, of course, appreciate scenes in nature with an aesthetic attitude, and frequently the qualities in nature take on humanlike formal-expressive significance. Thomas Hardy, for instance, begins a chapter in his novel *Tess of the D'Urbervilles* by referring to the sun as "he." We say such things as "The flowers smiled gaily in the field" and "The day awakened under dark shrouds." The presence of formal-expressive qualities is thus especially relevant to the internal order that is a condition of aesthetic objects.

Furthermore, tension is not a necessary ingredient in the nonaesthetic internally related objects. Of course, one could insist that each part of an organism must maintain its own distinctive function for the sake of the organism as a whole. Yet unification is the dominating principle, and it is the unity of the whole for the sake of which the parts function in their own ways. Certainly, in a work of art, this unity of the whole, is served. But the power of the work also comes from the contrasts.

The second point that needs to be made concerns a condition established by the fifth level that has not yet been mentioned. The order encountered at the aesthetic level imposes a demand on attention. This demand is under the guidance of what I called earlier a *center of relevance* and what may also be called *the focal control* or *controlling focus* of the order of the work. This idea is a focus of control should be developed in the context of art.

The condition is called *focal* because it approximates a unique determination of the components that are controlled by it. Its identity is not fully determinate, although it functions as if it *would* become completely determinate in the long run. As a focus, this condition governs the relevance of some formal-expressive elements, actual and potential, and the irrelevance of others. There are degrees of relevance. A broad nose, for instance, is relatively irrelevant – that is, inappropriate – as an element on the figure of Jesus in an El Greco crucifixion. But a longer nose is not irrelevant, although it would be less appropriate than is the actual length of the nose in the painting. The use of an organ in place of the chorus in the final movement of Beethoven's Ninth Symphony is less relevant than is the chorus itself, given the lengths to which the symphony must go in order to contrast with and complete what went before the introduction to the "Ode to Joy" theme. The controlling focus functions similarly for attempts to interpret works of art. And by *interpret* I have in mind various kinds of interpretation, including formal analysis, descriptions of what critics claim is expressed, interpretations of rendering (as are those of performers of music and drama), and even impressionistic commentary.

The controlling focus of a work of art is not a condition that can be defined and spelled out as if it were a set of definite rules. It is more like a gravitational pull that remains open to changes that may occur in the future of the work as audiences become more familiar with it and return to it with richer experiences. Focal control, however, does require one general rule, that at least minimal coherence be exhibited so that the attention of audiences can identify the work as a work and as aesthetic. This leaves open the possibility that even a work of art randomly produced by a computer might have coherence. But having coherence is not enough. There is another condition that must function so as to ground coherence and, in turn, the controlling focus. This other condition is the peculiar sort of referent that a creation signals. The idea of such a referent was introduced in Chapter 3 and will be considered again when the application of reference to nonverbal expressions is taken up in the next chapter.

The final point to be made before again concentrating on tension in the arts concerns the way that internal relatedness demands attention. The way that an internal order attracts attention suggests that an aesthetic object appears with an "ought," a normative condition that invokes value judgment. This is not to imply that the work needs to be a masterpiece, or even be clearly good rather than bad. The object's internal order may turn out to demand that it does not merit sustenance. It may, when considered more intensely, show itself as not what ought to be but as what ought not to be, for its internal order may break down at crucial points, or the expressiveness may trivialize its formal order. Some critics of Norman Rockwell might say the latter of much of his work. Nor does the point that the aesthetic object has normative functions mean that the work must affirm something good or bad in the world. To be sure, some masterpieces may be construed as normative representations of things in the world. For instance, David's neoclassical paintings and Raphael's madonnas may be interpreted as "saying" something about, respectively, nobility and spiritual value in secular and religious life. But these normative significances are extra-aesthetic, and although such significances may have relevance to what is aesthetic (as the discussion of metaphorical reference suggests), the aesthetic as distinct from extra-aesthetic normative function depends on the exhibiting of an internal order that ought to be or, in cases of poor art, that ought not to be.

Tension, Internal and External

In the reconsideration of interactionism, a distinction was made between inner and outer or external tension. Both tensions were seen to depend on the contrast between what is familiar and what is unfamiliar – between expected usage and expressions that are in some way incongruous with interpreters' expectations. The parallels between the structure of aesthetic works of art and verbal metaphors must now be considered specifically in terms of the manifestation of inner and outer tension.

It might be objected that attributing tension to all instances of non-verbal arts is a mistake. Tension is not obviously present in all works of art. A serene landscape by Constable, for instance, might seem to be devoid of tension. Nevertheless, if the extension of verbal metaphor to the arts is to be effective, inner and outer tension must mark off even the most docile works which exhibit the most harmonious organization and the least disquieting content or representational significance, that is, if the work is aesthetic and a creation.

To show why tension can be attributed to all aesthetic works that are creations, it is necessary to emphasize that in responding to verbal metaphor, attention is initially drawn to the special, unfamiliar way in which the metaphor brings terms together. This peculiarity alerts the respondent to the expression's nonliteral and possible metaphorical function. And when unfamiliarity is encountered in a nonverbal

expression – in innovative uses of color, in distortion of representational shapes, or generally, in a style – then, similarly, new aesthetic
significance is suggested. Innovation of this kind can occur in what
seems at first to be a tranquil landscape, as can be observed in a Constable landscape with its flickering speckles of light that exhibit an
innovative use of pigment and a subtle tension between the play of
light and colors that tend to be dominated by browns and greens un-
derneath the clouds.

As for verbal metaphor, the contrast of the unfamiliar or peculiar
with the familiar is evident in both the external and internal relations
relevant to the work. External tension is found in the difference between the new style of a created work and its antecedents. For instance, the innovation in style in Constable's work is evident in the
contrast between the way the artist manipulated the elements of the
medium – the movement exhibited in the flakes of light – and the
way the other artists had done so before. As a consequence of such
innovations, we now see Suffolk as much if not more through Constable than we see Constable through Suffolk. Constable has effected an
external tension found in his audience's ways of seeing. In this respect, there is an external tension that parallels the stylistic shifts in
language brought about by effective metaphors in poetry.

Internal tension must be understood as dependent on the relations
of the work to its external context. This dependence is more obvious
in nonverbal art than in verbal metaphor. In verbal metaphors, tension was attributed to the joining of key terms from contrasting categories. The understanding of these categories and their difference is
made possible through attention to the meanings of the terms that
belong to them outside the metaphor. Thus, the tension said to be
internal to the metaphor, which brings these categories together, is a
function of the external significance as well as the new significance
that arises from the metaphorical expression. In the case of the arts,
this same kind of contrast appears at two levels.

The first level is found in the difference between the functions of a
medium's elements outside an aesthetic work of art and the internal
functions of those elements when they are components of the aesthetic level of the work. This difference, of course, exemplifies the
contrast pointed out in the discussion of metaphor, between elements
with antecedent meanings and the meanings of constituents in internal relations. In the context of the arts, the contrast is at the basis of
the framework within which aesthetic attention works. It parallels the
way that verbal metaphors provoke attention to the special, unfamiliar way they bring terms together.

Similarly, the special function that visual and sound qualities assume in an aesthetic work of art alerts the interpreter to the presence of something that is bracketed in relation to the everyday world. A line, for instance, formed within an aesthetic art work no longer functions simply to show perceivers where edges are, or to serve, say, as part of an arrow that points to something. A line in a painting functions expressively to carve out space and to lead gracefully or vigorously from one area to another, at the same time carrying its own integrity so that it has an intrinsic attraction. The color green in a landscape painting is not a hue signaling that traffic can proceed. Rather, the green in the painting has other functions, such as establishing contrasts, intensifying shapes, balancing other colors, and, of course, contributing to whatever representational significance may be part of the painting. But because attention is drawn toward such qualities in their internal relations rather than toward the antecedent meanings of the qualities, because attention is drawn into the bracketed world of the aesthetic object, the tension is best called *internal*.

In light of the analysis of aesthetic works of art into five levels, this internal tension can be understood as a tension emerging from the transformations of aspects of a work of art at one or all of the first four levels as they are constituted at the fifth level. Again, this contrast is said to be internal because it is focusing on components in terms of the fifth level that exhibits contrast. Thus, with respect to the aesthetic level, components do more than simply assume functions not found at previous levels. In aesthetic, internal ordering, the elements that become aesthetic components affect one another from the exigencies of their own various functions at different levels. Antecedent significance must be attended to simultaneously with the immanent, aesthetic significance. In other words, the qualities or elements that become constituents in aesthetic works of art do not completely lose their identities as things with functions appropriate to the other levels. This is one reason that they are part of an integration rather than a synthesis – a point made in connection with verbal metaphor and that applies also to the arts. But it is this retention of a certain self-identity, at the same time that an element interacts internally, that furnishes an internal tension in an aesthetic object.

The second level of internal tension parallels the inner tension between key meaning units or subjects in verbal metaphors. In this case, the tension is a species of the contrast between the aesthetic and the other levels of works of art. Yet this is such a prominent species that it deserves consideration in its own right.

The difference between the two subjects itself indicates the sense in which tension, as a species of the contrast between levels, occurs. The difference is based on the difference between what is aesthetic and what is not aesthetic. However, as in the case of the contrast between levels, the aesthetic subject functions for the aesthetic object as an image that alludes to its antecedent, extra-aesthetic source. Recalling the example of Cézanne's *Mt. St. Victoire*, it can be said again that the image of a mountain that served as material for Cézanne functions as a background presence that contrasts with the painted image. The parallel with verbal metaphor should be evident if we recall that it is not the referents of subject terms that interact; rather, it is the complexes or systems of meanings implied by the subject terms. The image of an actual mountain interacts with the aesthetic image (visual meaning-complex) of the mountain of the painting.

But the role of these images is more complex than has been indicated thus far. There are other elements that may function as subjects. This is easiest to see in the case of representational components. Yet formal-expressive functions of elements can give an element the function of a subject, that is, can make it provoke background images suggesting extra-aesthetic sources. A dominating shape in a Kandinsky nonobjective painting may suggest power, which may clash with a sweeping line that suggests grace. Similarly, in music, the quasi-technical term *subject* indicates that nonverbal qualities function in ways similar to the ways that subjects in verbal metaphors function. Musical themes, musical phrases, "statements," all attributed to specific patterns of sound, imply that musical meaning units are expressive in a way that includes preaesthetic images – conceptual, emotional, and sometimes visual. None of these should be confused with the musical meaning itself, any more than verbal metaphors in poetry should be thought of as identical with, or as significant only insofar as they refer to, some object of experience that served as material for the poem.

The proposal being made about the subjects of nonverbal arts is comparable to Virgil Aldrich's thesis that there are visual metaphors.[20] He says that visual metaphors may inform the contents of works in the visual arts, painting being the kind of art form he uses for illustration. He distinguishes three main concepts that work together to produce a visual metaphor: the material, the subject matter, and the content. The material is the shaped qualities – for instance, colors or values, texture, line, and mass, that form the painting. The subject matter is what is portrayed. The content is the outcome of interacting material and subject matter. Adopting the seeing-as theory of metaphor, Aldrich observes that an aesthetic response to a painting is seeing the content or meaning in a certain way, that is, seeing the material as the subject matter or seeing the subject matter

[20] Virgil Aldrich, "Visual Metaphor," *Journal of Aesthetic Education* 2 (1968): 73–87; and his "Form in the Visual Arts," *British Journal of Aesthetics* 11 (1971): 215–26.

"bodied forth" by the material. The interanimation of material and subject matter brings about a "transfiguration" of both the material and subject matter in the content or emergent meaning: "the embodied image in which [material] and [subject matter] are transfigured or 'expressively portrayed'."[21] The subject matter is seen as an image of what it is apart from the interanimation, although when apprehended through the work of art, the subject matter interacts with the work. Aldrich's subject matter plays the role of the primary subject in my proposal, which has sources in extra-aesthetic conditions.

One of Aldrich's examples is particularly appropriate to the point of this discussion. Leonardo's *Mona Lisa* is said to have as its subject matter a woman with whom we are not acquainted, the wife of Francesco del Giocondo. This subject matter "illustrates the concept of 'a woman with a subtle (sly? knowing?) smile, a look of feminine self-sufficiency and enigmatic invitation on her complacent oval face, etc.' "[22] What is important is that Aldrich claims that a concept of a woman (not an individual referent) is illustrated. Moreover, if the painting is looked at with respect to the expression manifested in the painting, rather than with respect to that represented, then the meaning (visual) units, the painting and the subject matter, interanimate each other. This interanimation gives birth to the created meaning, what Aldrich calls the "content." Aldrich describes the content in the case of *Mona Lisa* as "the woman prehended in the picture."[23] Accordingly, for him, the painting is a visual metaphor.

In a later article, Aldrich offers an example of his basic thesis which more clearly illustrates visual metaphor. He considers a painting by Kokoschka, *Courmayereur et les dents des geants*, 1927. The painting shows houses with angular roofs set against angular mountains. Aldrich describes the interanimation that constitutes the visual meaning of the whole as a fusion in which there is a partial "denaturing of house and mountain."[24] The part of the mountain is "domesticated," and the house becomes mountainous in character. This outcome is parallel to a verbal metaphor that says, "The roof is a part of the mountain."

Aldrich's view does more than concur with my proposal regarding the isomorphism of metaphorical structure in verbal and nonverbal expressions. Aldrich offers illustrations that suggest how the major visual meaning units of works of art interact. Yet a distinction must be made between his account and mine. Aldrich speaks of the content or meaning outcome as a fusion, as a synthesis in which the components that interact lose themselves for the sake of the unity into which

[21] Aldrich, "Visual Metaphor," pp. 76–7.
[22] Ibid., p. 82.
[23] Ibid.
[24] Aldrich, "Form in the Visual Arts," pp. 215–6.

they are brought. I am not convinced that he means to affirm the complete loss of their identities, for he does say that subject matter, although "liquidated" in the content, can nevertheless be distinguished from the content. Still, he repeatedly insists that in aesthetic cases of seeing, subject matter and work are "at the mercy of the content." Thus, it is not clear that he sufficiently acknowledges the tension generated by the contrasts between components pointing back toward antecedent significance and the same components pointing inward toward their internal, aesthetic functions.

Another writer, Albert Rothenberg, refers to Aldrich to help illustrate his own theory and also places more emphasis on this tension. As part of his extensive study of creativity from the standpoint of his own psychoanalytic approach, Rothenberg proposes the concept of "homospatial thinking," a process of superimposing two different, even partially incompatible forms, on each other so that they appear simultaneously in the same space.[25] One of his most powerful examples is Leonardo's *Cartoon for St. Anne,* in which the bodies of Mary, St. Anne, and Jesus merge into one unit. At the same time, however, Rothenberg identifies the outcomes as integrations and stresses the tensions that are at work for aesthetic attention. As pointed out for verbal metaphor, tension and integration are mutually dependent. I shall now turn to this third feature of metaphor, integration.

Integration

The general conception of integration was explained earlier, and the basis for the application of this conception to the arts was indicated in the discussion of tension in this chapter. It is the contrasts between constituents and antecedent meanings that yields tension, and it is the retention of these contrasts throughout the life of an object while it is attended to aesthetically that ensures that the whole to which attention is given is an integration rather than a synthesis. *Synthesis* has been interpreted as applying to what is perfectly unified such that its parts are submerged and lose their own integrities. By contrast, an integration sustains both the individuality and the cooperative actions of the parts in a community. For example, the house-image in the Kokoschka painting referred to earlier retains its integrity as a domesticated house when it interacts with the mountain in which it is embedded, even though it "is part of this mountain." The mountain-image also retains its mountain quality, even though it is domesticated and "is this house." And as I insisted earlier, this bidirectionality of significance enables the whole to endure as an integration with its own appropriate tensions.

[25] Rothenberg, *The Emerging Goddess,* especially pp. 268–328.

The metaphorical structure of nonverbal expressions needs more sustained illustration than our discussion has offered thus far. In conclusion, I shall focus on several examples and interpret them in terms of the three key features of metaphor, verbal and nonverbal: the presence of two subjects, tension, and integration. The interpretation will concern primarily the interactions of components rather than the referential function of the work, because the application of the proposal concerning metaphorical reference to art will be taken up in the next chapter.

An Example: Representational Painting

Vermeer's *Young Woman with a Water Jug* is a fairly well known work which does not exemplify an obvious tension such as might appear if the painting displayed either a startling or dramatic subject or an agitated form. There are nuanced tensions internal to the delicately composed overall form. But tension is not the prominent aspect of the painting. Consequently, the Vermeer painting should show more emphatically the integration exemplified in the contrasts of formal-expressive components with extra-aesthetic images of subject matter.

The title indicates one of the subjects or key meaning units of this painting, the figure of the young woman with a water pitcher, which is a dominating shape that serves as one of the composition's major organizing determinants. The figure shows a young woman with simple but delicate features that are delineated by an economy of shapes and lines. Her gesture indicates that she is glancing toward an open window, and this suggests movement toward the boundary of the painting, a feature that enhances the sense of open space so important to the work. The subject matter or extra-aesthetic image, then, is that of a woman, though none in particular, who engages in domestic chores. But this preaesthetic, envisaged image undergoes a change by virtue of interaction with the painting's formal-expressive components. These components include objects that surround and establish a careful spatial arrangement that frames the shape of the young woman. It is especially important that they also include the painted shapes that constitute the woman's aesthetic image — shapes that are relatively flat, bold (with respect to the woman's clothing), and silhouetted against the wall behind her. The wall is divided by the rectangular map in the upper right-hand corner and the prominent blank space, the substance of which is a pervasive light. Other components that affect the interaction that yields the aesthetically informed figure of the young woman are the pictorial table, with its warm, rich red and delicate designs, and the translucent window shape with its tracery. The window, map, and table covering show relatively intricate designs that surround the figure of the woman, at her sides, in front, and behind her. The outcome is that the woman is a kind of axis from which radiates the linear movement that brings the major shapes together.

All these components are expressive as qualities that give stability, quietness, and slow movement within the picture. The table covering introduces a rich warmth. The window introduces clarity and distance in being open to the outside, and of course, it serves as a source of light, which is a pervading quality of the whole, making both the foreground and the background intimate with each other. The shape of the young woman is given a place that works cooperatively with the other objects to strengthen the powerful sense of space as a medium of interlocking shapes that work laterally as well as in depth.

The point of this consideration of the painting thus far is to illustrate a way of interpreting the work in terms of the interaction of components so that one of the key extra-aesthetic meaning units is taken up as an image that is controlled aesthetically and that thus is transformed into a contrasting internal subject. However, as indicated earlier, there is also at least one other internal major term – that is, other than the extra-aesthetic woman-image – which helps compose the whole. In the case of the Vermeer, a second key meaning unit of this kind is not obvious, at least if one expects the key term to be somewhat representational. Furthermore, the attempt to identify a second key term here is subject to interpretation with which different interpreters might quarrel. However, it seems to me that there is clearly a second subject, something that helps account for the work's main substance, something that cannot be accounted for by noting exclusively the main subject of the figure of the woman as it interacts with other components. It is the control of another dominant factor that mobilizes the components interacting with the shape of the woman.

My proposal is that this second subject is space that is constituted by the spread of light over the carefully organized space of the room. Thus I would venture to say that the second key term can be referred to by a verbal metaphor: "Space that is light and light that is space." Whether one accepts this way of identifying the second subject, the point can still be made that the main metaphorical interaction is between two subjects: the figure of the young woman and the light and space that produce the work's pictorial import. Thus, if Kokoschka's mountain can be domesticated and his house can be made mountainlike, then the young woman with the water pitcher can be made an object controlled by space and light, constituted by space and the interplay of light and dark portions of the woman's dress; and at the same time, space and light can be affected by the woman so that the very character of space and light in this work is qualified by the woman's figure, as it is also qualified by the other objects portrayed.

Unlike Aldrich's interpretation, an extra-aesthetic woman, or a generic woman, in the world is not seen as the aesthetically presented woman of the painting, which is constituted by space and light. Instead, the interaction is internal so that the aesthetically presented woman-image is the image of light and space and the aesthetically presented light-and-space-image is the woman-image. It is this whole that is relevant to the world.

I do not intend to deny the function of extra-aesthetic significance in the appreciation of the significance of a work of art. Rather, my proposal depends on construing formal-expressive qualities as significant and relevant to the world in the way that a representational figure that is a subject is significant and related to an extra-aesthetic subject matter. Thus, although it can be said that light and space exhibited in the Vermeer painting are expressive in contributing to the quiet movement and quality of airiness and cleanliness, and although it can be said that colors contribute to the warmth and strength of the work, nevertheless, we discern these against the background of an awareness of extra-aesthetic encounters with expressive qualities in everyday experience.

What has been said about the presence of the painting's subjects should be enough to show that the second feature of metaphorical interaction, tension, must be present. The presence of external tension is evident in the relation of Vermeer's style to the tradition preceding Vermeer. Vermeer's uniqueness in his own century was in part based on his way of merging keen observation and care in dwelling on the objects exhibited in his paintings with an objectivity or distance from the very things that engrossed him. Perhaps just as important was Vermeer's command over the composition that made his organizations both simple yet structurally stronger than those of some of the other painters who concentrated on similar subjects.

More important to interpretation that focuses on works of art themselves, rather than on their relations to contexts, is the internal tension and its foundation in the tension exhibited in the contrasts between external and internal functions of components. These contrasts were indicated in the discussion of the presence of two subjects. What was said implied the kind of internal tension founded on the contrasts of components between constituents and antecedent elements. Thus light and space is transformed (though not lost) as it is taken up into the painting and made substantive to resonances of colors and shapes presented as abstract forms and as representational figures that make up the precisely controlled composition. Internal tension was also suggested in the remarks about the relation between the extra-aesthetic woman-image and the aesthetically presented woman. But this is also intimately bound up with the tension present in the forming of the aesthetic woman-image through the interaction of light, color, and space.

Just as tensions were implied in the interpretation of the Vermeer painting, so the idea of integration was implied in the descriptions of the composition viewed as a whole that depends for its character on the distinctiveness of each component. The spread of light must sustain the power of light in its own terms, in terms of some of the traits of light known independently of the painting, if it, as a constituent, is to enter the constitution of the woman-image and the surrounding objects. Map, window, wall surface, table, and pitcher, each in its own location, stand with their own integrity in order to constitute the areas that radiate and contain the woman-image. And most importantly, the space–light subject term retains its distinctive function as the woman-image subject retains its own function in the interaction. The outcome is the visual metaphor.

An Example: Nonrepresentational Painting

Mondrian's *Painting 2: Composition in Gray and Black (1925)* is like the Vermeer painting in not exhibiting an obvious dramatic tension in its overall form. Further, it not only does not exhibit a startling subject, but it also seems to have no subject whatsoever, if "subject" refers to representational images. There are, however, shapes that function outside the painting in extra-aesthetic contexts and that also function aesthetically and as formal-expressive components within the painting. In this minimal way, there is a tension, at least to the degree that there is contrast between formal-expressive functions and extra-aesthetic images. And there is the subtle internal tension controlled by the equilibrium distinctive to Mondrian's genius. Yet as an example of the visual arts, this work by Mondrian surely represents the extreme test case for the proposal that the features of multiple subject terms characterize a metaphorical structure that belongs to all media of nonverbal expression.

Some confirmation that the presence of multiple subject terms appears in Mondrian's nonrepresentational work is found in the words of the commentator, Kermit Swiles Champa, who, in discussing examples, refers to specific rectangles as motifs. He says that before Mondrian's 1921–3 period, diagonal edges and the "aggressive overall shape of the 1919 lozenges" function as motifs, or as formal-expressive components that have dominant roles in the visual intelligibility of Mondrian's painting.[26]

[26] Kermit Swiles Champa, *Mondrian Studies* (Chicago: University of Chicago Press, 1985), p. 105.

In *Painting 2: Composition in Gray and Black (1925)*, there are at least three shapes that function as interacting subject terms: a black rectangle in the upper-right corner; a large light square covering the major portion of space of the painting, from the right of center to the left margin and most of the space from top to bottom; and the second largest, gray rectangle set vertically under the black rectangle at the upper right. The light gray rectangle below the black, however, is not heavy enough to support it, and so a tension is established by the weight of the largest rectangle at the left which counterbalances the black rectangle, preventing it from thrusting downward. Other shapes enhance this interaction, but the key shapes functioning as major subject terms dominate the composition as a whole. The integration, then, is found in the equilibrium that pervades the composition without extinguishing the shapes' power to act with the tensions of imbalance, balance, and counterbalance. The way this work has reference will be considered in the next chapter.

An Example: Music

Illustrations of the presence of the three key conditions of metaphor in music require acknowledgment of one basic difference between the examples of music and the examples of the kind of nonverbal expressions considered thus far. The features to be found in music are present in what is intrinsically temporal. Of course, it takes time for attention to pass over the components of a painting, and it takes time to "read" a verbal metaphor. But the object of attention in these cases offers its features at once so that there is visible, aural, or cognitive presence ready for one's attention to survey. If one apprehends music through reading a score, the same kind of relationship between attention and its object will hold. Yet the object of attention is a series of inscriptions that are instances of sign types, that is, types of notes that make up a code for virtual patterns of sounds. And these sounds are not spread out spatially as are the colors and shapes of a painting. Consequently, the presence of the two main meaning units, the tension, and the integration must occur in sequence in which the functions of components that constitute these features are intrinsically before and after — not in front or in back, to the side, or below or above — one another. Yet the meaning units can be discussed as if they were laid out before us in the way colors and shapes are in the visual arts, and the difference in the manner in which the metaphorical structure of music and the visual arts is displayed does not make a difference in the structures themselves.

Let me sketch briefly how the three key features of metaphor can be distinguished within a part of a piece of music, for example, the opening of the last movement of Beethoven's Ninth Symphony. The identification of the subjects or main meaning units in the last movement of this symphony obviously cannot be isolated from the work's other movements. There are few if any other symphonies in which the themes of the earlier movements are made as explicit as they are in the last movement of this symphony. The main subject or theme of the final movement, however, is set to Schiller's "Ode to Joy" and is a melody that was only barely adumbrated earlier. This theme functions as a key meaning unit that plays a dominant role in the course of the whole last movement. Yet it does so in light of other meaning units, some of which are crucial to framing the main theme, or, in the musical metaphor, a major subject term. The crashing opening (described by some as a "horror fanfare") itself is a forecast of something gigantic to follow.[27] Arising as if in spite of the thunder of this opening are reminders of the past, the main themes (subject terms) of the three preceding movements each separated by reiterations of the negating fanfare. The result is a kind of dialectic that builds toward a demand for some resolution. The resolution, though not complete synthesis, is given in the "Ode to Joy" theme which emerges out of the bass string voices and rises to the heights made possible by the other strings and finally the human voice.

Let me interject here that I shall put aside as irrelevant the criticism that Beethoven weakened the work as a whole by introducing a chorus to bring the main theme to fulfillment. Even if the criticism were correct, and I do not think it is, the theme and its development can still be identified and seen to function in ways like the major components or subjects of verbal metaphors.

For the purposes of my proposal regarding the metaphorical structure of music, what is important to notice is that the last movement of Beethoven's Ninth Symphony presents a main musical meaning unit that functions in tension – that is, in various degrees of contrasts – with the other musical meaning units, in particular, the opening fanfare and the themes from the other movements. Also, the ode theme itself is varied in the forms in which it is presented so that there are additional contrasts, especially between its instrumental and its vocal presentations.

There is, of course, external tension or contrast in the difference between Beethoven's innovations and the instances of the musical tradition that preceded him, and even between his innovations here and his own earlier works. This latter contrast is perhaps most strongly evident in the relation of the achievement reached in the Ninth Sym-

---

[27] See Anthony Hopkins, *The Nine Symphonies of Beethoven* (London: Heinemann, and Seattle: University of Washington Press, 1981), p. 273.

phony and those anticipations of the ode theme in earlier works, such as the Choral Fantasy.

That integration is present should be clear from what has been said about subjects and tensions. The ode theme must have its own integrity, and this integrity is attested to by its presence in earlier works by Beethoven and in different aesthetic contexts. This is not to suggest that a component of music must appear elsewhere in order to have its own distinctive function. What is important is that when the same ode theme enters the composition, it interacts with its context, and it takes on enhanced, if not distinguishable significance, in relation to the whole of the work. But it takes on these other musical roles because it contributes its own integrity to that with which it interacts.

Interaction in verbal metaphors is not insulated from the world out of which the metaphors emerge. Metaphors generate extralinguistic, extraconceptual conditions. We shall consider next how nonverbal interaction may also have such relevance to the world. And in that context, we shall, in the next chapter, explore the issue of how Beethoven's Ninth Symphony, as well as other examples considered, are relevant to the world.

5

Metaphorical Reference and the Arts

The Problem

Aesthetic and Extra-aesthetic Significance

Even the most intransigent aesthetic purist would not deny that great works of art have some relevance to extra-aesthetic human experience. The relation of art to life may be quite tenuous and the connection circuitous. But there is an impact of some kind. Throughout its history, art has had religious, moral, and political functions. And this has been true after as well as before the advent of art for art's sake movements. Plato saw the power of art (or at least some art) and the danger it could pose for moral and political life. Painting and music in the medieval period served the Church. Michelangelo labored on his paintings in the Sistine Chapel out of his willingness to fulfill the wishes of his pope and out of his own commitment to a religious conviction. Composers in the nineteenth century worked with patrons, loved ones, and political heroes in mind. Their compositions not only were dedicated but sometimes also were given forms that reflected their extramusical ideas about their sources of inspiration.

While granting such connections, the purist might insist that we ought not to understand aesthetic objects in terms of psychology, religion, morality, politics, metaphysics, or, most generally, the practical purposes of art. To do so is to misunderstand the distinctive function of the arts, or at least of what we now call "the fine arts." Thus, while agreeing that art can have extra-aesthetic consequences, the purist may insist that these consequences are not what gives art its own value as art. They do not give art its own distinctively aesthetic right to exist.

It seems to me that there is a fundamental insight in this injunction against treating works of art as instruments for purposes other than art itself. The injunction is ignored at the peril of losing one of the highest realizations possible for humans, that is, the capacity to appreciate the intrinsic qualities and internal relations found in perceptual objects, in the interactions among dramatic characters, and in patterns of sounds. Such appreciation is an achievement that is integral to if not definitive of what it is to be human. A long tradition in the philosophy of art supports the purist – a tradition that emphasizes that the significance of a work of art must be immanent within it. This tradition rests on the principle that each art work has its own internal integrity and is therefore autonomous. The interdependence of symbols and what they symbolize, in the case of aesthetic objects, has been insisted on by a relatively long line of theorists, including Croce and Collingwood, among the earliest in this century, although the idea can be traced to nineteenth-century romanticism and to Kant. Such writers remind us that if symbols are construed as vehicles for conveying messages, or information for practical purposes, those symbols are then "transparent" or dispensable, once their significances have been understood.

Such is not the case with aesthetic achievements. In art the "vehicle" is indispensable. The meanings and what the work may refer to are integral to the work itself. By contrast, a practical sign need not have a form that is unique in the way it informs us of what it refers to. A barber pole is only one way to refer to a barber shop, and its form is used only as a device or vehicle to tell us what is behind the doors where it appears. A word such as *electron* could be replaced by other words that would equally well refer to the particles for which the word is a sign. But a Monet painting of water lilies has a form that is indispensable in offering us the significance of the work.

Nevertheless, as already emphasized, at least some works of art show us things about the world outside those works. They give us insights. But they also seem capable of performing this function without being dispensable vehicles. And they realize the distinctively aesthetic function on which the purists insist, but in a way that cannot be appreciated apart from an extra-aesthetic function. Thus, the extra-aesthetic consequences of some works of art are possible only in and through the intrinsic aesthetic aspect of those works. Dante's *Divine Comedy,* for instance, had an origin outside art itself. Dante drew on religion for material and inspiration. To be sure, this material was transformed as it functioned aesthetically, giving us a poetic masterpiece. Yet the outcome also aspires to something beyond itself and succeeds in contributing to a perspective on the world. And it succeeds in this way because of its own aesthetic power, that is, its poetry, just as it succeeds in aesthetic power in part because of its religious content. Kafka's novels not only exemplify originality and strange worlds of their own; they also suggest visions of our common world. But they would not do this without being what they are – aesthetically fashioned works.

Paradoxically, then, whole works of art offer insights or seem faithful or appropriate to something, although what they are faithful to may be their own aesthetically determined creations. T. M. Greene formulates the point in another way. He observes that the artist's approach to things in experience is "highly individual, yet never wholly idiosyncratic"; yet the artist's outlook manifests "significant originality in proportion as it is simultaneously new and sharable, individual and universal."[1] How is this possible? How can a work of art be intrinsically and immanently significant, significant in its own terms as an independent, autonomous integration of components, while at the same time offering an insight into the world?

It will not do to argue that the aesthetic and extra-aesthetic functions of works of art are distinct and functionally independent of each other. Such a proposal would conflict with the widely held view that content and form are interdependent if not fused. What is said depends on how it is said, and how something is said is intelligible only in terms of the form or the ordering of the components of what does the saying. This fusion of form and content, of course, is at the basis of the insistence on autonomy and immanence of meaning. If we accept this principle of form—content interdependence, as I think we must, then the question we face is how a work of art can, in its aesthetic function, affirm a kind of significance that can be assessed as fitting or unfitting, as insight or lack of insight.

The Problem of Truth and Art

An obvious version of this question concerns truth and art. Is the attribution of fittingness or appropriateness (already said to be relevant to verbal metaphor) to a work of art a way of characterizing it as true to something in the world? There are reasons for giving an affirmative answer. If art can offer insight, then it can offer knowledge of some form. And knowledge concerns what is true. But if a work of art, in its aesthetic function, is called true, it must be true in a special sense. That "truth" must be given a special sense, if it is applicable to art at all, has been implied by those who regard art as truth-value neutral, when truth was taken to be subject to verifiability and predictability tests. As one theorist, L. A. Reid, put it:

If a work of art is to be in itself in any sense "true" (as distinct from containing, assimilating, and transforming truths in more ordinary senses), it cannot be true by conforming to anything which is *other* than, external to, itself. If not, and we are to call it "true" at all, the only thing left is for it to be true to "itself." The measure of its truth must, somehow, be intrinsic to it.[2]

Reid illustrates his contention with an analysis by Robin Mayhead of one of Donne's "Holy Sonnets."[3] Mayhead's analysis identifies specific

[1] Theodore Meyer Greene, *The Arts and the Art of Criticism* (Princeton, N.J.: Princeton University Press, 1947), pp. 444–5.
[2] Louis Arnaud Reid, *Meaning in the Arts* (London: Allen & Unwin, New York: Humanities Press, 1969), p. 229.
[3] Reid's discussion of Mayhead is on p. 232.

formal aspects of the poem, including various uses of letters, words, and phrasings that force the reader to respond with rapid and slow readings of the passages. Certain word repetitions give an "impression of urgency" and of Donne's awareness of the closeness of death. Reid's point is to show how good criticism finds internal truth standards in the interactions of elements within the work under analysis.

I think Reid is correct in his claims about truth in art. However, his illustration and general account of how aesthetic truth standards are internal to the work do not answer our question about significance. For it is still puzzling how a work of art, called true in terms of standards intrinsic to it, is *in light of these standards* fitting or appropriate to something not found in the art work, that is, to something in the world. The special form of truth in which Reid is interested is essentially determined by expectations and criteria of what is appropriate in the internal relationships – the coherence of elements with one another and the whole, or as he puts it, "how each part is integral with other parts and with the whole."[4] However, the point I am stressing is that somehow a work of art regarded as an aesthetic whole, even as a world of its own, as is sometimes suggested, is fitting or appropriate with respect not only to itself but also to the world "outside," that is, to a world known independently of the work. This is the way in which a work such as Goethe's *Faust* or a Cézanne landscape may be thought to provide insight into life or nature.

The Proposal

Preliminary Statement

To attack this problem, I shall focus on the way a work of art may be said to refer to something not found exclusively in the integrated form and content of the work itself. In brief, I shall try to show that the answer to the question concerning the appropriateness of an autonomous art work to the world can best be understood according to the conception of reference introduced in Chapter 3. I want to explore the idea that a work of art, as a nonverbal metaphor, refers to something that is creatively designated or fixed by the work. Thus, the interaction of characteristics said to belong to works of art when they are regarded as aesthetic objects designates a new, unique individual that we take to be the referent of the work. Let me reiterate that my discussion concerns works of art that are creative and revelatory, that offer new insights. It is not necessary to assume that the concept of art is normative and that unless a work is creative or is a creation it

[4] Reid, *Meaning in the Arts*, p. 234.

should not be called art. I assume only that some works of art are regarded as having created insights, although I believe that some things called works of art do not.

It is a new referent, then, that is the condition of appropriateness or inappropriateness of the work of art to the world. This unique thing is a condition that constrains the meanings and interpretations that we regard as relevant to the work. These constraints provoke the attributions of *fitting, appropriate,* and *insightful,* or if the work is judged negatively, the antonyms of these. At the same time, however, the referent is something that is created. Thus it is considered unique. It cannot be completely understood by ideas that are antecedently known.

As observed in the discussion of metaphorical reference, the proposal does not require that a referent be a particular object that can be located in space and time. Nor need a referent be designated by a pointer or sign such as an arrow that is exclusively or primarily indexical. I am, however, assuming the Peircean view that all signs have some degree of indexical function. A formula expressing a law is indexical to the extent that it indicates a resistance to be encountered in instances of the law. And even a mathematical concept meets with constraints or a core of reaction when thoughts are directed from the abstraction to its instances. Thus, a referent may be thought of as the dynamic extension of a sign or of whatever has meaning.

It is important to keep in mind that for works of art and verbal metaphors, because what is designated is unique, it is not the referent of any of the representational components of the work. Nor is it the referent of any formal component, such as a color, a line, a shape, or a combination of these, insofar as they function within nonrepresentational works. For instance, an expanse of blue in a nonobjective painting might be said to designate blue in the world. But even if this idea could be justified, when the referent blue is combined with other such referents, it would not be the unique referent creatively designated by the work as a whole. For instance, the referents red, white, and black of a Mondrian abstraction do not make up a totality that is the referent of the painting.

For additional illustration, recall the relationship between a meaningful thing (a symbol) and its referent that is not an instance of art. We may once again consider a barber pole that has as its referent a barber shop. Neither the meaning of barber poles nor what they refer to as barber poles is unique. Furthermore, barber poles do not create the barber shops to which they refer, as works of art create their referents. On the other hand, a madonna by Giotto, done in the style he originated when he advanced beyond some of his inherited conventions, does not refer simply to Mary and Jesus (or Christ). If Giotto's painting referred only to these referents, it would inform us about something identifiable in history or in theology that, once recognized, would leave the painting dispensable. The painting is not like a code. The style of the painting as it is specified in Giotto's achievement creates what it signifies: The unique complex of meanings that constitute the painting determines specifically what the painting refers to. We, the viewers, discover a specification of the madonna and child as a referent that can be found nowhere else. The painting is not a window with a transparent surface for viewing Mary and Jesus. The meaning of the work is presented on the surface, not somewhere else. And the significance or import of the work includes the unique referent of the meaning. Because of this, we are privileged to a new insight, here visual, into the madonna and child (otherwise known historically and theologically) such that we visually encounter something new, a madonna–child referent that is unlike anything encountered before.

Insofar as this proposal applies to signs and their referents in general, it should be applicable to scientific creation as well as to art. What perhaps appears least plausible in saying that a scientific creation creatively designates a new referent, however, is the idea that the object of a scientific theory is unique and, consequently, that what science is about is not general or lawful. Thus, when we focus on the uniqueness of the creative achievement itself, the idea of creating new referents seems more straightforwardly applicable to the arts than to the sciences. The role of metaphor in science already has been considered briefly, and I hope that what was said indicated that accommodations can be made to fit the proposal to the growth of scientific theory. In any case, the main issue here concerns art rather than science. The idea that some works of art create new individuals that give those works relevance to the world can be examined more closely through a consideration of one of the consequences of the proposal. Let us then look more closely to see whether the apparent relevance of some works of art to the world can be clarified by the proposal that works of art as metaphors create new individuals as their referents.

A Consequence of the Proposal

The consequence to be considered follows from the point that the kind of referents in question must uniquely satisfy the meanings of the works of art that create and fix them. The unique integration of interacting components of a work of art designates a corresponding unique referent, one that can satisfy no other unique cluster of qualities or organized meanings that make up the work. A suggestion in one of C. S. Peirce's accounts of indexical signs supports and extends this point about the interaction between a work of art and its referent.

The index, he comments, refers to its object by virtue of being really affected by that object.[5] If there is such reciprocity between work and referent, then there will be an autonomous relation determined by the uniqueness of both the ordered meanings or qualities of the work and their referents. This is to say that the idea that what works of art refer to are creations, outcomes that satisfy only those clusters of qualities that constitute the work, indicates that the referents have a unique relation to the works of art that fix them. No other cluster offers the same referent, for it is unique to the cluster. The unique specification of the madonna–child referent of the Giotto painting can satisfy only that painting.

A consequence of the proposal seems to be that if referents in art are so intimately bound up with the work's qualities or meanings, then these referents must be ingredients in a larger aesthetic whole. They are part of an aesthetic situation composed of two poles, the work of art – the work as a meaning cluster – and its referent. The referent would then be immanent in the object of appreciation, in that it would function within a situation defined by the work and its referent. Within this whole, the referent interacts with all the other components to yield the work's significance. The referent, then, would seem not be independent of the aesthetically apprehended work of art.

I think this way of regarding the relation of work to referent as an aesthetic situation is correct. However, the point needs qualifying. The referent is in one way alienated from the other components and does attain a certain independence. The referent of a work of art is not itself another quality or meaning. And to this extent it functions in some way separately from full incorporation into the larger aesthetic whole. As already suggested, in the remarks about how referents need not be spatial objects but, rather, resistances, referents function as conditions of resistance or as constraints for the meaning of the works that refer to them. In this capacity of resistance, a referent is intelligible only with respect to its effects, that is, with respect to the significance that it helps determine as relevant to the whole that it also helps constitute. What Giotto's madonna refers to is a condition that constrains and directs interpretations so that some are more relevant than others. And this constraining condition is a factor in influencing and controlling the future of the tradition. Masaccio had to respond to conditions of this kind in creating his own style, which was in part an outgrowth of Giotto's.

In resisting and constraining the meanings relevant to the work, the referent transcends the immediate object of aesthetic attention.

[5] See especially Charles S. Peirce, *Collected Papers of Charles Sanders Peirce*, ed. Charles Hartshorne and Paul Weiss (Cambridge, Mass.: Harvard University Press, 1931), vol. 2, especially paragraphs 304, 305.

This is not to say, however, that because of this transcendence, we "see through" the work or can dispense with it. The organized visual qualities are indispensable to our discerning the referent in its uniqueness. The referent hovers between immanence in an aesthetic object and independence of that object. Its relation to the aesthetic object is constituted in its making relevant the object's meanings. It is a norm, an indeterminate norm, for these. And in its individuality as a resistant and constraining focus – in its resistance to being "swallowed up" by, or reduced to, the whole whose senses it makes relevant – it transcends its sign and is directed to what is extra-aesthetic and to what intrudes into the world. Of course, what the world must be like by including referents of works of art is a question that deserves attention in an ontology. The question here has been confined to the function that these referents have for the works that designate them.

As in the case of verbal metaphors, the interpretive function of the referents designated by works of art helps account for the nonverbal version of the so-called problem of paraphrase. The recognition that each attempt to describe and analyze a work is inevitably incomplete – because it always falls short of showing the work's significance – is evidence that a unique referent is at work as a center of relevance, requiring and constraining our paraphrases but not fully determining them. No matter how long one studies a Cézanne painting, for instance, the particular meanings that we identify – visually and perhaps in verbal expressions – are never sufficient to exhaust it. The determinateness of the significance of a *Mt. St. Victoire* – for example, Mt. St. Victoire as an architectural source of strength, which is one meaning that approximates a characterization of the painting – requires continued discriminations of relevant meanings in an ongoing interpretation. But the control on these future attempts is the referent as a center of relevance.

To return to the point made earlier about the way the referent and the work, though distinguishable from each other, nevertheless form an aesthetic whole, it should be said that the referent is independent of this whole to the extent that it functions as a focus of relevance to future works and interpretations. At the same time, it is unique in this function. There is no other individual or focus of relevance that satisfies the relevant meanings for which it, the referent of the work in question, is the focus. The work that gives birth to this referent is like a complex genetic coding, but a coding subject to mutation in the future.

The function of the referent for interpretation is not confined to its being a link between immanence and transcendence. In addition to their interpretive functions, the referents of works of art contribute to the effect that art may have on life. They also function as foci of constraints and prompting for our responses when we cease interacting with works of art in aesthetic experiences. The individual referent is an indeterminate norm for us, too, as it is for a work of art within an art tradition or style. The work controls our emotional and cognitive responses through the referent's unique determining force. If the referent of a Giotto madonna is of religious significance, it is so in a type of religious experience known only in terms of the painting's qualities.

The idea of the creative, designative power of art shares some ground with Carl Jung's theory of symbols, and so it should be helpful to compare my proposal with his.

Jung's view was summarized earlier in the discussion of the relation of symbols to metaphors. Recall that Jung distinguishes between signs whose referents that can be known independently of their signs and symbols whose referents can be known only by means of their symbols. Art belongs to the latter kind of symbol. Thus, for Jung, there is a correlation between the symbol and its significance, which is a unique referent. The only access to this referent is through the symbol; for example, the cross for Christians has a unique meaning that can be known only through the cross.[6] My proposal might seem to be a version of Jung's theory. However, there is one major difference between Jung's view of the reference of a symbol and what I think needs to be said about the reference of a work of art.

As was pointed out earlier, Jung's purpose is to show how symbols reveal universal psychological forces, that is, fundamental types of disposition by which humans have for centuries oriented themselves. These are in the collective unconscious, and various symbols expressed by human achievements throughout history reveal these forces. If symbols function in this way, then they do not symbolize unique referents. The referents turn out to be universal types that Jung has identified apart from the symbols themselves, that is, through his psychoanalytic theory. But my proposal is that creative designation yields a unique referent that cannot be antecedently classified or discovered by a theory. To characterize the referent of a work of art with reference to general terms could only be to identify the cluster of qualities or meanings exhibited in the work of art. But although resisting and transcending generality, the referents I have in mind, which are uniquely dependent on the interacting components of works of art, must still be sufficiently independent of those meanings, which are immanent in those works, to ground the attribution of faithfulness, and they must do this without losing their uniqueness so that they are turned into universal, antecedent realities.

---

[6] The consideration of Carl Jung is based on his *Psychological Types,* pp. 601–10.

Creative Reference and Nonrepresentational Art Forms

The intimate connection between the dependence and the independence of created referents is easiest to see in the representational arts. Thus far I have tried to illustrate the point primarily by referring to a Giotto painting and earlier to verbal metaphors and works of literature. More extensive examples might be given for literature. For instance, I think it could be said that *Oedipus Rex* offers an insight into human nature by creatively designating a new, unique integration of freedom and necessity in human agents. This unique integration comes to be known with respect to the internal interactions of components within the drama itself. But this unique integration is also known *through* as well as *within* the drama; thus, what is known, the individual to which the drama refers, transcends the work of art at least to the extent that knowing it as a focus of relevance has an impact on things and events experienced apart from the work. Thus, our vision of human freedom to some extent has been modified in and through Sophocles' work.[7]

It is more difficult to see how aesthetic immanence and transcendence are present in works of art in media or art forms that are not representational. Instances of abstract or nonobjective painting and sculpture, and absolute music seem prima facie to bear their significances wholly within their forms and to be closed to reference. But if the proposal is to apply to all art, then both abstract and representational art must be referential, or relevant to an extralinguistic condition, or the world.

One response to this issue, of course, is to deny that nonrepresentational painting and absolute music pose such a problem. If a meaningful expression does not represent, it might be claimed, then it does not refer. However, I do not think this is a proper way out of the difficulty. Abstract art and absolute music are often said to "speak to us." And even if we object to using the term *speak* in this way, we cannot easily reject the belief that there are examples of such art that give us insight into ourselves and the world. Thus, for example, I assume that a Mondrian composition is fitting and appropriate to something more than itself. It is relevant, at least, to the world's visual structure. A Mozart symphony reveals complex dramatic forces that parallel life conditions. Susanne Langer went to great lengths to explain this kind of significance in music. Furthermore – and this is my main point – nonrepresentational works of art can somehow be fitting not only to something "there" in the world but also to something individual and new.

[7] I have urged this interpretation in my "Sophocles and the Metaphysical Question of Tragedy," *The Personalist* 47 (Autumn 1966): 509–19.

Reference and Nonrepresentational Painting

In my remaining remarks, I shall attempt to show how my proposal fits two nonrepresentational arts. I shall discuss first a nonrepresentational painting and then spend somewhat more time on absolute music. If reference can be found in music, it should be found in all forms of nonrepresentational art. I want to suggest that some constraints are external to the purely formal properties of painting and music – constraints that have a function like the extralinguistic and extraconceptual conditions present in the representational arts.

It was said in Chapter 4 that Mondrian's *Painting 2: Composition in Gray and Black (1925)* would be considered again in order to illustrate that nonrepresentational painting may have reference. This painting should be particularly appropriate for this purpose, for it has no overt representational value, that is, no formal-expressive component that portrays or contributes to portraying a specific person, thing, or event in an extra-aesthetic place or time in the world. It does, however, include formal-expressive components, as already suggested by the application of interactionism to it. With respect to the way subject terms function together to yield an integration, the complex that constitutes the painting has a formal-expressive dimension.

In the case of representational painting, such as the Vermeer painting considered in Chapter 4, reference is informed by the interrelations of formal-expressive components so that the referent is a unique object that serves as a condition for the integration exhibited by the work itself. As a condition of the work, it is a controlling focus that must be relevant to the components' formal-expressive interrelations. The referent functions as a controlling condition of the exhibited components or images – the young woman, the open window, the table, and so on.

Similarly, the referent or a nonrepresentational painting focuses the exhibited abstract components – the gray, white, and black rectangles found in the Mondrian painting. Colors, rectangles, lines, and colored lines and rectangles, of course, are encountered outside paintings. It is tempting to say that these are portrayed as abstract images in the painting. And it surely is true that we can identify types of many, if not all, abstract shapes in paintings in the extra-aesthetic world. But even if one does, which may suggest that aesthetic abstract shapes represent extra-aesthetic shapes, it is important to keep in mind that no creative, aesthetic work has a previously knowable referent in the world, whether the work be abstract or representational. Even a portrait that works aesthetically and that is not a purely imitative image such as are many snapshots, has a referent to which the sitter for the portrait is made more or less relevant by virtue of how the portrait exhibits an image that shows something not otherwise identified in the extra-aesthetic subject or sitter. It is neither preaesthetic nor extra-aesthetic things that serve as the referent of a creative metaphor or a creative work of art. It is a unique individual. Accordingly, the created referent of a creative nonrepresentational painting is not any abstract image exemplified in the painting, but rather, it is the focal control that is a condition both of the relevance of the images one to the other and of the relevance of the work as a whole to the world.

The proposal at issue here implies that a nonrepresentational painting can be relevant to the world and that most if not all such paintings, when they are creations, do show us something that has a role to perform in the world. It may be suggested, as will be considered further in the discussion of music, that the world includes human reality, psychodynamic processes, a "life of the mind," that may be the locus of some nonrepresentational paintings. However, there also may be a visible part of the world that is the locus for created referents.

The Mondrian painting, I think, presents a unique specification of abstract visual images – visual conditions and forces that are exhibited in the painting and that as exhibited give access to the referent, the condition that gives relevance to the work. In this case, the referent can be described – inadequately, as always, because words are not the medium of the painting – as a specification of a visually discernible equilibrium in the world. This description is certainly not original. It was suggested by Mondrian himself, who regarded his work as being concerned with aspects of reality. Thus, he stated: "Every expression of art has its own laws, which are in accord with the principle of art and life: that of equilibrium. . . . In both [expressions of past and contemporary art] is [sic] tried to express equilibrium, always in a different way. . . ."[8] And as one commentator observes, Mondrian's intention was "always to put the very essence of life *into his* work. . . ."[9] The sense in which conditions of this sort can be said to be referents of nonrepresentational art should be further clarified in a consideration of music.

Reference and Music

In the case of music, I shall appeal here to considerations that seem to me to be related most directly to the determination of referents,

[8] Piet Mondrian, from a manuscript printed in typescript with handwritten corrections in *Piet Mondrian, Exhibition November–January 1965* (Basel: Galerie Beyeler 1964, p. 1).
[9] Frank Edgar, *Mondrian*, trans. Thomas Walton (London: Thames and Hudson, 1968), p. 137.

namely, the considerations that a performer – specifically, in the discussion to follow, an orchestral conductor – must take into account when "translating" the score into a performance. The performer, I think, is closest to whatever conditions must be met in order to interpret the score. Furthermore, I assume that the composer himself or herself may be the performer, actual or virtual, and that the act of composing is done with an ear for a possible performance (if only in a later act of reading the score with attention to virtual patterns of sounds). What, then, constrains the orchestral conductor's "translation" of a score? What constrains the interpretation of a musical composition?

Before attempting to answer this question, let me make clear that the term *interpretation* as I use it is the equivalent neither of a characterization of the "form" of a composition, such as might be given by a critic who analyzes the structure of the music, nor of the emotional responses and other extraformal associations, such as those of some commentators writing for a disc or tape brochure. This is not to say that interpretations in these senses play no role in the kind of interpretation at issue here. Indeed, I shall emphasize the extent to which an interpretation depends on certain kinds of extraformal meaning. In any case, interpretation in this context consists first of what at least some conductors do during rehearsals and, in turn, during public performances – that is, select tempo, direct the performers to play rhythmically (rather than by mechanically beating time), select intensities of crescendos, determine the length and emphasis to be given to pauses, decide on the appropriate emphasis to be given to various orchestral voices, and so forth. Such considerations should serve what may be called the *overall conception* of the piece of music to be performed. By overall conception, I mean the sort of thing Wagner probably meant by *melos,* and what Felix Weingartner considered essential to an intelligent and emotionally appropriate performance:

It is this homogeneous conception of the essential nature of a musical work that constitutes what there is of specially artistic *[sic]* in its interpretation; it originates in a deep feeling that is not dependent on the intellect, that cannot, indeed, even be influenced by this, while it itself must dominate everything that pertains to the intellect, – such as routine technique, and calculation of effects.[10]

In giving so much weight to the overall conception, I accept, as does Weingartner, that there is an objective identity to which interpreters

---

[10] Felix Weingartner, *On Conducting,* trans. Ernest Newman (New York: E. F. Kalmus Orchestra Scores, 1905), p. 17. The term "melos," the "quintessence" or "spirit of the art-work" is attributed to Wagner by Weingartner (p. 9). Weingartner encountered it in Wagner's "Über das Dirigieren," to which I do not now have access.

(including audiences as well as performers) attend. If one regards such an object of attention as what the composer intended – Weingartner seems to refer interchangeably to the composer's intentions and the music's overall conception – it would be a mistake to reduce the intention to psychological conditions or to something subjective. The composer's intentions are a function of what can be found in the music, and what can be found in the music is understood through the score (with at least some indications put there by the composer for the performer) and through additional interpretive criteria to be mentioned later.[11]

In any case, what I mean by *interpretation* includes more than what can be formulated by an analysis of formal structure – whether the analysis consists of probing for underlying levels or chordal sequences or simply concentrates on what is evident on the "surface," such as what can be noted in the development of melodic themes.[12] An interpretation by the conductor can hardly ignore what may be called *expressiveness*, at least as expression is said to characterize music in Langer's theory. I doubt (despite what Stravinsky admonished) that any professional performer believes that his or her interpretation can be based on nothing but playing the notes or following them in accord with formal instructions alone. Such a performance would seem mechanical, or it would be interpreted in my (and Weingartner's) sense, because the performer would be expressive in spite of what he or she might claim. For instance, as already suggested, such things as a tempo marking of *allegro* must be interpreted by the conductor. This interpretation, I assume, would be to determine just what the speed should be in the context of the whole – that is, in a context that consists of the sections that may come before or after the passage in question, the presence or absence of pauses, the particular instruments, orchestral color, and so forth. As Weingartner puts it, "No slow tempo must be so slow that the melody of the piece is *not yet* recognizable."[13] It is considerations such as these that make the performer's, and in partic-

---

[11] To tackle the many issues associated with the hermeneutical circle would require another study. Suffice it to say that I do not think the circle is closed. And what I say about intentions as they relate to the problem is not, it seems to me, inconsistent with what E. D. Hirsch has said about the author's intention – although I think the independence of what Hirsch calls "intentions" from psychological and biographical factors or mental processes is easily overlooked. See E. D. Hirsch, *Validity in Interpretation* (New Haven, Conn.: Yale University Press, 1967).

[12] One kind of formal analysis that I have in mind that probes "below the surface" was proposed by Heinrich Schenker and is based (in part) on identifying hierarchical structures of related tones within harmonic patterns. A book that provides explanations of Schenker's analyses and comparisons with other approaches is Maury Yeston, ed., *Readings in Schenker Analysis and Other Approaches* (New Haven, Conn.: Yale University Press, 1977).

[13] Ibid., pp. 28–9.

ular the conductor's, job more that of a critic than that exclusively of a technician.

However, the main issue here concerns an extramusical condition that I suggest helps control the conductor's interpretation. A referent such as what I have claimed for representational art would fulfill this function. And if the proposal applies to music, then the interpretation of the composer's indications on the score is dependent, in part, on a unique referent.

What was said earlier about referents as unique restraints on interpretation was suggested by Peirce's view that a referent is something that is indexically singled out. A sign that refers does so because of its indexical function, as distinct from its iconic and symbolic functions, the latter two of which pertain, respectively, to qualities and general meanings. What is referred to is not itself general. It is individual. When it is attended to through the symbolic and iconic aspects of the sign, it is an indexically identified referent; it is singular. And every meaningful experience, or every sign situation, includes reference as well as symbolic and iconic aspects. Further, the singular is encountered with a certain resistance. It reacts against the will in that it is an indeterminate and uncontrollable, albeit a controlling, aspect of the sign's significance. It will not succumb completely to the generalizing demands we place on it. This resistance is the referent's dynamic aspect, its constraining otherness. And with respect to its constraining action, the referent serves as a condition that is dynamic. In applying this conception of reference to music, it is necessary to consider how some of the conditions for interpreting music, in the sense of interpretation just described, function in the same way that dynamic referents function for verbal signs when they are considered as indexes.

It should be evident from what has been said already that an interpretation of a piece of music is not itself a standard for the music. Rather, the music is the standard for the interpretation. Each interpretation requires a consideration of qualities that the work contains, such as the conditions of proper tempo. One test for these interpretations is the coherence of the sound patterns with the overall conception of the piece being interpreted. A performance should exhibit the contribution of the elements of melody and/or harmonic structures to the unified whole (the melos).

I have noted Weingartner's point about the conductor's dependence on the "homogeneous conception" of the work. It is this conception that enables the conductor to bring "something into the light that had really been there all the time."[14] Of course, what this conception is, is subject to controversy. And some disagreements about what

---

[14] Ibid., p. 18.

constitutes a work's homogeneous conception may never be settled. Weingartner strongly disagreed with some conductors. From his point of view, they went to excesses in varying tempi and even revising scores when they wanted to achieve an overall effect that suited their own perspectives. There are obvious differences among many twentieth-century conductors. Some, such as Leopold Stokowski, treated some compositions as built of lush and swelling melodies and textures. Herbert Von Karajan is considered to represent an approach to conducting different from that of Arturo Toscanini, who strove for clarity of structure, crispness, and dynamic precision as a way of giving form to expressiveness. But all conductors must read the score and decide, in terms of the virtual sound patterns it signals, what to stress or minimize. Aaron Copland, in commenting on how performances of his work may vary, puts it this way: "But each different reading must itself be convincing, musically and psychologically – it must be within the limits of one of the possible ways of interpreting the work."[15]

In light of the proposal about the referents of art, it follows that what different interpreters of a score attend to manifests some resistance or constraint, which alerts the interpreters to the limits with which Copland and Weingartner were concerned. The greatest evidence that they remain within these limits is suggested when different interpretations of the same piece do not hide the fact that it was written by the same composer. To be sure, performances may be so varied that the composer's particular style is lost; then we can recognize a composition as by a particular composer only if we already are familiar with the composer in question and the particular melody or some part of the composition that remained intact. But this is not to recognize a style. Apparently, Weingartner regarded some of Hans von Bülow's performances of Georges Bizet as excessive departures from a proper interpretation of the score. Weingartner thought these departures so great that the performances could not be recognized as being of Bizet's work.[16] In any case, if we can recognize a composer's style in a composition that we have never before heard, then there must be at least some general constraints encountered in sound patterns. And different constraints mark the various styles of different composers.

There is, then, an identity or focus of control that serves as a basis for conductors' differences over interpretations. This identity must be founded on more than internal, purely formal coherence. Conductors work toward a "homogeneous conception" that is not merely formal. Attention paid to expressive aspects of the work suggests this

---

[15] Aaron Copland, *Music and Imagination* (New York: Mentor Books, 1952), p. 58.
[16] Ibid., pp. 22–3.

extraformal condition. Expressiveness is integral to the overall conception. And the constraining factor of expressiveness is evidence of a focus of relevance, a referent, that is not confined to the coherence of the work's formal aspect. This transcendence of pure form is necessary for music (and all art) that has relevance to the world.

It might seem strange to consider musical referents as functioning in both the world and interpretation. How can the referent of a musical composition be external to the performed music as well as the composer and interpreter? Here it should be recalled that sorts of referents vary with respect to the functions they have in controlling attention. For some objects, such as those interpreted by scientific theory, pragmatic tests, and regular observations provide access to these differences of function. Referents that function as conditions of obdurate objects are ordinarily regarded as space–time objects that order perceptions and concepts in fairly regular, repeatable ways. Referents that function as conditions of illusory objects are much less repeatable, at least in ever-widening communities.

In the case of the referents that function as expressive conditions for musical compositions, some of the constraints at first, at the inception of a new composition, must be unique, although they may become fairly repeatable if they arise and affect the musical tradition to which the composition may contribute creatively. At least some of the new constraints instituted by the introduction to the twelve-note technique in this century are now, in contexts of compositions written in such scales, anticipated and repeatable. Some of these make possible new expressive possibilities. Thus, the point here is that musicians working together on performances of twelve-note technique compositions or traditional tonal compositions interact with one another, as is perhaps most obvious in the case of chamber music groups. They not only call attention to details of the score, the resources of their instruments, and their particular competencies, but they also note expressive requirements.

Recently, I heard a radio progam in which three critics discussed a piece of (absolute) music on first hearing, in this case, of the performance rather than the composition. One of the critics panned the performance on the grounds that the performers played with nuances that conflicted with what the music was "about." The way in which music is "about" something is hardly more sound patterns themselves; rather, it must be something expressive that serves the kind of function referred to as the *overall conception,* whose focusing condition is the referent, the transcending source of constraint on the appropriateness or inappropriateness of the critic's judgment. And as already said, conductors interpret in the way of the critic, but for large groups of musicians in orchestras. Expressive requirements are the ways that musical referents are manifested to musicians and audiences. And such manifestations are given to those who are responsive in comprehensive ways, including emotional and intellectual reactions.

Let me suggest that referents of music, which I have said give focus and constraints for expressive aspects of music, seem intimately associated with what may be called *human reality* – the dispositions that yield patterns of behavior and patterns of feelings and thought or, more broadly, that manifest mental processes regarded as what comprises something called the *human spirit,* or which I shall also refer to as the *reality of human subjectivity.*

In the case of music, the world is not invariantly external or independent of human reality, as may be the case for many referents of the representational arts. Although the unique referent of a landscape is not an independent thing-in-itself, its controlling focus or referent enables the painting to present the viewer with something that is appreciated for conditions other than those of the appreciator's feelings and cognitive processes. The landscape painting's relevance to appreciation, of course, includes interaction with human feeling and cognition. Yet it also functions as what is ordinarily (in a sense congenial to a form of realism) regarded as independent of mind. It is at least as relevant to nature, or the natural world, as it is relevant to an appreciative, responsive consciousness. Thus, we may learn to see a place in a Cézanne way of seeing.

Some musical compositions may share this kind of reference with landscape paintings. Some music manifestly transforms yet suggests natural sounds. Part of Beethoven's Sixth Symphony makes this explicit. And at least some parts of examples of absolute music may consist of sound patterns that bear remote connections with the actual sounds of nature, such as the sound of flowing water or the rhythm of the heartbeat and of breathing – connections that are much more remote, of course, than are the patterns of color, shape, line, and so on in a landscape painting in their relation to patterns in nature. But in general, the overall conceptions of instances of absolute music exhibit their expressive power in a way more directly connected with feelings or, as suggested, with mental life, with "the life of the mind," than do the representational (nonverbal) arts. It was recognition of the music's power to present symbols of the life of the mind, specifically, the dynamic structures of emotion, that inspired Susanne Langer's theory of music, and of art in general.

One of the obvious difficulties in supporting this proposal that there are musical referents that constrain interpretation is that formulas or rules for the way these constraints are encountered cannot be given. With respect to music, novel, specific criteria at work when external constraints affect interpretation are not available in advance. Yet, as in the cases of theory and the visual arts, some general guidelines may be suggested, although being general and available before innovation occurs, they will not be specific. And it is imperative – if the acceptance of creative advance, or newness in the strong sense that can be attributed to unpredictable intelligibility, is not to be forgotten – to recognize that the musical referent itself is not given directly in the external constraints that may guide our expectations about the expressive needs of a piece of music. Not only is it new, but our access to it, as with verbal metaphors, is through the senses, which in the case of music are patterns of sound.

The guidelines for the interpreter's expectations about the focus of expressive significance are, I think, tied to the expectations that guide interpretations of formal conditions. However, beyond paying attention to notations in the score and deciding whether they were put there and intended by the composer and whether they contribute to the coherence of the work, an interpreter considers other works by the same composer of the piece being interpreted. How were these interpreted in the past? Are past renditions of these other works clues to the work at hand?

Attention is also given to the period in which the work was produced. If the period is classical (postbaroque), there will be some clues that prevent an excessively romanticist interpretation of Mozart. The musical referent in this case, however new it may have been for Mozart's time, would not have constrained the expressiveness of his music in this way, although as some conductors have concluded, Mozart's pieces – his piano concertos, for instance, and other nonoperatic works – may be shown to be more dramatic than others in the past have thought them. A romantic rendering of Mozart would yield a performance constrained more by a referent of the conductor's convention than of Mozart's, or what gives his music its special coherence and charm.

The case is different for Beethoven, at least in his middle and later works, which advanced the tradition in the direction of romanticism. Other issues are relevant, such as the tone qualities of the instruments and their resources, what audiences of the period might have listened for, whether these considerations should be selected rather than adopting a concern for what the composer might have written – in the same style of the period – and whether the composition had been written for new kinds of instruments and a different audience contemporaneous with the interpreter.

At bottom it is the homogeneous conception, the overall, extraformal expressive direction that must be found. The role of this extraformal condition is perhaps better seen in the interpretation of a living composer's work in a way that departs from the score but calls forth an agreement from the composer that the departure improves the musical "intent." It is this overall conception that, when the music of the past is to be interpreted, affects such choices as those of consistency with the past or with a contemporaneous audience; and it is this that is the most direct manifestation of the musical referent. The convergence of the various explicit general guidelines points to this conception, and in turn, this conception is a clue to the referent, which for music is a focus of human reality.

It must be emphasized that what I call the reality of human subjectivity, the life of the mind, or the structure of mental activity, which serves as a reference condition for music, like the referent of every creation, is unique. The controlling condition of a piece of music, although often verbalized in words suggestive of emotion or psychophysical processes, is not a condition that can be identified completely through antecedently known structures of emotions. The reality of human subjectivity as a referent of creative music is one (the original) of a kind.

Let me emphasize that this reference to something in human reality need not appear explicitly as a ground for interpretive decisions. To speak of the musical referent in this way is to characterize it in terms of an incipient ontology of art, which is not to say that conductors attend to constraints of which they would necessarily think in these terms.

The reason I have turned to this point is that I want to emphasize that a created referent of a musical composition may serve as a controlling focus when the referent is regarded in terms of mental activity rather than in terms of an extramental thing in nature. The ontological question of systematically distinguishing referents according to the kinds of reality to which they might be thought to belong – or as I would prefer to say, according to the contexts in which they function – need not be undertaken at the moment. Nevertheless, I want to avoid suggesting that the reality of the musical referent is subjective in the sense of being a function of only private consciousness. Nor do I intend to suggest that it is largely social or cultural in the sense that it is a function of conventions or general beliefs only internal to the social contexts of interpreters in any given period. The referent, as manifest in the homogeneous conception, must transcend the bounds of any finite community; if it did not, evolution through creative metaphors (here musical) would be denied. Each creative achievement leads its interpretive context, advances its tradition, so that the constraints on interpretation must have another source, one that is added to and that enhances the conventional and communal constraints obvious in interpretation.

What has been said about the referents of verbal metaphor and the visual arts is transferred to musical reference; consequently, the condition for constraints must transcend what is extraconceptual in that the condition for constraints is mind independent, relative at least to the composer and interpreter. I do not wish to contend that there are no musical referents insofar as human reality is a determination of general, if not universal, structures of human thought, attitudes, and normative dispositions. Yet I am committed to the view that such reality, even though it constrains interpretation in terms of human mental conditions, is independent in some respects of those social influences that affect the ways we envisage what it is to be human. There must in some respects be an independence from musical conventions and whatever structural properties of musical sound there may be that connect these conventions.

Moreover, there may be musical referents that have some independence from the determination of human conditions themselves. Some musical referents may have a locus in nature, a spatial–temporal as well as a biological realm. This status is appropriate not only to some program music, for instance, Schubert's Trout Quintet, but also to nonprogrammatic or "absolute" music. It seems to me that this is suggested by the fact that there is an overlap or family resemblance between program and absolute music and between many texts and their accompaniment in songs such as those of Schubert. And the resemblance between musical sounds and sound patterns may only very remotely, if at all, resemble sounds in nature in order to be considered programmatic or suggestive of sounds and movement in nature. The character of musical sound patterns as interpreted, I believe, is a focusing of constraints whose condition is not always located in human ways of functioning. The rhythms of nature, forces, continuities, breaks in continuities, the waxing and waning of natural processes, growth, decay, swelling and diminishment of clouds and sea, and the like as these are encountered in experienced resistances express such transhuman sources of constraints as they affect human intellect and feeling. And this sort of independent referent may be what is both created and discovered through creative musical metaphor.

What must be insisted on is that nonrepresentational art — specifically, music — has a controlling focus that gives unique specificity to the work that it transcends and yet that uniquely gives relevance to interpretive appreciation. A center of resistance constrains and gives a focus for musical qualities. This focus of relevance is not simply the series of additional identifiable sound patterns to which future interpreters may attend. As identified, such sound patterns would be in themselves repeatable apart from the composition. By contrast, the focus of relevance is unique. The focus itself resides in the referent that controls the patterns of qualities that are required and of qualities that are rejected as inappropriate.

There is another way to consider why it is important to acknowledge unique referents that transcend yet are relevant to the clusters of general characteristics enumerated in interpretations. In order to introduce this other approach, let me emphasize still again a point that I trust is already clear. If the ground of the relevance of meanings is not exhausted by meanings that are to be applied in future interpretations, then this ground is not simply the coherence of those meanings known to be relevant at any given time. It is not a unity of the work regarded as a principle of unification, if such a principle is thought to reintroduce something that is ontologically like the very meanings that are said to cohere. The ground of relevant meanings for the work is not another meaning alongside its meanings. Nor is it nothing but its meanings, which would imply an immanence that would render the unity unable to control those meanings. Thus, it should not be said that the referent is simply the work of art itself. If it were, the work would be relevant only to itself rather than to the world. The grounding unity must have some transcendence and have a mode of being that is distinct from meanings alone. It is dynamic. This reiterates the point that the referent of music, like the referent of representational art, is not simply a singular but is an individual or an active center of resistance. The acceptance of the presence of creativity and thus of real spontaneity in the world requires acknowledgment of this dynamic transcendence of the intelligibility of things at the moment of spontaneity. And the acceptance of real spontaneity that contributes to the intelligibility of the world requires acknowledgment of the relevance-making function of the created referent.

This idea that the referent of a piece of music is an individual that functions as a focus of human reality has a kind of confirmation in the suggestion that music expresses the composer's personality. Again, this is certainly not to say that interpreters attend to a personality while interpreting a piece of music. Yet as Mikel Dufrenne has pointed out, there is a legitimate significance in this imputing of personality to music. One can identify a significance in music that is personality-like or quasi-subjective.[17] Such personality which is sometimes thought to be expressed is not what could be known by psychological inquiry into the composer's life and motivations. Rather, this personality is constituted by, and is apprehended only in and through, the work. It can be known only in terms of the work. A Mozart symphony creates a Mozart personality — a Mozart musical personality — as much as

[17] Dufrenne, *Phenomenology of Aesthetic Experience.*

Mozart creates the music. And this Mozart is certainly unlike the historical Mozart.

The significance of music applies to a referent that now can be regarded as a dynamic personality, or in terms of the point that the referent of music is a unique focus of mental life, the musical referent is a dynamic individuation of human reality. When those who speak of the personality expressed in music, and sometimes erroneously, I think, seem to construe this personality as something accessible chiefly in psychological terms, they have hold of something fundamentally important to music. They discern the driving center of relevance of the works they try to understand. Just as an individual is an individual known through the meanings that that person rejects, adopts, and projects, so the referent of a musical composition functions as a center from which emanates the meanings of musical patterns, harmonies, systems of tones, and so on. This musical personality projects its relevance-giving power into the future, permitting some, but not just any, variation in interpretations. And just as created human beings have impacts on their contexts and just as they can grow and sometimes create their own futures, so pieces of music or, generally, works of art can create their futures. This is one reason, I think, that Kant says that the genius makes the rules and that the created work of art is exemplary. And it is one reason, perhaps, that Kant finds *Geist* in the outcomes of the works of genius. They do function as if they had *Geist* in the sense of soul, but they do so because they present us with referents that are emergent, dynamic individuals.

Concluding Remarks

The purpose of this chapter has been to suggest how my proposal regarding creative reference can be applied to the arts as well as to verbal metaphor. This task parallels the move from the treatment of the interactive functions to the consideration of the referential function of verbal meaning. A conception of both reference and meaning is required to form the account of interactionism which (1) does not neglect the idea that metaphor, verbal and nonverbal, is relevant to the world and which (2) recognizes that the world includes extralinguistic, extraconceptual conditions. It was proposed that a metaphorical structure is constituted by interacting meaning units that yield an integration characterizable as a family resemblance. The integration – which is to say, the metaphor – generates and sustains tensions. Internal tension arises from incongruities with antecedent meanings or contexts. But in turn, internal tension generates not only contrasts or external tensions with the past that is relevant to the metaphor but also the possibility for new, consequent meanings. The interacting constituents that condition internal tension enable new meaning through the creation of a new referent that functions as a controlling focus for interpretations. The realism that frames the proposed account of created referents rests on a presupposed ontology. Although this study has had as its chief goal the common functional structure of verbal metaphor and the arts, from the standpoint of philosophical reflection, the account needs a closer approximation to completeness through the development of the presupposed ontology. It seems to me appropriate, then, to point in the direction of that ontology. Thus, an adumbration of it will be the topic of the last chapter.

6

An Outline of an Ontology Evolved from Metaphor

The preceding discussion of metaphor and art was initiated with what I called a *metaphysically neutral* approach. The point of framing the discussion in this way was not to repudiate metaphysical or ontological commitments but, rather, to postpone them in order to characterize metaphors when attention focuses on them for their own sakes and for the sake of seeing their relations to other phenomena. Thus, an account of the way in which metaphors and aesthetic objects function when we attend to them could be given regardless of whether we believe that what appears for attention is or is not mind independent. However, it was also pointed out that metaphysical or ontological neutrality could not be maintained once the question of verbal and nonverbal metaphorical significance, with respect to reference, was raised. In addition, it was said that the sketch of an aesthetic theory included a commitment to a view of the ontological status of art works in terms of their functions in experience. The suggestions made concerning these issues clearly implied, if they did not explicitly affirm, a form of realism, as the claim was made that constraints on interpretation indicated the presence of something that was not wholly mind dependent. Consequently, the discussion could no longer be confined simply to a description of the way objects of attention function for attention, but it required extension to the question of the conditions for those functions.

Ontology and Metaphysics

Some brief remarks are necessary concerning the way I use the terms *ontology* and *metaphysics*. The two terms might, for the purposes of this conclusion, be used interchangeably. Both kinds of study are systematic examinations of the significance of the expression *what is* or of the term *being, significance* referring to both meaning and reference. The principles and assumptions that govern these kinds of examinations have led to a variety of forms – from Aristotle through Scholastic philosophy, to contemporary analysis and existential phenomenology. And what falls under the notion and scope of what is thought to be is as various as are the approaches to the topic. Yet if ontology and metaphysics can be distinguished within this tradition, the distinction must be based on the aim of the examination.

The aim of ontology may be thought of as describing what is, whereas metaphysics may be thought of as explanatory. Ontology concentrates on structures and traits; metaphysics concentrates on principles and on reality as such or on ultimate conditions that provide understanding of the structures and traits of things. Even if metaphysics and ontology can be distinguished in this way, however, they will necessarily overlap. Obviously, on the one hand, description can be extended to conditions (even an ultimate condition), and on the other hand, explanation describes what it explains. In this obvious way the adumbration of an ontology to be offered will overlap metaphysics.

The following attempt will not treat *what is* as monolithic or as characterizable by one property but as a multiplicity of discriminable identities that have traits and relations. What is, is both the actual and the physically and logically possible world. The focus, then, will be on describing or identifying the traits of what is, once the role of metaphor in the world is recognized. But such a description cannot avoid conditions that function as principles on which some or all of what is in the world is based. If these conditions are viewed as explanatory principles, then the undertaking may be construed as metaphysics. However, I shall not propose that what is to be described here is explanatory. My purpose is not to arrive at explanations that offer the possibility of predicting things or events or that permit specific descriptions of things or events to be deduced but, rather, to propose hypotheses about what must be acknowledged as part of the world. Yet, insofar as what follows includes statements about traits or aspects that are universally pervasive, what I am calling an ontology may be understood as continuous with metaphysics.

Before beginning the task at hand, I shall suggest a brief response to the recent discussions of whether it is necessary to accept the claim that metaphysics is now dead and whether it is possible to retain some form of realism rather than a relativism. A response is appropriate in the light of the realism already proposed in this book. What I shall say is intended, first, to indicate further ways of answering the questions raised earlier about the status of sources of constraints on interpretations and, second, to circumscribe the framework for the kind of realist ontology to be sketched and the consequent limitations that must be placed on its justification.

I shall begin with some remarks about Joseph Margolis's recent discussion of this issue.[1] Margolis proposes to overcome the conflict

---

[1] Joseph Margolis, *Pragmatism Without Foundations: Reconciling Realism and Relativism* (Oxford, England: Blackwell Publisher, 1986).

between relativism in its traditional and most recent forms (contemporary versions of what he calls "Protagorean incommensurabilism" as well as those in the fashionable idiom springing from some of Derrida's thought) and realism (including that of Peirce). His aim is to undercut both sides of the dispute with "robust relativism." A lengthy treatment of this proposal and the issue in general would require too much space and, I think, a diversion that is not essential to the purposes of this last chapter. Yet there is an obvious aspect of Margolis's position that is immediately relevant: his questioning of the principle – conviction, presupposition, or regulative ideal – of the convergence of inquiry in the future as a basis for affirming realism and the objectivity that is made possible on the basis of a commitment to convergence. My own view is that some form of the idea of convergence is needed in order to account for the conclusion *that* (not necessarily *how* in particular cases) metaphors and their interpretations can be more or less appropriate to something extralinguistic.

I propose to treat in two ways the possible challenge to realism raised by Margolis's view. First, I shall indicate briefly why the question of realism versus relativism needs to be recast. Second, I shall append to this book an essay on the way Peirce's realism and his conception of convergence can be related to some of his suggestions about how signs may function metaphorically. The outcome of using Peirce's ideas in this way throws light on how the interpretation of metaphors and art, on the one hand, and scientific inquiry, on the other, depend in distinct ways on convergence. It seems to me that the relation of the requirement of convergence to metaphors may be consistent with Margolis's robust relativism. In any case, the Appendix is relevant to the topic of this book, for it develops the proposal that referents of metaphors are both created and independently dynamic. It is not included as part of the main text, however, because its focus is on an interpretation, albeit also an application, of Peirce's writing.

As I have just suggested, whatever label is properly applied to the ontological commitment I wish to recommend – realism or some kind of modified relativism – the issue, I think, needs to be recast. The issue should not be thought of in terms of traditional realism or foundationalism versus relativism, or even its recent radical form of deconstructionism. These perspectives or points of view, or at least the labels for them, carry the weight of expectations such as that realism is committed to some antecedent structured objects and that relativism leaves no room for independent conditions of thought. It may be possible to avoid or minimize prior assumptions about such prior commitments. Thus, I believe that the issue should be thought of as whether there are constraints on inquiry, creative achievement, and interpretation, and if there are, what the loci of these constraints on thought are. I take for granted that there are constraints. We do meet with resistances that condition or restrain the ways we respond and act. Even a solipsist cannot avoid recognizing such resistances. The view I have proposed in this book locates some of the constraints on thought – on metaphorical thought, in particular – in its referents, which are to be understood as at least partially independent of thought. To this extent, the view is a kind of realism, and I shall continue to refer to it as such. The view affirms objectivity and a condition that is on the side of the object and that regards the object as not wholly dependent on past, present, or future thought. This is not to deny that there are restraints coming from the side of the activity that creates and discovers objects. Pursuit of the question of locating all constraints that function for inquiry and creativity, should, I think, be directed toward sorting out biological (including genetic conditions) and behavioral conditions as well as conditions that are independent of human organisms that engage in constructing some of the fruits of inquiry and creativity.

The radical character of creativity that I have insisted on in this book, given the domination in our tradition of a form of Kantianism or Hegelianism (linguistic and conceptual idealism) or of the opponent of these, deconstructionism – or to return to Margolis's way of proceeding, some form of foundationalism as opposed to radical relativism – may easily lead to construing the proposed realism in this book as social or as requiring that the source of constraints lie in a future or foundational community consisting of, or at least inclusive of, interpreters. Thus, what is called *reality,* or more specifically in the context of my account of metaphorical reference, what is called *the individual* that focuses constraints, would be a condition of human intelligence. The source of constraints, it might be said, is a projection of society or communities, perhaps comparable to what a "social reality" is for Emile Durkheim. This alternative to the realism I have already suggested may seem especially apt in light of the claim that there are musical referents. And as I have just indicated, the idea of creativity in the strong sense may seem to imply that creations, and thus referents of created outcomes, must be fully constituted by the creator. According to this alternative, anything other than and independent of the referent that might be called *real* could not be created but could only be discovered.

Moreover, if the referent is held to be created and also held to be what accounts for the attribution of *fitting* or *appropriate* to the creative expression, then it must be the creation of a source not confined to an individual creator or metaphor utterer. The referent that has been said to be an existent individual must be a focus of social or communal projection that both influences the way the creator or metaphor utterer thinks and is manifest as the constraints on the creator, and on the wills of large segments of societies or communities generally. In order to clarify my proposal and suggest an answer to this alternative, which is, after all, a version of idealism, I shall consider the possible forms that may be taken by the alternative view that reality is dependent on social and communal conditions and propose that the constraints on creation and interpretation, or the objective condition of insight, must be partly independent of communal reality.

I have assumed that the alternative, social–cultural realism, proposes that what is regarded as reality is the object of the beliefs, attitudes, and commitments of a larger community. Such objects must be either dependent on or independent of the larger community. If the community is limited to time periods and place and if the objects of belief are said to be dependent on the community, we have a form of cultural relativism. If the community is thought to be more general, consisting of a fundamental human condition such that the constituting source functions according to universal categories, or, somewhat more weakly, according to an overall common orientation – perhaps something like what Kant thought of as the *sensus communis* – we have either a Kantianism or a full-blown idealism. According to a Kantianism, there would still be an independent unconditioned condition, more fundamental than the objects of beliefs themselves. According to the idealism, nothing would be "left over," and reality would be constituted by mind or by human, though universal, resources. These resources might be described as innate dispositions toward certain general categorization and/or genetic coding and environmental conditioning. For the Kantianism, the constraints that I have insisted on and that presumably would not be denied by any of the versions of the alternative under consideration, would have an ultimate locus in the independent condition. But they would be unknowable insofar as they are located there. They are encountered only in the effects of the independent condition, that is, the objects of belief and thought of a universal human condition.

There is a sense in which this view comes closest to the proposal I have been suggesting, because the individuals that have been said to be referents of metaphorical creations have not been said to be encountered directly; they are encountered only in senses or meanings that comprise interpreted objects. However, my proposal construes these individuals not as things-in-themselves that are in themselves unknowable. Instead, they bear a direct, dynamic relation to the senses that they constrain and that give us at least an indirect access to the individuals. This relationship between senses and referents as dynamic individuals is discussed further in the Appendix. The extent to which it can be distinguished from a form of Kantianism will be settled there, insofar as I know how to decide the issue. Because I rely a good deal on C. S. Peirce's thought as a basis for my view of referents, it may help to point out that the issue at stake takes the form of a tension in Peirce's own philosophy between a conception of truth as a correspondence between thought and an independent object and as a kind of coherence of convergent interpretations. The Appendix will offer what I think is a way to bring together these two poles of a conception of truth into a viable theory of interpretation.

What is important at the moment is to differentiate my proposal from a form of idealism for which there is nothing real that is independent of mind. The possibility of showing this is most delicately problematic in the case of musical referents, which have been described in terms of human reality, and which therefore seem to fit an idealist model. But although I have tried to explain the sense in which musical referents are not wholly, at least not always, mind dependent, given what has been said about referents of visual nonverbal expressions as well as verbal expressions, it is important to pursue further reasons for not falling into a linguistic or conceptual idealism. This does not mean that I can refute one alternative and demonstrate the truth of the other. I do not think such fundamental views can be subjected to either inductive or deductive proof. At best, reasons, or what may be called *grounds,* may be offered for preferring one over the other. These grounds can serve as a basis for constructing what I call a *picture* of our world. What grounds, then, are available for deciding between affirming a mind-dependent or a mind-independent position?

Let me suggest three reasons. First, some form of realism coheres better with everyday experience, even of qualitative objects such as musical sounds, for which things are encountered and imposed on attention. Surprises, shocks, resistances appear to us without our conscious determination of them. Another way to put the point is that a realism, at first a naive realism, seems consistent with a large range of pretheoretical experience. In using the term *pretheoretical,* I do not mean to imply that elementary, ordinary experience is somehow pure and completely non–theory laden. I refer only to ordinary experience as pretheoretical with respect to interpreting its ontological source. After all, idealistic claims that nothing is mind independent are theories, just as realism is at the level of ontology. Ordinary, everyday experiences themselves do not carry with them the ontological commitments of idealism. They carry with them intuitions of both realism and idealism with respect to particular experiences: of obdurate objects publicly shared and seemingly independent of particular perceivers, for instance, and of evanescent objects believed to be illusory and seemingly mind dependent. My first reason is hardly conclusive, for there may be conditions of which we are not aware that are, as some forms of idealism would have it, responsible for resistance and the appearance of some objects as independent. The point is mentioned, however, because I think it is easily overlooked that realism makes just as much phenomenal sense as idealism does, if not more at the pretheoretical level.

A second and perhaps somewhat stronger reason for preferring the mind-independent view lies in the acknowledgment that we encounter resistances that cannot be readily interpreted if they can be interpreted at all, as mind dependent for individuals. Whole communities occasionally encounter resistances sooner or later, no matter how thoroughly their beliefs are welded into a unified way of constituting the world. The point that there are such resistances was crucial to Peirce's view that reality is not a purely intelligible system of constructs unified by societies. Resistances are fundamental to the constraints on observations in the interpretation and application of scientific theory, as well as in the interpretations of ordinary experience. We make errors not only as individuals but also as communities. The point here is that shared resistances place restraints on more than individual interpreters. Thus, if one insists on idealism, its form must apply beyond the limits of particular communities. Indeed, resistances for whole communities are the basis for both cross-cultural understandings and misunderstandings. And this suggests that different communities can understand one another and we can compare and relate them only on the condition that there are constraints that transcend particular communities. This second point, of course, does not decide the issue for the idealist who affirms common, universal human ways of experiencing, for these, rather than some extramental reality, could be the source of the shared resistances. What reason is there for not preferring this form of idealism?

In answering this question, I believe the strongest reason can be given for accepting the mind-independent view. In brief, the reason is that unless there were something that transcends all human construction in constraining interpretation, the affirmation of new insights would need to be abandoned. If genius does sometimes give us these creations, then it does so by transcending communities. And because these advances beyond such limits are insights, perspectives that reveal something no one and no community revealed before, then the control on the creator must transcend antecedently intelligible human construction. This is to go beyond whatever limits that may have been based on even universal structures of human intelligence. The very structures of human reality must be modified, sometimes ever so little and sometimes dramatically, as in the cases of Copernicus and Einstein, and in the arts, in the cases of Giotto, Cézanne, Beethoven, and

Stravinsky, each of whom stretched and broke fundamental limits within their own appropriate media. If it makes sense to say that genius is innovative, that it creates and is insightful, giving us appropriate, fitting creations, then there must be a condition that constrains the creation and that cannot be reduced to prior ways of organizing experience.

What evidence supports the claim that creating may go beyond the limits of any available structures of intelligibility? I think Peirce's conviction that there is or would be a convergence toward a future consensus in scientific theory in the long run suggests a clue. Without settling the question whether it is any longer reasonable to propose that such universal agreement would be reached in the long run, it seems to me nevertheless significant that convergences do develop in finite contexts. Further, the efforts to pursue inquiry, to be ready to be surprised by unanticipated and unpredictable resistances on observation and thought, suggests that there is at least a regulative ideal of future convergence of contexts in which limited consensus has been attained. In the interpretation of art and science, this regulative presupposition, I think, serves as a justification for continued interpretation. If there is a condition on which this presupposition rests, then it must be the sort of extralinguistic, extraconceptual source of constraints affirmed in this book.

It might be countered that the condition I have claimed is mind independent or extralinguistic and extraconceptual does not account for the way constraints are encountered by whole communities and individuals any more adequately than does a mind-dependent condition that transcends all particular communities and even universal constituting structures common to humankind. The latter condition would fulfill the requirements of providing a referent for insight that goes beyond the limits of all communities. I accept this point. However, I also think it implies the same fundamental commitment on which I have been insisting. If the source of constraints is ultimately independent of all bounded mental activity, its function must be like that of the real, extraconceptual individual, the referent, that focuses the new intelligibility of creations. But why regard such a condition as mind dependent? I see no reason to do so that has any functional impact on the account of how creative metaphors can create something new to which they are fitting.

To repeat what was said at the outset of this chapter, the question in the final analysis is not how to label one's position as idealist or realist; the question concerns the locus of the constraints on interpretation. If anyone willing to agree that some fundamental condition must account for constraints that surpass antecedent organizations of our ways of interpreting experience and wants to call this condition mind dependent, that person must have a preconception of some more fundamental source. For instance, one might move in the direction of certain culturally oriented psychoanalytic views, such as that of Carl Jung. But in this case, the source in question would be just as mind independent as mine is, insofar as it constrains fundamental, universal archetypes of the human mind, which it would need to do so long as the emergence of newness in the world is not deliberately or inadvertently rejected, as I think it is by Jung.

One might instead be committed to another kind of so-called mindlike, if not mind-dependent, source: a source that is said to be divine and that is responsible for the dynamic condition of new constraints. In this case, it seems to me, there is no reason to construe such a source as mindlike, at least in any way in which humans understand what this means, unless the one who makes such claims either reduces what is divine to some form of finite intelligence alongside other intelligences or somehow manages to have access to divinity. For the first alternative, the finite, so-called divine intelligence must be just as subject to surprise and resistance as other, human intelligences are. For the second alternative, it seems to me, the proposer implies a special privilege. I trust it is clear that this book is not based on claims of special privilege to the source of constraints on creativity, and obviously it is not about divine creation or divine metaphorical expressions.

There is still another consideration that is of particular relevance to what I have said about the source of constraints. This has to do with the sense in which normative factors bear on the way constraints are effective and even on the source itself. To treat this issue adequately would require another book. However, I shall address it at the conclusion of this chapter, proposing the direction in which the issue must lead.

Constraints, then, appear to have an origin in what is other than purely social reality as well as the human agent. And as maintained earlier, some of these must be extralinguistic and extraconceptual for a view that affirms that novelty can enter the world. At the same time, there are requirements that clusters of constraints must meet if they are to control the acceptance and rejection of what is created and discovered. These requirements include coherence among the relevant restraints, some degree of consensus on the part of at least a minimal community of agents, and an increment of uncontrollability – that is, those requirements of coherence and agreement occur in a context that is not completely controlled by those who create and discover. There is room for surprise and error. This view, whether thought of as a form of realism or objectivized relativism, is not consistent with infallibilism. Nor is it a form of foundationalism of the sort that Peirce rejected.

This much I would like to insist on as a framework for the following ontology: It seems to me that such a view presupposes a comprehensive convergence, at least for inquiry outside the arts, as a regulative ideal. It also seems to me that particular regulative ideals of convergence must be presupposed for interpretations of metaphors. Whatever arguments for these claims I can offer are found in the Appendix. Suffice it to say here that I offer my ontology not as a proposed closed system supposed to be necessary to all possible worlds. Rather, it is a picture of what I think must be described as the most pervasive ingredients in the actual world characterized as including moments of irreducible novelty that are sometimes originated in acts of creating metaphors.

What must the world be like if creative metaphors are integral to and constitutive of it? This issue arises in the light of the proposal that there is a metaphorical reference to unique objects and that metaphorical referents are in the world. Further, what was said about the function of these unique objects as constituents of the world implied an ontological commitment to something mind independent in the world. The specific question to be answered, then, is What kind of world is it that includes unique individuals that are made possible by metaphors but that also are in some respects independent of language and thought? The answer I shall offer will be a sketch of an ontology in which metaphor plays an integral role.

It is essential to insist that the discussion will be only a sketch. To propose otherwise would be pretentious. The topic is obviously matter for another book. Nevertheless, some suggestions limited to what will be little more than an outline are appropriate. The conception of philosophy that has guided my inquiry leads to the larger topic, and enough has been said to show that a fully developed account of metaphor extends to the way metaphorical insights both advance our understanding of the world and contribute to creating this understanding.

The Constituents of the World

A world that includes the outcomes of metaphors must be understood as a totality of identities. The term *identity* is chosen rather than *object, thing, entity,* or *event,* all of which denote the referents of the term *identity* as I use it. *Identity* is used in order to carry the idea of whatever is or could be. Thus it covers both mental and natural events and physical things. It may refer to consciousness itself. Choice of the word *thing* might suggest that this beginning of reflection gives priority to physical, durable entities. Although reflection does begin with what are taken to be physical entities, they do not exhaust that with which reflection begins. Consciousness and processes are also given for initial moments of inquiry. *Object* might have been selected as a term that approaches a neutral starting point. However, the term is not used because it might suggest that what constitutes the world is exhausted by intentional objects. For similar reasons, *phenomenon* was not selected, as the term is associated with the phenomenological approach that is left behind. *Event* was not chosen because it seems more appropriately used to refer to what can be identified in terms of temporal properties. The issue of terminology is raised because my purpose is to begin "in the midst of things" as they are found when we are mature enough to have been trained to think in accord with learned ways of classifying what is experienced. No term is perfectly neutral with respect to the absence of a host of prejudices. Even the term *identity* may suggest what is unitary as a singular, whereas singularity is only one way in which identities are presented for reflection.

The identification of those identities classified as objects (intentional), as things or physical entities, as mental events or acts, or as natural events depends on how they function. An identity that manifests durability in the form of the same or similar properties, invariant from moment to moment, is here called a *thing*. It persists so that at least some of its characteristics endure independently of changes in perceptual perspectives for a community of observers. A thing also persists or can be identified without reference to time, although it may have temporal relations that are relevant to it if its relation to others things – and events – is to be understood. The properties of a piece of marble can be identified apart from temporal considerations, although its place in earth's history can be identified in part with reference to its age. Predictions concerning a thing can be made with the expectation that the exercising of human will and the undertaking of actions will not affect all the properties predicted. The properties are relatively stable from one moment to the next.

An identity that functions as an imaginary object is relatively unstable, and predictions about its properties depend primarily on expectations concerning the mental processes or the conditions of observation associated with it rather than the properties of the imaginary object itself. If psychotic hallucinations can be predicted, such predictions will depend on identifying mental conditions. A mirage can be predicted if certain meteorological and geological conditions as they relate to perception are known.

Events, natural and mental, are identities that must be characterized with reference to time and in which various things are related to one another in terms of time. The growth of a plant is understood with reference to its properties at different times. Commemorated events are obviously identified with reference to specific times.

Identities may be abstractions. Unlike physical objects, their properties sustain an independence from whatever exemplification in things they may have. Abstractions that serve as rules for natural laws, or mathematical objects that are applied to things, are exemplified. The law of gravity is exemplified in the behavior of bodies in relation to one another, and sphericity is exemplified in the shape of the earth. Yet these abstractions are invariant in relation to their instances.

The number of identities constituting the world is indefinite and perhaps infinite with respect to their cumulation over time. The kinds of identities also may be infinite insofar as creativity will be present in the future evolution of the world. However, there are some fundamental aspects common to all identities. These are aspects of the way identities function for inquiry that concerns the world. They might be thought of as categories, but I shall not try to discuss them in such terms. In part, the basis for the description I shall offer lies in Charles Peirce's conception of indexicality, a point already made in the earlier discussions of reference. It also will have some parallels with his three categories. A more fundamental dimension of Peirce's view is directly related to what follows. And although I shall not here discuss this part of Peirce's philosophy, the Appendix offers in Peircean terms the key to the following description of identities that constitute the world.

Three Fundamental Aspects of Identities

It should be obvious from what has been said about the use of the term *identity* that a description of the world's constituents is not exclusively a description of a collection of particulars, whose intelligibilities are embodied or exemplified in the world. But the point needs to be amplified through recalling what was said earlier in this book about referents: They were called *individuals,* which are centers of relevance to meanings. Thus, they are intelligible complexes of meanings that gain extralinguisticality by being conditions that focus resistance or constraints and that are not entirely dependent on the interpreter. There are resistances that no single interpreter and no group of interpreters can overcome by an effort of will or an act of thinking. The source of these resistances is the extralinguistic and extraconceptual condition to which language and thought are relevant or irrelevant, faithful or unfaithful, appropriate or inappropriate, accurate or inaccurate.

Referents are directly relevant to identities. They are ideally determinate constituents of the world. An identity has three fundamental aspects: intelligibility, constraint, and presence. Intelligibility as a condition of knowing was discussed earlier in this book. In this context, the interdependence of intelligibility and meaning must be highlighted. Every identity that is recognized has an aspect that serves as its intelligibility. Each identity, by being discriminable, is capable also of being intelligible to some degree. As intelligible, an identity is a meaningful complex or a cluster of interrelated meanings. Not all the meanings are contingently related to one another; otherwise, they would not constitute the identity. There are some constraints on their interrelations. Some constraints may be a function of inner coherence, whose determination is linked to requirements located in interpretation, such as the standard of consistency expected of a valid argument or an analytic definition. Such constraints may be called *purely formal.* But other constraints, which may be called *material,* are conditions located in something other than the interpretive process itself. These constitute the second fundamental aspect of objects.

The second aspect is the basis for recognizing that an articulation or expression concerning the identity is relevant to the world. Thus, perceptual judgments are constrained by conditions external to the one who judges – conditions understood by such means as theories of light or sound as well as by directly encountered resistances to arbitrary identification and characterization of the properties of the objects perceived. Similarly, constraints lie at the base of theories which are tested by predictable consequences – things or events to which theories are related and that are not themselves determined in every respect by the inquirer.

The second aspect of identities might be called their *facticity,* because insofar as identities function in accord with this aspect they may be understood as facts. However, the term *fact* or *facticity* might suggest something fully determinate, an entity or referent of theory, that is fixed and describable and determinate independently from all descriptions. That there are such independently fixed identities is, of course, questionable. Thomas Kuhn argued, for instance, that what scientists accept as evidence depends on the inquirer's fundamental presuppositions (paradigms).[2] Although Kuhn's thesis regarding paradigms does not in itself contradict the view that there are identities independent of theories, it does emphasize that the evidence for them depends on such assumptions. This dependence also calls attention to the fallibility of inquiry, for presuppositions change and theories are not final.

The question of whether and what independently fixed identities

[2] Thomas S. Kuhn, *The Structure of Scientific Revolutions,* 2nd ed., enlarged, *International Encyclopedia of Unified Science,* ed. Otto Neurath (Chicago: University of Chicago Press, 1970).

must be thus cannot be settled by the evidence of predicted consequences. The view I am suggesting assumes that the interpretation of identities is fallible. However, the possibility of being fallible and of suspending judgment about independently fixed identities implies corrigibility rather than arbitrariness.

And this condition of corrigibility is a function of resistance related to further resistance in the future. Because what is at issue is relevance to the world, I think it is plausible to regard the second aspect of identities, that is, the condition of constraint or resistance, as facticity.

It might be objected that if purely formal constraints are not exhaustively the conditions for the relevance of certain (empirical or independently real) identities to the world, then some identities, that is, abstractions that submit only to internal or analytic constraints, will seem separated from the world. What is the status of such identities? Is there a realm of forms "outside" the world? The answer to this requires recalling the point that the world may include more than so-called external and enduring things. There is what was called *human reality* or the reality of the mind (mental events and acts), and there are other domains of identities (those subject to purely formal constraints that are in a domain of abstract possibility). The point here, however, is that purely formal constraints such as logical and mathematical principles may be relevant to a part of the world that involves overt process and action. When an insight is said to be relevant to the world, it is a world of process and action, a world as a place for dynamic interdependent things and events. On the other hand, an insight that meets purely formal conditions may be just as, if not more, rigorously constrained as are insights that meet material constraints. But the insight concerns an organization of abstract possibilities that are not directly determined within a dynamic field of material or perceptually functioning resistances.

The third fundamental aspect of identities is their sheer presence. Whatever is intelligible and offers resistance must be whatever it is, prior to being in relation to or to being interpreted. Presence does not itself require an interpreter, but only the possibility of being related to something else, of resistance in its relation to another, and of intelligibility or of interpretation. Presence is simply the condition of possible discrimination. Its character in any instance cannot be at issue, because once an instance of it is both discriminated and considered, it is brought into relation and is no longer sheer presence. Or to make the point even more figuratively, once presence is discriminated, it recedes into the background and leaves what is discriminated in the foreground. Presence is the condition of the other aspects of the identity that is manifest. In any case, it is the first aspect, intelligibility, and the second, constraining condition, that are of chief importance in this discussion.[3]

It should be noted that meanings, or the nodes of interpretation, are presented immediately for attention. But once presented, they initiate interpretation. Attention is driven forward regarding them in relations, internal and external. What is interpreted partly depends on the inquirer or interpreter. On the other hand, with respect to the second aspect, that is, the identity as a constraining center, what is interpreted is a real or an independent focus for the meanings or interpretations that are presented as a referent.

It has been pointed out that referents designated in terms of what is intelligible need not be physical things' identity. The identities that make up the world include events (physical and mental), types (such as word types, as distinct from word tokens), and tokens or inscriptions and specific verbal utterances. They also include generals or repeatable identities that are instanced in, for example, particular events, physical things, and verbal tokens. The kind of identity to which interpretation can refer is a function both of the perspective and approach of the interpreter and of the identity as a focus of resistance. In effect, then, pragmatic tests, rigorously controlled or loosely applied, must be among the techniques used by a community of interpreters who cooperate in identifying and characterizing identities that are objects of inquiry and interpretation.

Basic Classes of Identities

Not only do all identities manifest the three aspects, but they also can be classified into two basic kinds: artifacts and natural identities. The latter can be further classified into active identities or agents and what is passive or what are natural things. Artifacts that are products of human agents are of primary concern here. Artifacts need not be physical or even strictly perceptual, observed outcomes, although they must be capable of being instanced in such things as performances and imagined perceptual and conceptual objects. Literary products, for instance, are immediately inscriptions or utterances, but their significances include possible instances of perceptual and conceptual objects.

---

[3] Readers familiar with Peirce may recognize in this account of the first and second aspects of objects the two categories of Firstness and Thirdness. Thus, the sheer presentation of a phenomenon (or what I call an *identity*) as something to be interpreted is the phenomenon in its immediacy, which is its Firstness. But this way of regarding the phenomenon is prescinded from a richer encounter that includes an ongoing interpreted and interpreting process. The latter is the Thirdness relevant to the phenomenon. Secondness is the aspect of the object that I have called the *second aspect*.

The process of making artifacts requires a relatively strict, deliberate control on the part of the producer, a point to be considered further. By contrast, although natural things may be consequences of other natural things or processes (as in the case of animals and plants), natural things and events do not produce, nor are they produced by, rules subject to change by whim (I assume that mutations are not whims), by reflective judgment (in Kant's sense), or by conscious deliberation. Plants reproduce themselves according to natural laws, and so when they change, they do so as part of evolutionary growth. Similarly, animals reproduce according to biological laws. In the case of human reproduction of offspring, deliberation may affect the conditions under which reproduction takes place. And recently, some instances of such processes seem to overlap the kind of production that occurs when artifacts are made — test-tube techniques that contribute to reproduction, for instance, although basic laws of embryo development still prevail. Thus, although humans and animals are products of parents, they are not artifacts, because at least until now there have been fairly extensive restrictions on the calculation and control of parents and society regarding the specific traits of offspring.

Nonetheless, natural things may contribute to larger contexts in ways that may be considered productive. They may serve as conditions of significance. The components of metaphors, verbal and nonverbal, function in this way. Such functions, of course, are important increments in a total process that may consist of the production of artifacts or of a productive process in nature, if the component in question is a natural thing rather than part of an artifact.

There are subclasses into which natural things can be divided that follow from the distinction between active identities and passive identities that function as things. The basis for this distinction is the consideration of whether or not an identity is responsible for its action. Responsibility for producing artifacts is, of course, particularly important here. Where there is responsibility, there is agency, and the responsible identity either is itself called an *agent* or is regarded as activated by an agency that is internal to the identity. Passive identities are acted upon, although they may be parts of systems and processes to which they contribute as components. Yet they are not made by virtue of functions that originate within them. For instance, although general ideas, emotions, elements of a medium, and so on contribute to works of art, responsibility lies with the agent that incorporates these in production.

For this view, human beings are active identities that contribute to the intelligibility of the world. They do so in two ways: as intelligible components of the world — that is, by contributing their own intelligibilities to a larger context — and as objects that are responsible for adding new intelligibilities to the world. This latter contribution occurs because humans sometimes are responsible for artifacts. And their artifacts are projects that affect the constitution of the world. At this point, the question of the role of metaphor in the world should be evident.

The Role of Metaphor in the World

Metaphors and Their Constitutive Function

Metaphors are either verbal or nonverbal artifacts. But they are constituted in a way that distinguishes them from other artifacts. This further distinction is between what, on the one hand, is made or produced by repeatable, structured activities that conform to preestablished rules and which accordingly is predictable and what, on the other hand, is generated by activities that are not governed fully by preestablished rules and which is not fully predictable. In other words, some artifacts are simply made, whereas others are created. Creations exemplify value and what I elsewhere called *Novelty Proper*.[4] We cannot discuss here the complexities of the idea of Novelty Proper. However, it must at least be said that Novelty Proper is newness of a kind or uniqueness of a type whose token exemplifies for the first time the intelligibility of the kind or type. This form of newness is called *proper* because it is appropriate to expectations concerning the strongest kind of newness, or newness attributable to instances of creativity that contribute to the advance of a tradition and that sometimes initiates these traditions themselves. The point here is that in the ontology being adumbrated, new instances of intelligibility are integral to the intelligibility of the world. And if metaphors are instances of new intelligibility, then metaphors function in fundamental ways in the constitution of the world.

The contribution of metaphors to the world, however, is not simply the sort of contribution that might be ascribed to advances within a language or within a nonverbal medium or art form. Because metaphors create referents as well as complexes or integrations of meanings (styles), they contribute through created referents to the constitution of the world. As said earlier, they create referents that function in somewhat the same way as do new children as they affect their own contexts and the future of the environment to which they belong. They are active forces in the world. Of course, some are less so than others, just as children who mature may become mere conformers

---

[4] The term *Novelty Proper* and a discussion of the presence of value in the outcomes of creative activities is offered in my *A Discourse on Novelty and Creation*.

rather than creative agents of the kind most dramatically exemplified in genius.

This point can be formulated in a slightly different way, in terms of what has just been said. The referents of metaphors are identities that are artifacts, and in this way they constitute a class that is obviously unlike children. But these artifacts have two aspects, intelligible structure and focal resistance, which, as metaphorical referents constitute evolving intelligibility. They advance our understanding of the world as it includes both identities that can be characterized as independent of interpreters and identities that function in the way human interpreters do, as both passive and active. It is in this latter capacity that metaphors create and discover human realities, as was suggested in the discussion of the referents of music. And they, like human realities, are components of the world, just as are nonhuman realities, for which creators of metaphors are also responsible.

With respect to the second aspect of identities, focusing resistance, created referents are dynamic centers of relevance that offer resistances to arbitrary interpretations. But as created, these foci are components of evolving reality insofar as that reality is not yet available to fully explicit interpretation. Thus, metaphors create individuals that serve not only negatively as conditions resisting innumerable possibilities of intelligible meanings but also positively as propulsions toward affirmations of relevant intelligibility for the future. In such capacities, they should not be divided into a class of identities that are artifacts of the sort (if there are any of this sort) that do not interact with natural identities. They make a difference to the interpretations of such identities, and in particular, they make a difference to the emergence of natural identities in the process of evolution.

This stronger claim, which was introduced briefly in the earlier chapters on reference, probably is the most controversial of all the suggestions I have made in this book. One may well ask how creating new intelligibility can be understood as something that is inseparable from creating something independent, at least provisionally independent, of intelligibility. There are two considerations that I shall address in response to this question. The first has to do with the relationship between two of the aspects of identities, and the second has to do with the relations of the constraining aspects of different identities to one another.

In order to explain both considerations, I shall again raise the issue concerning the relation between works of art and their referents: Is this relationship itself aesthetic? It should be clear, in the case of created aesthetic works of art, that this is to ask whether the relationship is metaphorical. It should be obvious, too, that the relationship originates as metaphorical, because metaphors and their meanings are internal to each other (meaning is immanent), and it is through the internal interaction of expression and meaning that the unique referent is denoted. The referent of a metaphor is intelligible through this unique determination by the metaphorical meaning. Thus, the metaphorical expression and its referent as interpreted or as intelligible are components in an integration. They are interdependent but interacting poles of an aesthetic object. But as pointed out earlier, the referent of the metaphor escapes complete inclusion as immanent. It does so by virtue of its other aspect, the constraining resistant center of relevance, which is the ground for saying that a metaphor is appropriate to the world.

What, then, is the relationship between the two aspects of the metaphorical referent? It is obvious that one way in which they are related is a function of the referent's "near side" or intelligibility. This is the power of the uniqueness of intelligibility relevant to created referents. Consequently, unlike identities that are not instances of creativity, metaphorical referents do not, as intelligible, take part wholly within an established system or web of intersecting meanings known independently of the immediate cognition or interpretation of these referents. In these cases, the community of inquirers or interpreters has a ready-made system of interpretation within which the referent can be included. In the case of the new referent, the intelligibility contrasts with the ready-made web of interpretation and forces an adjustment of it. The metaphor disrupts accepted rules and introduces new rules for finding the world intelligible. This function of metaphors is not confined to a purely linguistic or conceptual medium. The previous discussion was an attempt to show how nonverbal data can function metaphorically.

The idea of metaphorical functions may also be extended to the world that is interpreted through metaphor. The main reason for proposing this extension has been indicated in the point that new rules of interpretation, and correlatively of what is interpreted, that are generated by creative metaphors are not arbitrary. Nor is a metaphor controlled wholly by the system into which it enters and that it initially affects. The other side of the referent, the focusing resistance, plays its own role. After all, the relation between metaphor and referent is an integration, which implies the integrity of the components, and in this case, the integrity of the two poles of the metaphor in relation to its referent. What sustains the integrity of the referent pole is the constraining aspect of the referent. As was stated, this side is dynamic, propelling its interpreted meanings and serving as a condition for the force that adjusts antecedents and current intelligibility.

In the evolution of science, this claim about the role of the constraining side of referents is borne out to the extent that metaphors help form new scientific theories. As was indicated earlier, I am not alone in making such a suggestion.[5] If theory is relevant to the world and if metaphor helps create that theory, then metaphor shares with theory whatever creative power it has. One might reduce this power to the power of discovery. And there is a dimension of creating that, I think, involves discovery, for the extralinguistic and extraconceptual resistances limit the conditions for the change made through creative theory construction. But if the world is not a static structure waiting to be described by inquirers who are active only in terms of being attentive, if it is instead something dynamic that evolves, then the condition of resistance is not simply waiting to be discovered. It must be dynamic and part of an evolving reality that interacts with creative inquiry and helps create the metaphors that interact with it creatively.

The point probably can be made with less difficulty in the case of creation in the arts. The constraints that are relevant to metaphors that contribute to the creation of the new rules or intelligibilities limit and propel the development of the media proper to the different arts. But when the works of art exemplifying new rules are relevant to the world, their metaphors have new referents. Thus, it was said that a unique human reality was made possible in and through Beethoven's Ninth Symphony. As a creation by Beethoven, it made the symphony relevant to human reality because it contributed to that reality. It introduced into the musical world and in turn the world of human aspiration a unique structure integral to what it is to be human.

Responsibility for Metaphor

When applied to creative activity, the earlier point that some identities are agents responsible for what they produce suggests a paradox. If there is something unique in a creation that is not in every respect under the control of the agent, then what does it mean to say that the agent is responsible for a created outcome? The answer depends on seeing first that responsibility can be neutral with respect to accountability. That is, it can be merely causal, or the function of a condition that contributes to what needs to be known as a basis for predicting a result. Human responsibility is sometimes also accountability; that is, it is the kind of responsibility according to which the agent is praised or blamed on condition that the agent could have done otherwise.

In the case of creative activity, or, specifically, metaphor creation, the answer to the question concerning the paradox also depends on

[5] Mary Hesse has discussed the role of metaphor in science in several places. What I take to be the classic statement is found in her "The Explanatory Function of Metaphor," in *Revolutions and Reconstructions in the Philosophy of Science* (Bloomington: Indiana University Press, 1980), pp. 111–24. Richard Boyd's view of metaphor in scientific theory was touched on in the reconsideration of interactionism.

seeing that the primary source of responsibility must be twofold: the agent referred to as the human creator and the external or extralinguistic–extraconceptual focus of resistance. The role of this second source of (causal) responsibility is, of course, consistent with the preceding account which suggested that the world, insofar as it is not exhausted by its intelligible structure is dynamic. If the world is dynamic, then it seems appropriate to regard it as being to some extent responsible, along with the creative agent, for controlling the articulation of verbal and nonverbal metaphors. This responsibility of the world, however, is different from human responsibility because we would not hold mind-independent aspects of the world accountable for their responsibilities for creative achievements. I leave aside the question of divine responsibility, much less accountability. Obviously, if I were to say that a divine source is responsible for all acts and events, then the idea that something independent of human agents can be responsible would be more obvious, though no less controversial.

My point can be formulated with reference to the concepts of spontaneity and freedom. A human creator who is responsible must act out of a condition of freedom. There must be at least the degree of freedom an agent must have in order to act in ways that transcend established mental and behavioral conditions so as to break with old rules and introduce new rules. This kind of activity presupposes an increment of spontaneity in the creative process. On the other hand, mind-independent foci of the world must also include increments of spontaneities. In these instances, however, it does not seem relevant to attribute freedom to those foci of resistance, for accountability – implying the freedom to do otherwise and to be conditioned by remorse – is beside the point.

The question of responsibility and the function of metaphor in creation and interpretation needs to be explored at length. A study of the problem extends the ontology I am suggesting into normative considerations. Indeed, apart from this specific issue, a purely descriptive ontology is, I think, impossible, unless it is so limited that the function of selectivity and the possibility of hierarchies of the various kinds of reality are ignored. In any case, if certain aspects of identities that constitute the world exemplify increments of spontaneity, which interact with the normative aspects of human creativity, then normative conditions will be integral to the ontology. Moreover, answering the question of responsibility and metaphor would require examining the distinction and relationship between moral and aesthetic responsibility. Insofar as the creative agent's attention is directed only toward the interacting meaning units of the object to be created, responsibility seems to be aesthetic. But this aesthetic concern is inextric-

ably bound up with the extra-aesthetic aspects of the developing outcome, which also introduces constraints, and these constraints are not
wholly aesthetic. They are moral, social, and religious, in that the
system of intelligible structures of the world's identities contributes
to the community of interpretation that follows the created achievement.

What has been said about accountability and the need for a development of an account of metaphor (which is an account of creativity
as well) in the context of normative considerations suggests that a full
account would extend beyond an ontology, at least if the ontology
were undertaken as it has been in this chapter. Or to put the point
another way, further development of the ontology would require the
development of an axiology. But the axiology would comprehend
considerations appropriate to social psychology and certain directions
in which psychiatric theory and humanistic psychology may be given.
The ways in which a creator or metaphor constructor is affected by
cultural context and psychological dynamics of which the agent is not
fully aware, are considerations that would help us better understand
the conditions under which the individuation of effort and created
outcome take place. This is not to say that metaphor construction could
be reduced through such explanations; otherwise, as has been emphasized repeatedly, the strong sense of creativity and the origin of
fundamentally new outcomes would be rejected. Yet we should be
able to circumscribe the unique identities encountered as metaphors.

The first step in moving toward the axiology that, along with the
ontology would form the larger framework for social–cultural and
psychological considerations, was suggested in my *A Discourse on Novelty and Creation*. To develop those suggestions further would require
another book. However, I shall indicate the general points that specify the axiology proposed there. I stated that the creator is most generally directed by a concern for bringing something into being. This
is a normative concern, for it functions as an ought – it is a demand
that the creator may either enjoy or experience as a burden. In either
case, the demand is presented as an obligation. The demand appears
as what was called *the value of being*, and this fundamental ought-to-
be lures the creator. The value of being, however, is unindividuated;
it remains unspecified and indeterminate until normative specificity
is brought about in the outcome. Specified value is what is distinctively
attributed to the creation. This value is what is new. Consequently, it
cannot function only as a lure, because it must be brought into being
or given the specificity, by the creator, that qualifies the kind of value
it is.

The act of creating is bidirectional with respect to the particular norm that guarantees that the outcome is a creation and not simply something different. I have suggested elsewhere that the condition under which such bidirectional action takes place in creativity is what Peirce called *agape*. The creator must work out of concern for a creation-to-be that the creator permits to unfold, something like the way a parent's love is a condition for the self-development of children. And the creator's responsibility is comparable to, though not identical with, a parent's accountability for what children do both on their own and under the guidance of the parent.

This characterization of the creator's normative activity points once more to the need to consider psychological and social–cultural factors. It also suggests, I think, that a more complete account possible for metaphor or creativity in general invites the cooperation of persons working in fields both within and that may be related to philosophy: Specifically, for the purposes of this book, these fields would include social and individual psychology, psycholinguistics, philosophical anthropology, and philosophy of culture. To pursue this task would be an enormous undertaking.

Extraconceptual Metaphors: Real Individuals

This last consideration points to another issue from which an ontology that includes attention to metaphor cannot be divorced. To what extent does aesthetic or metaphorical interaction pervade the world insofar as it is mind independent. If the relationship between aesthetic object and its referent is metaphorical, is there not a sense in which there must be a metaphorical structure that is in the world? If so, then it is a mistake to regard metaphorical structure as only linguistic or conceptual. There are mental processes that can be studied for their metaphorical structure. And there are products or outcomes of these processes that can be studied for their metaphorical structure – the major part of this book has been such a study. But because there is an interaction between language and the world and between thought and the identities of the world, the world itself must include the structures that condition linguistic metaphors. The world itself must be integral to metaphorical interaction, at least in its evolutionary dimension.

It should be obvious that I do not mean to say that the world that shares metaphorical structures with language is a collection of things in themselves. The world is a complex of identities, some of which function as things that are not interpreted as mental events or as nothing but intentional objects. Further, all referents of meanings are twofold with respect to their functions for interpretation. One side of referents is the controlling focus that resists mind-dependency. Consequently, when I say that the world includes metaphorical structures, I mean that the world with respect to the controlling foci of referents and with respect to identities that are not mental events or exclusively intentional objects includes metaphorical structures. This point may be seen in light of what I shall call "levels" of the worlds that I shall discuss later.

Illustrations of the way some philosophical views assume, explicitly and implicitly, that the world or the reality about which they inquire and for which they offer interpretations exhibits metaphorical structure can, I think, be found in various examples of opposing perspectives. Phenomenological descriptions, existentialists' accounts, rationalist theories such as those of Leibniz and Spinoza, Plato's dialogues, and Wittgenstein's late work contain metaphors – and sometimes these form crucial components of their views – which purportedly are about reality insofar as it is intelligible. Even the notion of family resemblance, which, I think, is a powerful metaphor that brings together the ideas of differences and partial identities as components of an interacting web, applies to the world insofar as the world is the limit of language.

Most fundamental to the metaphorical structure of the world is the interplay of identity – as sameness, which is not necessarily pure unity or mere numerical identity but is a general commonality or controlling condition – and difference. An ontology that develops its picture of the world discursively must assume the contrast between sameness and difference. Thus, an ontology amplifies these two conditions as they interact. The tension of sameness and difference, then, is at the root of all ontological discursive pictures. From the interaction of these springs the various emphases given to the terms that make up ontologies. But once interaction is affirmed, some instances of it may yield more than purely discursive accounts. And this implies that the resulting accounts may include references to complexes of metaphors ascribed to reality. Complexes of metaphors may be constituents of the world.

The suggestion that the world has metaphorical structure should not be taken as a claim that an ontology with metaphor is committed to asserting that all identities in the world, or all relations among identities of the world, are metaphors. Instead, the proposal is that only some aspects of the world are metaphorical. This leads to the last bit of commentary on the outlines of an ontology with which I conclude this book. I propose that the identities that compose the world can be regarded as levels correlated with the kinds of attention that inquirers direct toward them.

Levels of the World and the Effective Place of Spontaneity

These levels that I propose are roughly parallel to the levels of the work of art.[6] The first, most basic level is the physical level. It is called most basic because it is a necessary condition for all the others, whereas they are not necessary conditions for it. At the same time, this level is not a sufficient condition for the others, because the other levels include principles or rules that make them intelligible but that are neither present in nor the result of the principles or rules constituting the physical level. This first level includes objects of theory — molecules, atoms, subatomic particles, energy, regularities or laws of matter, and the like. At the same time, there are observable characteristics available to commonsense perception, such as perceived weight, size and texture, all of which imply interpretations that are themselves based on theory.

The second level is the biological level. It differs obviously from the first by virtue of the presence of life. Exactly what is meant by the term *life* is, of course, a complex issue. Suffice it to say here that the order of identities that can be characterized as living manifest some degree of self-development and reproduction. (The attributes to which I appeal are generally those distinguished by Aristotle.) Many of the rules and principles according to which biological identities function are also objects of theory. Traits available to commonsense observation belong to the biological level, as do perceptual and derivative notions drawn from biology and probably medicine — for instance, traits such as observed growth, responsiveness, adaptability, and communication.

The next level is psychological. What is added here is reflexivity or self-consciousness. Whether some nonhuman animals are self-conscious and can be included here is open to question. (If there is a reliable distinction to be made between human and nonhuman animals, it must be made in terms of the next, fourth level.) In any case, the capacity to distinguish and order the lower levels and to reflect on what does or may occur when attention is directed toward the world is distinctive of the psychological level. Further, at this third level, identities are potentially, if not always actually, identities that function as agents, that is, as manifesting actions for which one can suppose a source of initiating condition — an agent responsible at least in the nonaccountability sense.

[6] My account of the levels of the world, or of reality, which I shall distinguish, owe much to certain aspects of Nicolai Hartmann's ontological strata, although I adopt them in a very simplified form for the purposes of this sketch. See, in particular, Hartmann's *New Ways of Ontology*, trans. Reinhard C. Kuhn (Chicago: Henry Regnery, 1953); and Hartmann's *Ethics*.

At the fourth level, not only is there reflexivity but there also is the manifestation of normative selection, selection made at least apparently on grounds not restricted to training and habit. Self-consciousness here functions according to norms adopted self-consciously by the agent. This level, then, might be called *the spiritual level,* although the term should not be understood as necessarily religious in any traditional sense of religion that is tied to specific doctrine. The normative traits of identities at this level (at which they are agents) are aesthetic, moral, social (and political), and religious. And insofar as an agent selects, rejects, adopts, and repudiates these norms, accountable responsibility, spontaneity, and freedom are present. Obviously, it is at this level that created artifacts are produced and aesthetic works of art or metaphor are created.

The point of distinguishing the four levels of identities is to find a place in the world for metaphors and also to extend the suggestions about the place of the sources responsible for producing metaphors. By viewing creative agents as functioning at a level conditioned by, yet not wholly dependent on, other levels at which identities function, we can propose an ontology in which a case can be made for the interaction of what is free in a self-determining, creative sense with what is thought to behave according to regularities or laws of physics, biology, and psychology. The most important development of an ontology with metaphor must examine this difficult issue. But I think the lines are drawn so that an account can be given for the injection of freedom into the world as it is known according to the regularities that are or can be objects for scientific inquiry. The result would be what may be called a *developmental teleology,* which is an account that considers the occurrence of various kinds of teleogical functions, aesthetic, moral, and so on, as instances of spontaneity or as self-determined. The question of establishing the reality of freedom and showing its effective relevance to the world is best approached through an ontology that takes spontaneity as it is found in creative acts to be a fundamental ingredient in the world. The result of the effort would give the proper place to metaphor and the source responsible for it.

The primary purpose of this book has been to propose a way in which the intricacies of metaphorical action and its outcomes are pervasive at the aesthetic level of human expression. And insofar as this effort approximates an adequate picture, I believe that the way toward pursuing the long-range project of constructing an adequate ontology has been prepared. Let me summarize the main points of my sketch of this ontology.

My proposal concerning metaphorical interaction and reference required considering the interaction of attention and its object with respect to the conditions of aesthetic phenomena, specifically of art, and to the general conditions of intelligibility expected in interpretation in domains outside aesthetic phenomena. Consequently, the framework for a primarily descriptive ontology could be suggested. The framework hinges on treating the world as a complex of identities that function in distinctive ways. Their functions can be interpreted with reference to fundamental aspects that any functioning identity has: intelligibility, constraining focus, and presence. Further, each identity can be classified as something natural or as an artifact. Metaphors are artifacts, but they are outcomes for which some natural identities functioning as agents are responsible and accountable. In turn, metaphors, although artifacts, function like natural agents in affecting the world by enhancing its intelligibility and by adding to it the presence of constraining foci. Instances in which metaphors thus contribute to the world are instances of creativity, which is to say also that they are instances of evolution. The framework for the adumbrated ontology, then, is directed toward describing the world as fundamentally evolutionary and as manifesting its evolution in metaphorical interaction and reference that is verbal, nonverbal, and extra-conceptual. This is to say that evolution in the world as well as evolution in thought and language is the outcome of metaphorical interaction that is adequate and effective because it is referential.

Appendix: Metaphorical Reference and Peirce's Dynamical Object[1]

The most striking part of Max Black's form of interactionist view of metaphor is the announcement that some metaphors may be said to create rather than to discover similarities.[2] At the same time, Black insisted that some metaphors may be adequate or "faithful" as cognitive insights that show us "how things are" in the world. However, in explaining how a metaphor can create similarity, which is the kind of thing ordinarily thought to be part of the world, Black said that similarities are not independent of cognitions. They must be understood as perspectives on the world. The perspectival view, however, "explains away" what was exciting about Black's original claim, as it turns out that what is created is idea or experience rather than something ideas create. Furthermore, Black's explanation does not explain whether the world given for metaphorical perspectives is itself a system of more perspectives or is something like a Kantian unknowable thing-in-itself.

The following discussion will try to explain the creative insights that some metaphors seem to offer us, without sidestepping the ontological issue raised when we ask what the created perspectives are. I shall attack this issue using some of Peirce's ideas about the referents of signs. Peirce's conception of the object of a sign suggests a way to preserve the creative and insightful function of metaphors without forcing us into either a linguistic or conceptual idealism (for which the world is exhausted by some final system of perspectives on themselves) or a neo-Kantianism (for which the world is an unknowable reality independent of perspectives). Instead, we are given a way to

---

[1] An earlier version of this appendix was presented on May 1985 to The Pennsylvania State American Philosophy Group. A short version was also presented to the Semiotic Society of America meeting in 1985.

[2] Max Black's development of interactionism is found in his *Models and Metaphors: Studies in Language and Philosophy,* vol. 3, "Metaphor," pp. 25–47; and more recently, in "More about Metaphor," pp. 431–57. It is reprinted in a slightly modified version in Ortony, ed., *Metaphor and Thought,* pp. 19–43.

The problem that I shall discuss was first considered in my "Metaphors, Referents, and Individuality," *Journal of Aesthetics and Art Criticism* 42 (Winter 1983): 181–95. However, I did not develop the way that Peirce's view of Immediate and Dynamical Objects as referents is particularly useful in attacking the issue.

retain both creativity and a form of realism, or objective reference, that has a function in controlling specific changes in theory and interpretation.

This proposal hinges on an account of the peculiar sort of reference that can be attributed to a metaphor. Thus a central question must be addressed: What kind of referents can carry two functions: being created, and being independent of the language and thought that creates them?

Before trying to answer this question, however, let me emphasize that the issue here has important implications that might not be immediately obvious. If creative metaphors can have ontological objectivity, then we have an alternative to various views that deny that independent grounds can be found for interpretations of texts. In short, an account of metaphorical reference bears on some of the views recently proposed by deconstructionists, as well as a variety of other postconstructionist views. Let me also note that I bypass considerations of other approaches to the relation of reference to metaphors, particularly those of Nelson Goodman and of Israel Scheffler.[3] Although these "extensionalist" views do include considerations of what metaphors apply to, they deliberately exclude the ontological issue as it arises when one poses a form of realism as an alternative to nominalism.

The following considers some of Peirce's discussions of how signs function indexically and metaphorically. I shall use a few quasi-technical terms that appear in Peirce's semiotic: "ground," "Dynamical Object," and "Immediate Object," and the perhaps more familiar terms, "secondness," "symbol," "index," and "icon." I shall not attempt to define all these terms. Instead, I shall characterize icon, index, and symbol and let the meanings of the other terms emerge in the context of the discussion. Attempts at definitions, particularly in light of the purposes of my discussion, would be both rash and fruitless. The conceptions drawn from Peirce's writings are too complex to be defined adequately here, if anywhere. Indeed, the meaning of each term could be approximated only in a study of its own. Furthermore, the import of each of these terms need not be fully captured. Only those aspects of Peirce's semiotic that are relevant to my discussion are at issue. Indeed, the justification for characterizing the terms integral to what follows – and a justification is proper for those readers familiar with Peirce – is that my interpretation of them needs to be acknowledged at the outset.

---

[3] Goodman, *The Languages of Art;* and Scheffler, *Beyond the Letter.*

Terminology

The three most familiar kinds of signs, icon, index, and symbol will be treated as three functions of signs. This functional approach is justified, I think, because Peirce regarded any genuine sign as exemplifying all three classes of signs. Each genuine sign is at the same time an icon, an index, and a symbol.[4]

Insofar as a sign functions iconically, its meaning is found in some form of direct, or unmediated, relation of the sign to its object. The relation depends on some quality intrinsic to the sign and required for the sign to refer to the referent. There are three kinds of iconic function. First, a sign may refer to an object insofar as it is an image of its object, as a picture may resemble its referent. Second, a sign may be iconic insofar as it has a structure isomorphic with the structure of its object, as a diagram represents its referent. And third, an iconic sign may refer to its object metaphorically, or by virtue of what Peirce calls a "parallelism" (2.277). The idea that a metaphor is iconic of its referent because of a parallelism, of course, is particularly important to my concerns. Unfortunately, Peirce does not expand this idea, and its significance for my purposes will require some interpretive extrapolation.

A sign functions indexically insofar as it refers directly to something singular, which may be an individual, a collection of individuals, or a continuum. As an index, a sign focuses and directs attention to its object. Attention is focused by a sign's indexical function when it is not degenerate, because of something that is, or results from, a dynamic relationship, such as that of a bullet hole to a bullet – where the hole is an index of a bullet. A personal pronoun is an index (though here degenerate) of the person who is its object, and a demonstrative pronoun is an index of the thing that is its object.

A sign functions symbolically if it is general or refers to something general. A symbol may be a type, such as a word type, or when it is embodied, it may be a replica or token that instances a word type. A

---

[4] In classifying signs, Peirce defined "icon," "index," and "symbol" by concentrating on the way they relate to their referents, as can be found in, for example, *Collected Papers of Charles Sanders Peirce* (Cambridge, Mass.: Harvard University Press, 1931–1958), vol. 8, paragraph 335. All references to the *Collected Papers* in the text and in the notes will follow the standard form, for example (8.335) for vol. 8, paragraph 335. The functional way of treating signs is also indicated in Peirce's discussion of how an object may be present to the mind, that is, in terms of the three kinds of signs (8.346). But in particular, Peirce's insistence that " . . . it would be difficult if not impossible, to instance an absolutely pure index, or to find any sign absolutely devoid of indexical quality" (2.306) suggests that the same experiential item can have three ways of being a sign, or three ways of functioning semiotically.

symbol may be a natural law or a formula for a natural law. However, what is important to my discussion is that whatever represents a complex of abstract qualities, which also are instanced by embodied qualities, is a symbol. For example, the word type of the expression "black stove," is a symbol of blackness and angularity, both of which are embodied in the stove. Blackness and angularity are generals that are embodied qualities in the stove. And these qualities, as generals, are symbols in the way that laws are symbols. These are also called *legisigns*.[5] They might be called *universals,* except that this term carries associations that Peirce wanted to qualify or avoid, because he thought that unlike what is usually thought about universals, generals can grow.

It is important to observe that a sign functions symbolically insofar as it is understood as a rule that determines interpretation. And this function depends on specification in a referent that can be identified and interpreted through its qualities. A quotation will bring out this dependence, as well as another way that signs function that is important to my discussion, namely, the way that signs function so as to refer to what Peirce calls *Immediate Objects.*

A symbol is a law, or regularity of the indefinite future. Its Interpretant must be of the same description; and so must be also the complete Immediate Object, or meaning. But a law necessarily governs, or "is embodied in" individuals, and prescribes some of their qualities. Consequently, a constituent may be an Icon. (2.293)

This quotation contains two points that are especially relevant to metaphorical reference. The first is that despite the generality of symbols, and thus the generality of their meanings, they are made determinate through embodiment in individuals. The second point is that what is called "the complete Immediate Object," which Peirce here calls alternatively "the meaning," is general. As such, the Immediate Object is a law or regularity of the indefinite future. The term "Immediate Object" will be considered further in connection with the other quasi-technical terms not yet discussed.[6]

Indexicality and Interpretation

In order to explore how Peirce's view suggests the special kind of reference characteristic of creative metaphor, it is necessary to focus on the indexical relation between signs and their objects. Consideration of this relation will be the occasion for introducing the other terms in Peirce's vocabulary that are important to developing the idea of metaphorically created referents.

[5] For example, see (8.334). A sign that is the nature of a "general type," is called a "legisign."
[6] In other places, Peirce uses lowercase and uppercase letters for the first letters of both words in the term, for example, "Immediate Object."

An example, initially one that is not a metaphor, will serve as a point of departure. What is the indexical function of the proposition "This red rose is large"? As indexical, this proposition focuses attention, first on the subject, "This red rose." Further, this subject calls attention to an individual, which is the referent of the proposition. The individual, however, is a referent in two ways. First, the individual is what Peirce sometimes calls an "immediate [or Immediate] Object," which, as suggested, is an embodied complex of abstractions – in this case, the abstract quality of redness and the complex of abstract qualities or respects by virtue of which it is interpreted as being a rose. In addition, the predication of "large" to the subject refers to the embodiment of the abstract quality of largeness. The expression as a whole, then, is indexical of an Immediate Object interpreted as an embodied complex of redness, largeness, and what it is to be a rose, which here serve as its meaning.

The referent as an Immediate Object is a system of connected abstractions that might be further attended to if one continued to interpret what the referent is. This can be seen in light of Peirce's conception of semiotic situations, all of which necessarily include interpretants that in turn are interpreted. As a sign, the proposition stands for or is *of* the Immediate Object, but *for* an interpreter. Thus the thing referred to is an object that is cognitive or known in one or more respects. And the referent is a cognitive object that consists of a certain complex of embodied respects, which Peirce also calls "grounds."[7] These are focused and given individualized locus in the large red rose. Of the respects in which the expression is a sign are embodied or determinate in the red rose, they will be the qualities by which it is known.

Insofar as the referent is an interpreted object, it is an Immediate Object that contributes to an interpretant. And its persistence as an Immediate Object depends on the continuing process of interpretation. Future interpretations may constitute the referent as something richer, such as, in the example of the large red rose, a member of some unusual class of interest to a horticulturist. The Immediate Object with which we started is left behind, so to speak. It is caught up in a growing interpretive web. However, it does not follow that the developed and developing objects of interpretation become increasingly subjective or dependent on finite interpreters. Nor do the interpreted objects fall prey to a linguistic conventionalism. They are not exhausted by perspectives or interpreted respects or qualities.

[7] The term *ground*, used for an embodied abstract quality that mediates a sign and its referent, was introduced early, in Peirce's "On a New List of Categories" (1.545–60). In (2.228), *ground* means the respect or idea in reference to which a sign stands for its object.

Peirce's idea of interpretive processes does not commit him to construing referents as purely linguistic or symbolic, arbitrary conventions. They are not arbitrary, for two reasons. First, at each stage of reinterpretation, or new interpretation, what is interpreted is an Immediate Object that is constituted within the interpretive structure of a sign relation. In each sign relation, the sign represents an object to an interpretant. This relation gives semiotic structure to each stage of interpretation. Consequently, no instance of interpretation is wholly self-contained and decisive for establishing a set of meanings arbitrarily. There is, then, an objectivity of growing interpretations converging on a larger, coherent community of interpretations.

Furthermore, it must be emphasized that an Immediate Object is, at any given stage, an embodiment. Thus, the Immediate Object is not a purely abstract general, or set of universals. It is the object as represented, but as represented in an instance or as an embodiment. And as an embodiment, it is a referent in a second way, as something dynamically related to the interpreter. Thus it forces itself on attention. It is something reacted to, which resists or constrains interpretation and which insists or persists in focusing attention for at least some minimal time. The referent, then, is what Peirce calls both a "Dynamical Object" and an Immediate Object.[8] The referent is resistant because it functions as a Dynamical Object. As pointed out already, as an Immediate Object, or as a complex of qualities, it is an object of interpretation. And because it is also a Dynamical Object, as well as a constituent in a sign situation, the referent is resistant to arbitrary and purely conventional interpretation. The referent as a

[8] In a letter to William James, Peirce stated: "We must distinguish between the Immediate Object, – i.e., the Object as represented in the sign, – and the Real (no, because perhaps the Object is altogether fictive, I must choose a different term, therefore), say rather the Dynamical Object, which, from the nature of things, the Sign *cannot* express, which it can only *indicate* and leave the interpreter to find out by *collateral experience.*"

Also, in a letter to Lady Welby, Peirce observed: "As to the Object, that may mean the Object as cognized in the Sign and therefore an Idea, or it may be the Object as it is regardless of any particular aspect of it, the Object in such relations as unlimited and final study would show it to be. The former I call the *Immediate* Object, the latter the *Dynamical* Object. For the latter is the Object that Dynamical Science (or what at this day would be 'Objective' science), can investigate. Take, for example, the sentence, 'the sun is blue.' Its Objects are the 'sun' and 'blueness.' If by 'blueness' he meant the Immediate Object, which is the quality of the sensation, it can only be known by Feeling. . . . So the 'Sun' may mean the occasion of sundry sensations, and so is Immediate Object, or it may mean our usual interpretation of such sensations in terms of place, of mass, etc., when it is the Dynamical Object" (8.183).

The function of the Dynamical Object will be considered later. The point here is to see that there is an Immediate Object that functions to provide representation and thus meaning. Thus, at the same time, it is necessarily connected with the Interpretant in particular, first as an Immediate Interpretant, which is what is expressed by the sign in the context in which it functions (8.314).

Dynamical Object constrains the respects in which an object is interpreted (in addition to the constraints of the system in which it functions).

The dynamical side of indexicality may be understood in terms of
Peirce's category of secondness. The way the referent is a Dynamical
Object is the way secondness functions in a sign. Secondness is the
resistance and constraint encountered as interpretation proceeds in
constituting the Immediate Object. The Dynamical Object functions
in one respect like a thing-in-itself; that is, in itself, it is neither constituted nor discovered by interpretation. It is what conditions interpretation from the other side, so to speak, of the object as immediate.
This is why the Immediate Object can be a locus for focusing, or a
condition for the relevance of meanings as the interpretation proceeds. As an Immediate Object, the referent gives a focus of relevance
for the respects in which the sign refers to the referent. But it does
this because the referent as the Dynamical Object is a focus of resistances that constrain the respects relevant to the Immediate Object.
The referent is thus individualized insofar as it is a focusing condition.

However, it is important that the Dynamical Object not be equated
with a Kantian thing-in-itself. It is true that Peirce suggests that for
nonfictive objects, the Dynamical Object be thought of as "The Real."[9]
And he also suggests that the Dynamical Object only be indicated –
never described or articulated as can the Immediate Object. Yet there
are differences between things-in-themselves and Dynamical Objects.
Let me suggest two of these differences.

First, although the Dynamical Object is not something that is itself
revealed as a cognitive object, or as something given complete interpretive determination, it is something that *would* be so determined
in an infinite long run, or if interpretation could reach an ideal limit
in the infinite future. Second, the Dynamical Object is not a Kantian
thing-in-itself because it bears a special relation to the Immediate Object of interpretation at each moment in the semiotic process. This
special relation is found in the *way*, or *respect*, the ground, in which
resistance constrains interpretation. Thus the Dynamical Object is
genuinely dynamic in reacting in certain ways as interpretations constitute the Immediate Object. As far as I know, this suggestion that
there are ways or respects in which resistance occurs is nowhere explicit in Peirce's writing. But I think it is at least not inconsistent with
what Peirce says.

That there are ways of resistance seems obvious if we consider what
it is to react to distinct occurrences. For instance, the presence of a

[9] See note 8.

perceived object when we open and close our eyes reveals something that resists by persisting; the object resists disappearing each time our eyes are open. But in the case of trying to lift a heavy object, there is a different reaction and opposition to our will from the counterpressure of the object. And in the case of compelled reaction of being surprised by a clap of thunder, there is still another kind of felt resistance. Of course, we know such differences in terms of the generals, the repeatable identities, or the meanings that constitute judgments about the experiences. Nevertheless, the generals are different from one another, and their differences are manifestations of different ways of resisting. If there were not differences in the ways of resistance, interpretation would be nothing more than discriminations and consequent identifications of distinct generals or meanings derived exclusively from the function of the immediate interpreter.

The proposal that resistances can be qualified in terms of respects was introduced to indicate why Dynamical Objects, which are centers of resistance, should not be equated with things-in-themselves or unknowable, unintelligible, ultimate conditions. But the proposal also has another purpose. It indicates one of the ways that interpretation is constrained as it grows and is embodied in Immediate Objects. The secondness attributable to every referent, as secondness or sheer otherness, is not itself intelligible. It is immediate and brute. Yet in being encountered in referents that are interpretable objects, secondness appears as modes of restraint. In this respect, what opposes arbitrary interpretation is not wholly unintelligible. Or put another way, referents, even as Dynamical Objects, are interpretable in certain respects. They resist in certain respects, and these respects are interpretable. They are evolving conditions that serve the embodied qualities that are constituents of Immediate Objects.

The respects relevant to both Dynamical Objects and Immediate Objects can be regarded as positive or negative, positive and negative grounds. They are positive when they constitute the Immediate Object. They are negative when they function from the side of the Dynamical Objects and play constraining or limiting roles in the growth of future Immediate Objects.

In order to explain this, it may be helpful to introduce the idea of vectors. Accordingly, we may regard respects as vectors. I use the term *vector* in a loose mathematical sense simply to indicate that resistances are directional and variably weighted. They are vectors in serving as conditions that constrain in roughly specific ways that show some possibilities to be irrelevant and some to be relevant. Thus restraints give force and direction to the constitutions of Immediate Objects. As a vector, each constraint or respect, each ground, that helps determine the referent has a kind of "weighting" in its importance in the interpreted object. Some vectors are of greater relevance than others are, depending on how the interpreted referent functions. In the large red rose, for instance, the constraints against embodying qualities that would constitute it as a tulip rather than as a rose are more relevant to certain kinds of classification than are the constraints that affect the inclusion of redness and largeness.

But the point about the different weightings of grounds is not as important at the moment as is the other point, that there are modes of resistance and grounds that are directional. They are directional as are antennas that resist signals from specific directions. Thus they are vectors that can control the Immediate Object in determinate respects. At the same time, they are directional in leading from determination by dynamical conditions to the growing determination that makes the interpretive process intelligible.

For convenience, let me call the respects, grounds, or embodied qualities that constitute the Immediate Object, *positive vectors*. They are positive because they function for the sake of the constitution of the interpretation that is relevant to the Immediate Object. They are the possibilities that have been selected and accepted as relevant. In this respect, positive vectors indirectly play a role in the telos that the referent has in relation to future interpretations.

The ways in which resistance is encountered in referents may also be thought of as *negative vectors*. As already suggested, the word *negative* is used to indicate that resistance is a condition of opposition to possible respects or embodiments that might have been introduced into the Immediate Object. A negative vector functions from the side of the Dynamical Object rather than from the Immediate Object. It is a partially determinate opposition to arbitrary interpretation. But because it is a vector — because the Dynamical Object resists in certain respects — positive directionality is served. Interpreting the large red rose as square encounters a negative vector. The negative vector in this case contributes to preventing the identification of the rose as square. It is a condition blocking the interpretation of the rose as something that embodies squareness. It serves as one among other conditions for eliminating what is not relevant. Similarly, interpreting the rose as blue would encounter a negative vector. As a negative vector, the embodiment of blueness is resisted. And in so acting as a constraint, it eliminates one among many possible positive vectors, or color qualities, that are exemplified in the Immediate Object. Both negative and positive vectors, then, help control selection.

Needless to say, interpretation in instances of this kind usually occurs too quickly for negative and positive vectors to be explicitly recognized as discrete, characterizable conditions. The judgment that this is a large red rose is, in Peirce's terms, a perceptual judgment, and a

perceptual judgment cannot display all the complex interpretive in-
ferences that are ingredients in it. We are not reflectively aware of all
the interpretive thinking that goes on in a perceptual judgment. In
any case, an object such as this large red rose is the referent of a sign
that has the form of a proposition, or a formal expression of a judgment. And the introduction of the idea of vectors is the basis of an
account of referents understood as complexes of qualities that, as positive, are intelligible constituents and that, as negative, are forces that
limit the relevant intelligible constituents. This way of understanding
the function of referents in interpretation leads us back to the original
question about how a referent can be created and still be an objective
condition for interpreting the expression that creates it. It therefore
is necessary at this point to apply this account to the referents of creative metaphors.

Metaphorical Referents as Immediate and Dynamical
Objects

Thus far, we have considered how referents function, regardless of
whether they are denoted by metaphors. The discussion has been
concerned with propositions, specifically expressions of perceptual
judgments, which are commonly thought of as literal rather than metaphorical. But the point of drawing on Peirce's ideas is to apply them
to metaphorical reference. Can what has been said about Immediate
and Dynamical Objects help resolve the puzzle of metaphorically created referents? An affirmative answer depends on two considerations.
The first concerns whether the account of Immediate and Dynamical
Objects can be specified so as to be consistent with the peculiarities of
the way that metaphors articulate meanings. The second consideration concerns whether the proposed referents of metaphors function
as both new and objective with respect to what is responsible for their
being new.

Before extending this picture of reference to metaphor, two preliminary comments are in order. The first concerns another attempt
to develop a view of metaphor that is influenced by Peirce's distinction
between symbol and icon. This view is offered by Paul Henle.[10] He
proposes the idea that metaphors contain iconic elements. However,
he overlooks Peirce's distinction between the second and third kind
of icons, between analogical icons and metaphorical icons. In consequence, Henle treats Peirce's view as if it construed metaphors as
analogies. Apparently Henle's own conception of how metaphors can

---

[10] Paul Henle, *Language, Thought, and Culture* (Ann Arbor: University of Michigan Press,
     1958), pp. 173–95.

be shown to be intelligible was so strongly fixed that he missed the subtleties of Peirce's view. But more important, Henle is not concerned with how metaphorical icons refer to objects, which is the main concern of my own attempt to develop one of Peirce's insights.

The second preliminary comment concerns a possible objection to my distinction between literal and metaphorical uses of language. It has been argued that all language is metaphorical and that the distinction between the literal and the metaphorical raises unnecessary problems.[11] I am inclined to be sympathetic with this objection. However, I must point out that what is important about the distinction is not the label *literal* used to refer to expressions set off from metaphors. Rather, what is important is the difference between, on the one hand, linguistic expressions considered meaningful on the basis of antecedent meanings and referents and, on the other hand, expressions considered meaningful on the basis of conditions that make their meaningfulness unique and, in part, irreducible to antecedent conditions. The distinction, then, need not commit us to an essential separation of literal from figurative or metaphorical language. All that is necessary is that there be a distinction between, on the one hand, contexts in which linguistic expressions require determinations that are, for practical purposes, taken as literal and, on the other hand, linguistic contexts in which the general metaphorical and creative character of language is taken as central. It is the latter that exhibits uniqueness and newness of meaning in metaphor and art. Even if it is insisted that all language has metaphorical roots that persist in what appears to be only literal usage, some language will nevertheless be used literally, or in what is ordinarily considered to be literal ways – that is, ways in which the individuality and uniqueness of the interaction of nuances of meanings is ignored for the sake of precision and repeatability of meanings as they appear in different contexts. Thus, we can and do, for various purposes, treat certain ranges of linguistic expressions as paraphrasable or translatable. Such expressions may be called *literal* with respect to the functions of those expressions that permit paraphrase.

Assuming that some articulations of meaning do function in special, figurative (as distinct from literal) ways, we must return to the question of what qualifications are needed for this view of reference. The necessity of making such qualifications should be obvious if we recognize that metaphorical expressions are like all aesthetic creations in exhibiting meanings that must be initially immanent to the metaphorical or aesthetic symbol. Unlike expressions such as "This is a

[11] Mary Hesse is one of the most recent theorists who believes that all language is basically metaphorical.

large red rose," which is used descriptively and supposedly literally, creative metaphors cannot be intelligible exclusively in terms of antecedent meanings and references to antecedent objects. Their meanings are peculiarly related internally to the expression that presents them, because the intelligibility of the creative metaphor is unique. This they share with the function of meanings in works of art. And this is one reason that they may themselves be regarded as works of art in miniature, as well as ingredients in larger works of art.

Susanne Langer's conception of art as presentational symbol is a well-known version of this point. And as L. A. Reid puts it, aesthetic meaning is found only in the concrete work itself, in what is "meaning-embodied."[12]

If metaphors function as aesthetic articulations of meaning or as miniature works of art, then it would seem that they have no reference beyond themselves. Eduard Hanslick said of music that if it refers, it must refer to itself.[13] Accordingly, it seems that metaphors, insofar as they are aesthetic creations, must be self-referential. Indeed, it seems that if they are creations – even if we leave aside the attribution "aesthetic" – they must refer to themselves if they refer at all. If they are creations, it seems that there could be nothing independent of themselves to which they could significantly refer. Or to put it another way, it seems that meaning and reference fuse with each other in the case of creative metaphors, and we are pushed back to an interpretation of metaphor something like the one that initiated the discussion – metaphors can create only perspectives – except that we now have perspectives that are on themselves rather than on a world consisting of either additional perspectives or of something independent of perspectives.

Seeing the issue in this way suggests again a point made earlier that needs repeating. The issue of metaphorical reference has ramifications beyond a theory of metaphor itself. Earlier, it was said that the issue relates to interpretation theory. But the issue can be seen now in the light of the basic question of the relation of art to the world or to life – that is, to the question of the truth of art.

The problem, then, is to see whether the conception of referents as Immediate Objects and Dynamical Objects suggests a way for metaphors to preserve both immanence of meaning, as rightly insisted on by a relatively long tradition in aesthetics, and relevance to the world. Yet, as was suggested, when we consider Immediate and Dynamical Objects in terms of the relevance of the metaphor to the world, we see that the same dilemma appears in another form. Thus, in the case

---

[12] See Reid, *Meaning in the Arts.*
[13] Eduard Hanslick, *The Beautiful Music,* trans. Gustav Cohen (New York: DeCapo Press, 1974).

of metaphor, at least when metaphor is aesthetic, the issue concerns whether there is a Dynamical Object controlling the Immediate Object.

In extricating ourselves from the dilemma, we should first observe that Peirce's conception of the Dynamical Object is designed to provide constraints on scientific theory. The Dynamical Object is what prevents theory from being radically relative. The Dynamical Object is a condition for there being reference that would be reached in an infinite future. It seems plausible, then, to conclude that for Peirce, metaphors in science have Dynamical Objects, even if these are only indirectly reached through a system of symbols. Are there also Dynamical Objects that constrain aesthetic metaphors in art?

Peirce explicitly affirms the conclusion that there are objects of some sort for aesthetic literary expressions. He observes, "The Object of a Sign may be something to be created by the sign. . . . The Object of the sentence 'Hamlet was insane' is the Universe of Shakespeare's Creation so far as it is determined by Hamlet being a part of it" (8.178). Yet if the significance of artistic metaphors is immanent and if the referents of creative metaphors are created – and the object here is indeed Shakespeare's creation – then we might conclude that the object Peirce affirms is only the Immediate Object. And if the Immediate Object is identical with the metaphorical expression itself (as sign type), then the autonomy of the aesthetic function and the immanence of aesthetic meaning will be retained. I think the point that there must be aesthetic immanence of meanings in the Immediate Object is correct as far as it goes. But I think the denial that there is a Dynamical Object is unnecessary and dangerous for aesthetic interpretation.

I shall next focus on this issue, considering how immanence of meaning can be maintained along with the claim that metaphorical reference includes what Peirce called the Dynamical Object.

Let me suggest that the conclusion that aesthetic expressions, or metaphors in art, have Dynamical Objects is consistent with Peirce's general position, and this can be seen if we consider the pervasiveness of his conception of indexicality. Although reference may be a minimal function of some signs, there is no genuine sign that completely lacks any one of the three functions of iconicity, indexicality and symbolicality.[14] Thus, even a sign that is identified as an icon – as meta-

[14] Douglas Greenlee suggests that a fictive Dynamical Object is a previous internal thought; see his *Peirce's Concept of Sign* (The Hague: Mouton, 1973), pp. 65–6. However, I think this interpretation overly restricts the Dynamical Object and implies its assimilation to past Immediate Objects. For Peirce, the Dynamical Object is not only efficient in relation to the Immediate Object, but it is also telic. In any case, when we deal with creative-created signs that are relevant to the world, we are not dealing with fictive objects.

phors are, for Peirce – has indexicality or reference, as long as it is intelligible, that is, as long as the icon functions semiotically, as an interpretable thing. Furthermore, Peirce's characterization of metaphor as the third kind of icon suggests, I think, that metaphors have references that are not confined to themselves.

A metaphor is an icon that, as noted earlier, represents "a parallelism in something else" (2.277). I shall return to the idea of *parallelism* later. Suffice it to say at this point that because Peirce says that metaphors represent something in something else, the reference of a metaphor is to something other than the sign itself. And if Peirce attributes a kind of non-self-referential reference to metaphors in general, then this kind of reference must be characteristic of metaphors in aesthetic as well as scientific contexts.

Putting this point in terms of Peirce's suggestions about the twofold referent, it can be said that insofar as a metaphor represents something other than itself and insofar as it is indexical, its unique Immediate Object must be embodied. It must be a concrete complex of integrated meanings. And its concreteness is its dynamical side. It must be remembered that an Immediate Object is an interpreted object. But to be interpreted requires a focus or condition of relevance. This relevance is in part a function of the interacting connotations, whose selection does not yield complete nonsense; otherwise the metaphor would not be meaningful at all, much less exhibit insight. But creative metaphors may also exhibit insight so that the condition of relevance cannot be confined to internal considerations. There is import, significance, or relevance to the world. And this requires the function of the Dynamical Object. Thus as Peirce says, the Dynamical Object is "really efficient" (8.343). Furthermore, the Dynamical Object resists being exhausted by the meanings that comprise the metaphor's Immediate Object. And such resistance and constraints on interpretation serve as the objective condition of the metaphor.

A metaphor, then, creates its referent insofar as the referent is its Immediate Object. And in this respect, it creates and refers self-referentially to its meanings. However, it can be said to be apt, faithful, adequate, inappropriate, unfaithful, or whatever, to an extralinguistic condition with respect to its referent's functioning as a Dynamical Object. The Dynamical Object is the objective side of the created referent, or of the referent as Immediate Object. Encounters with Dynamical Objects functioning and manifesting themselves as negative vectors alert the interpreter to the relevance that created and creative metaphors have to the world. And in serving future interpretation through negative vectors, the Dynamical Object has an indirect creative function. It cooperates creatively through its constraints with the Immediate Object. Further, as a constraining condition of interpretation, it is negatively vectorial – that is, it restrains in certain respects – consequently, it is a condition contributing to telic growth toward future interpretation, although this telos is not predetermined. It is *sui generis,* or self-developmental – in accord with Peirce's conception of developmental teleology ("The Law of Mind," 6.102–63).

It must be emphasized that the Dynamical Object is necessary as a condition of resistance to future arbitrary interpretations. It is the Dynamical Object that functions as an extraconceptual condition independent of capricious interpretations, even if those caprices are shared with whole cultures. In interpretation, something other than the embodied meanings themselves is operative. Thus, in terms of the issue as it was formulated at the outset, it can be said now that something other than perspectives is made possible, even if the perspectives in question are those that form the schemata of whole civilizations. Such perspectives or schemata do change and grow. And the Dynamical Objects of creative thought – a kind of thought that is often expressed in metaphors – are the cooperative conditions of these changes.

Problematic Consequences

Two interdependent problems should be addressed before these suggestions about metaphorical reference are concluded. The first problem concerns whether the Dynamical Objects of metaphors in science relate to their metaphors in the way that Dynamical Objects of metaphors in art relate to their metaphors. The second problem, whose clarification is inseparable from the first, concerns the possibility of testing artistic metaphors for their relevance to the world or to Dynamical Objects.

This account of creative, metaphorical reference may be thought to break down when applied to science. How can science create anything in the world? How can it create anything that is independent of the conceptual scheme or theory constructed by the scientist? The answer to this question already has been indicated by what was said about the objects of metaphors in general. Insofar as the referent of a scientific, creative metaphor is an Immediate Object, the referent is created. Thus a theory that is built on or made possible by a metaphor refers to an Immediate Object, which is the interpreted and interpretable object. This is the creation of the scientist and scientists who develop it.

Scientists create the objects of their theories just insofar as those objects would not have been intelligible things functioning in the world unless the theory had been created. For example, there would be no

DNA as an intelligible structure unless a theory of it had been created. Yet the creation of the Immediate Object or theory does not require that the theory be arbitrary. The theory is not merely a construct.

A scientific metaphor is a creation that has its relevance to the world in terms of both Dynamical and Immediate Objects. The Dynamical Object sustains the development of theory, functioning as a condition for empirical tests. The concept of DNA, for instance, is not pure fiction. It is a created interpretation, a theory, that is constrained by what is in the world, the Dynamical Object, conditioning the interpretation. Yet the Dynamical Object, constraining theory, is not itself a static, immutable condition. It contributes to what is an evolving universe. The DNA referent came into being at some time and changed functionally as life evolved. Or as another example, the development of the theory of gravitation – and I assume that this theory in its inception, at least, involved metaphor – created its referent as an Immediate Object.[15] This Immediate Object was the theoretically articulated complex of meanings that state the law. On the other hand, the law is embodied, and the same referent as dynamical was and is a component of evolving reality. The relevant component of reality, in this case, is now known as gravitation itself, which in certain ways that, before Newton, were not intelligible, affected persons and things through constraints and resistances to perception and understanding.

It should be obvious that this account implies an evolutionary ontology. But this is consistent with Peirce's cosmology, which affirmed the growth of reality in all its dimensions – physical as well as mental, both poles lying on a continuum. However, even if this ontology were not accepted, the account of metaphor could be retained. If one insisted on a view in which the Dynamical Object were construed as a condition that could not evolve, it would still function as a control on scientific metaphors that would then be at least epistemologically creative in creating referents as Immediate Objects, although ontological creativity would be denied.

The second question concerns whether there are tests for the truth-value or the relevance to the world of metaphors and their Immediate Objects in art as well as science. I shall discuss this question in accordance with Mary Hesse's "cognitive claims of metaphor."[16] Hesse accounts for the relevance (or what she calls the "truth-value") of metaphors in natural science by appealing, finally, to tests of prediction

[15]Owen Barfield has offered a relatively lengthy account of how the idea of gravitation evolved from various senses of "grave" and was adopted by Newton in what looks like a metaphorical construal of the term grave for the purpose of science. See his *Speaker's Meaning* (Middletown, Conn.: Wesleyan University Press, 1967), pp. 40–42.

[16]Hesse, "The Cognitive Claims of Metaphor," pp. 27–45.

and success in communication. There may be "truth-consensus with regard to metaphor within the scientific community" because of coherence and an "external grounding in natural reality."[17] And this grounding is tested by prediction. Thus, when Hesse's view is transferred to the present context of the created referent proposal, the issue concerns whether such tests can be identified for aesthetic or artistic referents that are created. However, Hesse thinks there is a special problem for metaphors that function outside science. She sees that the possibility of tests is problematic only when we turn to extrascientific metaphors – poetic, religious, and ideological – in which, she thinks, there is no "test in the natural world."

In addressing this question, it is important to emphasize that my account of artistic metaphorical reference understands referents, in their dynamical sides, to be independent conditions. These referents are of, or in, the world. Thus, the question here concerns what tests, if any, show the fit of artistic metaphors to such objects in the world.

One way of responding might be attempted by interpretive critics who are willing to accept certain types of Immediate Objects as decisive. I have in mind not those who are primarily concerned with evaluating works with respect to formal success but, rather, those who are concerned primarily with determining specific messages about the world or particular "truths" known independently of the works of art that are supposed to be offered to us by those works. When a critic raises such questions about the relevance of the work of art to the world to which it may lead us, the referents of criticism are antecedently understood Immediate Objects. Thus, a critic might approach works of art by looking for historical data concerning influences on the creator or by speculating about the consequences of works of art for society and the future community of interpreters. But this is to look for referents that are preinterpreted Immediate Objects of the past and the future. Similarly, attempts to paraphrase metaphors, and to explain fully the meanings of works of art, are attempts to find other Immediate Objects to substitute for the works being analyzed. Of course, there are tests available for this kind of criticism – descriptive tests for the correlation of what is discriminated in the work with what is said to be the referents (antecedent) in the world.

However, our subject is Immediate Objects that are created and that cannot be matched with previously interpreted Immediate Objects. Are there tests for the fit of these to the world? One ready answer is that because the Immediate Objects are creations, they are original, and they consequently originate their own standards. It is they that serve as models that test future reinterpretations of estab-

[17] Ibid., p. 34.

lished Immediate Objects. Such tests may account for the fit of a creative metaphor to the world in the future. But what tests are there, if any, of the fit of creative metaphors to the world in which they are invented and to which they are accepted as apt or fitting? If there is an answer, it must depend on finding tests that work for aesthetic Dynamical Objects, as, in a sense, they do for scientific Dynamical Objects, which function as conditions for predictability tests and convergences of theories. Specifically, the issue turns on whether there are tests relevant to the negative vectors functioning in the Dynamical Objects that constrain the consequences and future community of aesthetic interpreters.

The immediate answer to this question must be negative. First, with respect to the test of convergence, art cannot be assessed in such terms. There is no final convergence to be expected for a community of aesthetic interpreters. I want to pursue this negative response by indicating how it is suggested by Peirce's statement that a metaphor represents a parallelism. What Peirce says about metaphors and parallelisms must be looked at more closely. Peirce's statement that a metaphorical icon represents a parallelism needs to be quoted in full and in its context. In this quotation, Peirce uses the term "hypoicon" as a substitute for what he calls the "substantive" for the iconic representamen:

Hypoicons may be roughly divided according to the mode of Firstness of which they partake. Those which partake of simple qualities, or First Firstnesses, are *images;* those which represent the relations, mainly dyadic, or so regarded, of the parts of one thing by analogous relations in their own parts, are *diagrams;* those which represent the representative character of a representamen by representing a parallelism in something else, are *metaphors.* (2.277)

Presumably, diagrams belong to the mode of Second Firstness and metaphors to Third Firstness. As a Third Firstness, the interpretive component of icons comes to the fore. Thus the representative character of the iconic sign is explicitly mentioned, emphasizing that a metaphor must have a representing function and that it has a greater dependence on a future series of interpretations than does an image, which simply stands on its own by virtue of possessing a quality. However, what is important here is that Peirce had an insight that was not adequately recognized until recently by theorists of metaphor, namely, that metaphors are not analogies.

As indicated earlier, Henle apparently thought that for Peirce, metaphors depend upon analogies. This interpretation might be explained by Peirce's reference to a parallelism. Yet it is clear that analogical relations are attributed to the second kind of icon. Consequently, Peirce must mean something else by the parallelism that is attributed to metaphors. Metaphors are not (as are diagrams) comparisons or expressions that purport to match antecedent relations in the world.

Nevertheless, a metaphor is a representation of something — "something else" which includes the structure of a parallelism.

Peirce's use of the term *parallelism* is significant. It suggests, I think, that the terms of a metaphor are incongruous in relation to one another and must sustain a tension. Thus terms such as *Man, dream,* and *shadow,* brought together in "Man is the dream of a shadow," manifest a certain tension as long as the prior complexes of antecedent meanings for each term are attended to. This metaphor exhibits, as an expression that is an Immediate Object, a parallelism. And the something else represented is a Dynamical Object, which here functions as a dyadic condition of the metaphor's representing parallelism. Thus, as parallel, the representing and represented relation can never collapse or permit its terms to converge. The contrast or otherness of one term in relation to the other(s) is sustained as long as what represents it is a metaphor and as long as it conditions the tension of the metaphor. And as long as an icon is a metaphor, it cannot merge with its Dynamical Object, even in an infinite long run. Just as cosmic evolution inevitably includes increments of spontaneity, so metaphors provide the semiotic counterparts to these spontaneities in the evolution of semioses.

A parallelism differs from a condition of convergence (such as may be appealed to in science). Metaphors themselves, either independently or in art, represent a peculiar kind of referent that resists the convergence of its qualities as exhibited in a unity. The referent must remain dynamic. In contrast, scientific theory, as has been pointed out, converges — that is one of its tests. Convergence is what coherence exhibits as it increases with the evolution of scientific theory. And in science, evolving convergence brings Immediate Objects closer to Dynamical Objects and to interpretations in which new metaphors become less dominant, being replaced by frozen metaphors or "literal" expressions. But the aesthetic Dynamical Objects of the arts — with respect to their negative vectors — remain inevitably resistant to — although they are not irrelevant to — the manifestations of their Immediate Objects. Because of the aesthetic Dynamical Object, we cannot count on the test of final convergence of aesthetic interpretations in a Final Interpretant.

This idea of the kind of referent represented by a metaphor can be complemented by another suggestion that Peirce offers in one of his comments about his conception of would-be's or generals. And this suggestion also clarifies the problem of finding tests to assess the relevance of metaphorical reference. In explaining what he means by would-be's, Peirce says that the idea of an agreement that would be actualized, if inquiry were sustained long enough, is a kind of hope "for *will be*" (8.133). This introduction of hope, I think, reveals something about his conception of the infinite long run in which scientific theories would converge. The introduction of hope suggests that would-be's are something more than regulative ideals or ideal limiting concepts. If they were only limiting concepts, Peirce's view would be another form of Kantianism rather than a pragmatistic realism and, in turn, the synechism, which he thought would serve as the foundation of an archtectonic. But if a would-be expresses a hope, then it cannot be understood simply as something that cannot be realized in fact. Instead, the convergence that would be is a concrete end. It is what Peirce called "concrete reasonableness." Applied to the test of metaphorical reference, it follows that the creator of a metaphor, at least in science, envisages constraining conditions that consist of more than an ideal claim of what ought to be agreed to by future audiences. There is both an empirical claim and a regulative command. On the other hand, what I have suggested implies that there can be no such would-be functioning in artistic metaphors.

Metaphors in art are not relevant to an end that can be envisaged as a determinate culmination of teleological necessity. It must be remembered that Peirce's teleology is developmental. Each telos is *sui generis*. Thus a developmental evolutionary process does not have its source in a principle of eros, which aims at a determinate goal that lures the agents of the process. Instead, the principle is driven by what Peirce calls *evolutionary love* or *agape*.[18] Thus, what constrains the aesthetic creator and functions as an extralinguistic condition, is not a realizable, future, determinate object. The creator in art must be permissive and accepting of such a condition, letting it, the Dynamical Object, develop and resist the creator's control over the Immediate Object, and without hope for terminating the evolution of art in an indefinite future.

If we cannot expect convergence as a test of metaphors in art, can we expect predictability or something like it – for example, some kind of correctness or appropriateness in showing the import of the metaphor, or a kind of fulfillment of anticipated experiences seemingly indicated by the import of the metaphor? Again, the answer must be no if what would satisfy such tests must be defined in terms of Immediate Objects already integral to the objects of familiar signs. If such tests were relevant, then we would need to accept the view that paraphrases are adequate translations of metaphors and that metaphors are expressions of literal propositions, in which case the novelty that is necessary where there is creation would be denied. If there are tests, they must be satisfied by constraints other than those of the con-

[18]The role of agape is distinct from eros as an operative principle in Peirce's view of cosmic evolution. See my "Eros and Agape in Creative Evolution: A Peircean Insight," *Process Studies* 4 (Spring 1974): 11–25.

sistency and coherence within a system expected of Immediate Objects. I think Peirce's conception of the Dynamical Object does play a role here, as suggested in the point that the construction and interpretation of metaphors are not arbitrary. A Dynamical Object provides constraint on semiosis. Thus, when a creative metaphor seems apt, that to which it seems apt, its referent, is its referent as Dynamical Object. And the felt constraint of this object is the only test we can expect of art. Metaphors create their referents by virtue of their Immediate Objects and are apt, adequate, and relevant to the world by virtue of their Dynamical Objects. And being apt is tested by the constraints of the Dynamical Object. Of course, the proposal that such tests are all we can expect is open to the charge of relativism: Each metaphor creator and each interpreter may encounter constraints not recognized by others. However, at this point the test of convergence, or a community of agreement, in a limited form, can be called back.

Although the test of final convergence cannot be expected in art, the difference between art and science in this respect is not as great as it might seem. Scientific tests are not decisive independently from communities of scientists. The selection of expected or predicted evidence is a function of selected hypotheses and a system of accepted theory. Assent to the tests depends on the discrimination of trained observation and, of course, the anticipation of converging agreement that takes place under the control of the Dynamical Object of science. Similarly, the tests of interpretations of art may, at any given time, be decisive if communities of informed (trained) observers, especially critics, agree. Agreement is much looser in aesthetic interpretation. In fact, it can even include quite varied, competing interpretations, which are different specifications of a more general, common interpretation. The differences are to be expected if the independent control of the Dynamical Object sustains the parallelisms represented by metaphors or aesthetic experiences. Although critics and audiences look, listen, read, and imagine as participants in communities of appreciators, the controls of their referents should not be expected to lead to perfect agreement. We cannot expect agreements that are determinate enough to unite, at any assignable time, communities as large as the groups of scientists working as inquirers in our Western European tradition. Yet this imprecision of outcome is not the same as anarchy of taste. And agreement within specific contexts, if not in an infinite long run, is still a partial standard, joined with the resistances intruding into each interpreter's experience. Like science, interpretation of art undergoes evolutionary growth. Although this growth does not aim at a final end, it is a growth in which new referents are created and incorporated into families of the created referents.

Conclusion

The purpose of this discussion of metaphor and Peirce's conception of their objects has been twofold: (1) to demonstrate a way in which Peirce's brief remarks about metaphor reach far beyond his time and offer insights that had escaped theorists of metaphor during his own time and (2) to apply Peirce's view of reference for signs in general to an understanding of metaphor. This application required a certain amount of extrapolation, but I do not think I have distorted Peirce's general, mature philosophical view. In any case, it has always seemed to me that the most respect is shown to Peirce when his ideas are taken as seminal ideas that enhance our understanding of philosophical issues.

In particular, I have tried to characterize some of Peirce's ideas about reference and to apply them to one of the problems invoked by questions concerning the ontological import of an interactionist theory of metaphor. Signs refer in one or more respects to twofold referents: to objects that are both immediate and dynamical. Immediate Objects are objects as represented for interpreters so that they are the referent as an integration of meanings. Referents are also embodiments of meanings and, as such, are Dynamical Objects that sustain a resistance to, and impose constraints on, the respects or meanings that are embodied. Dynamical Objects serve as negative conditions (like vectors) that limit the arbitrariness of interpretation. Referents of creative metaphors are also twofold. But in the case of what is unique and what has no prefigured Immediate Objects to which the expression could refer, Immediate Objects that are metaphorical meanings must be integral to the metaphorical expression itself. Such an Immediate Object cannot be independent of its sign. Yet the referent as a Dynamical Object transcends the internal relations of metaphor and Immediate Object. The Immediate Object, then, is what is created, and the Dynamical Object is the control on the part of the world that makes metaphors either apt or inapt in their relevance to the world.

Dynamical Objects also serve as conditions of the parallelism that Peirce attributed to the representational import of metaphors. Metaphors do not represent by analogy, but by a unique relation of parallelism according to which the terms of the relation must remain apart, in a tension that is conditioned by the dynamical side of the metaphorical referent. These relationships of metaphors to referents are present in both science and art. In science, they function in theory contexts that develop toward a convergence in the infinite long run. In art, there are no such contexts. Each metaphor and its referent are unique, and the relation of parallelism is the efficient condition of novel intrusions in inquiry and in the world of inquiry. Creative metaphors are the cutting edges of knowledge, and they are manifest most purely in art. It is art, or the aesthetic, that functions in semiosis to reflect the spontaneities affirmed in Peirce's theory of cosmic evolution.

Index